ESSEX CHURCHES

Chelmsford

ESSEX CHURCHES

John Hough

THE BOYDELL PRESS

First published 1983
by the Boydell Press
an imprint of Boydell & Brewer Ltd
PO Box 9, Woodbridge, Suffolk IP12 3DF

ISBN 0 85115 174 4

British Library Cataloguing in Publication Data

Hough, John
Essex churches.
1. Church architecture – Essex (England)
I. Title
726'.5.094267 NA5471.E/

Printed in Great Britain
by St Edmundsbury Press
Bury St Edmunds, Suffolk

CONTENTS

LIST OF ILLUSTRATIONS

Plates

Photographs by Sarah Greenwell

Drawings and engravings

Plans

INTRODUCTION

Saxon Essex

Essex was a peaceful and prosperous part of Britain under Roman rule. Colchester (Camulodunum) was the most important settlement of the county; indeed Colchester was then the most important place in Britain. Although the Roman soldiers commonly worshipped Mithras, a cult of Persian origin, Christianity gradually spread to the west despite savage persecutions. In AD 312, the Emperor Constantine was himself converted after his victory over Maxentius at the battle of the Milvian Bridge; the faith of a minority thus became the religion of the Roman empire, and British bishops were present at the conference, convened by Constantine at Arles in AD 314. Christianity would seem to have thrived in Britain during the late fourth century and early fifth century, although no churches in Essex of that era survive; for it was customary to hold services in private houses or at wayside altars, protected by rough buildings. Perhaps some of the pagan temples were taken over and used for worship; there are certain interesting similarities between Mithraism and Christianity.

Following the departure of the Roman legions, the Celtic Roman population were harassed by repeated invasions of the Angles, Saxons and Jutes, and Essex was particularly vulnerable. The Celtic church retreated to the south-west where it survived in Wales and other centres, but Essex lapsed into paganism, isolated from both the continental and its own Christian church. It was not until the arrival of Augustine in Kent in AD 597 that Essex again espoused the Christian faith; he was sent by Pope Gregory at the invitation of Bertha, wife of King Ethelbert and herself a Frankish Catholic princess.

In AD 590 the king of the East Saxons and ruler of Essex was Saeberht, nephew of the Kentish king. Augustine had baptised Ethelbert of Kent and then appointed one of his monks, Mellitus, as bishop of the East Saxons at London, then part of Essex; here the foundation of St Paul's, and of the abbey of Thorney, later named Westminster, were laid. The king of Essex, Saeberht, received Mellitus with respect and encouraged him in his work; but after his death his sons, who remained pagans, quarrelled with Mellitus and the bishop retired to Gaul. Sigeberht was, according to the Venerable Bede, the next king of the East Saxons. His friend Oswiu, King of Northumbria, persuaded Sigeberht to be baptised by Bishop Finian of Lindisfarne; and after his conversion, Sigeberht returned to his kingdom, asking Oswiu to send him Christian teachers. Cedd, the brother of St Chad, was recalled from his work in Mercia, and came with another priest to work in Essex. These two enjoyed great success in converting the inhabitants. When he returned to Lindisfarne, Bishop Finian, hearing of his success, consecrated Cedd as bishop of the East Saxons. Cedd returned to Essex; he worked vigorously, ordaining priests and deacons to assist him, and built churches in several places. Cedd's two centres were Ythancester (Bradwell on sea) and Tilbury. The former is described as being on the river Pante (the Blackwater); Ythancester is the site of the Roman fortress of Othona, near Bradwell on sea (cf. p. 3). Tilbury – Tilaberg in Bede's time – was then a quiet remote place in comparison with the populous Ythancester, and Cedd founded a monastic establishment there.

Sigeberht was subsequently murdered by two of his relations; he was succeeded by Swithelm, whom Cedd baptised at the court of the East Anglian king at Rendlesham, Suffolk. In AD 664, while attending the synod of Whitby, Cedd caught the plague and died; he was buried in Yorkshire. Wini was Cedd's immediate successor. On his death in AD 675, Eorconweald was consecrated bishop of the East Saxons, taking up residence in London. An exceptionally holy man, he built two famous monasteries, one for himself at Chertsey in Surrey, and the other for his sister Ethelburga at Barking.

No sooner had the kingdom of the East Saxons become peaceable and Christianity firmly established than it was subjected to the invasions of the Danes, which began towards the end of the eighth century. By AD 838 the Norsemen had overrun East Anglia and Kent, burning and destroying wherever they went. It was not until 1016, when Canute defeated Edmund Ironside, son of King Ethelred, at Assundune, and assumed the sovereignty of the whole of Britain for his lifetime, that any lasting peace was established.

By this time there was no longer a kingdom of Essex or East Saxons; but the Saxon line was restored with the accession of Edward the Confessor in 1042, followed by Harold, Earl of Essex, son of Godwin, and the last Saxon king.

A number of Saxon churches survive, some from the earlier and some from the later Saxon period. Because timber was the most readily available building material in most parts of Essex, many churches built of local wood have vanished. A typical Saxon village church survives only at Greensted near Ongar with a nave constructed of half-round logs. 'There was a time', wrote the Venerable Bede, 'when there was not a stone church in all the land but the custom was to build them all of wood. Finian the second bishop of Lindisfarne built a church in that island AD 652 for a cathedral which yet was not of stone but of wood and covered with reeds (i.e. thatched).' At Hadstock stands a grander sort of Saxon church; and at Strethall, Chickney, Inworth, Little Bardfield and in Colchester Saxon work may also be seen. A number of dedications to saints such as St Osyth, Ethelbert, Edward, Edmund and Botolph suggest Saxon foundations. Cedd's church survives at Bradwell on sea, built of Roman materials upon the foundations of the great Roman fort. Cedd's mission of AD 653 to Sigeberht's kingdom establishes its date as mid seventh century, and it would seem to be the earliest church in the county, followed by Hadstock, possibly founded by St Botolph. Waltham Abbey, a later Saxon foundation of Canute's reign, should also be mentioned; it was lavishly rebuilt by Harold just before the Conquest, but how much of Harold's original work remains is much disputed.

Medieval Essex

After William's victory over Harold in 1066, Essex was to experience the severity and oppression of Norman rule. After his coronation at Barking, William received the homage of many English nobles and prepared for a military progress throughout the country. In due course he rewarded his followers, such as the Mandevilles, the de Veres, the de Clares, with large tracts of Essex land; the English were dispossessed and reduced to serfdom. All the administration of the country was conducted in Norman French. Beside these sweeping changes there was great activity in ecclesiastical building, and new castles were constructed at Colchester, Hedingham and elsewhere. The greed and cruelty of the Normans seems to have been matched by their energy and piety. They built or rebuilt a large number of churches in the county; apart from the monastic churches, these tended to be on a small scale, in proportion to small villages. Castle Hedingham is an exception, as this was the headquarters of the great de Vere family, whose influence lasted from the Conquest until 1703, when the 26th Earl of Oxford died.

William's Domesday survey of 1086 listed about 440 places of settlement in Essex, and the population of the county would seem to have been about 70,000. There were two boroughs, Colchester and Maldon, but the more important Norman church buildings were monastic. As much as forty per cent of the land in Essex was owned by the Church during the middle ages; and this fact alone illustrates its immense power and influence prior to the Reformation and to Henry VIII's dissolution of the monasteries. By the time of Edward III it is thought that one in fifty of the population was employed in the church and there was a vast hierarchy of clergy. There were about fifty religious houses of various kinds and sizes in Essex. The abbey at Barking was founded by Eorconweald for his sister in the seventh century; it became very rich and powerful, owning over 9,000 acres by the time of the Domesday survey. Only members of great aristocratic families were eligible to become its head, who ranked as the leading abbess in England and as a peer of the realm.

Some monastic churches, such as Hatfield Broad Oak, Hatfield Peverel, Blackmore and Little Dunmow have survived in part to become the present parish churches. Waltham Abbey, founded in Canute's reign, rebuilt by Harold and greatly enlarged by Henry II, was a mitred abbey; its abbot sat in the House of Lords and the abbey was one of the most important in England. Only its Norman nave survives as a parish church. At Tilby, the gatehouse chapel alone survives where the Cistercian monastery once stood and this also forms the parish church. Many of these religious houses owned parish churches; the abbey at Saffron Walden controlled nineteen. Unusually, the most important order in Essex were the Augustinian Canons, who had as their headquarters St Botolph's, Colchester with ten other houses.

The Reformation and its effects on medieval churches

By the sixteenth century the power and importance of these religious establishments was declining. Bicknacre Priory closed down in 1507 through poverty, and Latton Priory in 1534. Cardinal Wolsey dissolved six more and used the money to endow his new college at Oxford. In 1536 the rapacious Henry VIII, having broken away from Rome, set about closing the rest of them. Some have vanished completely and the splendour of their architecture has gone; in a few cases such as Blackmore we can see their remains incorporated into the present church. The greatest of Henry's acts of vandalism – and there were many – was the destruction of the major part of Waltham Abbey, which had been so lavishly enlarged by Henry II as an act of expiation for his complicity in the murder of Thomas Becket, and finished in 1177.

The ruthless destruction of the monasteries has left Essex with some impressive ruins of their former glory; in some cases only a few stones remain, in other cases a parish church was formed from the former Lady chapel or nave. At St Botolph's Priory in Colchester, founded at the end of the eleventh century for Augustinian Canons, there was a Norman church of considerable size, with a nave 108 ft long. It was built of rubble incorporating many Roman bricks and still makes a striking picture in its ruined condition. It has a grim and severe appearance and is worth comparing with Waltham Abbey which is roughly of the same date. Another Norman foundation by the Benedictines, St John's Abbey at Colchester, has disappeared, except for a gatehouse which has a very fine flushwork decoration of the fifteenth century.

No sooner had Henry VIII enriched himself and his friends at the expense of the monasteries than he set about suppressing the chantries and guilds as a further source of revenue; and then ordered that 'such images as had been abused to superstition be taken down'. This destruction of church fittings and goods continued through Edward VI's reign, when figures of saints, stained glass, church plate, stone altars, altar cloths and copes, were removed and sold; the rood screens and rood lofts with the figures of Christ, the Virgin Mary and St John were in many cases taken down and destroyed. This wanton destruction, although halted in Mary's reign, continued for a while under Elizabeth. When the Puritans came to power in the seventeenth century, most churches had been stripped of their many beautiful and irreplaceable fittings and goods; the wall paintings had been obliterated or whitewashed over, the stained glass replaced by clear glass and the rood lofts destroyed or burnt. All the colour and imagery of the middle ages had gone – even fonts were disliked by the Puritans and in some cases thrown out, in the final stage of 'image-breaking' typified by the activities of William Dowsing in East Anglia.

As we see them today, the churches are often pale and colourless within; and it is hard to imagine how splendid and colourful they must have looked before the Reformation. Their plastered walls were often painted with scenes from the Bible, as at Copford, so that an illiterate congregation could learn the stories. The rood screens were gilded and painted richly, the statues coloured; and candles burned before the shrines of saints. The majority of the parishioners, poor and simple folk, found their church a magnificent haven from the outside world; today we need considerable powers of imagination to conjure up the colour and beauty that has been lost through the activities of our Protestant forebears.

During the eighteenth century, an age of 'enlightenment' when religious observance was in decline, the fabric of many churches was allowed to decay. With the Gothic revival in Victorian times, an orgy of rebuilding took place. In many cases, this was necessary to save the churches from collapse; but a great deal of the restoration was done in bad taste and was accompanied by further destruction of the original architecture and internal fittings, such as benches and pulpits. Despite man's greed and religious fanaticism the Essex churches still contain an immense treasure of the county's history, constituting the material for a life time's study.

Medieval architectural styles

Materials

The materials available for building in Essex deserve consideration first of all. Because Essex was covered by large areas of forest, particularly in the western part of the county, the principal and most easily available material was timber, usually oak and elm. The forests round Waltham, Hainault and Hatfield Broad Oak stretched north beyond Stane Street, east beyond Chelmsford, and south to the marsh land near the Thames. For this reason, houses were mostly built of wood and plaster, with thatched roofs; and this was why the Saxons generally built their simple churches of wood. As the forests were cleared and villages grew, fields were cultivated and the flints and stones collected; these often formed the pebble rubble walls of churches, of which the majority in Essex are built.

The Romans seem to have been great brick makers and had left a copious supply available in the remains of villas and other buildings. Many churches in the county include these red tile-like objects in their flint rubble walls and quoins. It was not until the later medieval period that brick-making again became widespread. Fine church towers such as at Ingatestone or North Weald were built, and clerestories were added to heighten the naves as at Great Baddow. In the sixteenth century the first churches built entirely of brick appear, at Theydon Mount and Chignal St Nicholas.

The earlier church walls of pebble rubble were often coursed as at Little Leighs, but the practice later died out. Essex lacks good stone for building; geologically, it has a saucer shaped cross section filled with boulder clay and London clay, with chalk outcrops at the rim towards Saffron Walden and south near the Thames. The only two natural occurring stones other than chalk clunch, which does not weather well, are septaria and pudding stone. Septaria is mostly found in the clay beds of the north-east corner of the county in the form of an argillaceous limestone. The stone looks like a petrified clay in various shades of ochre or brown and it is used more frequently in the churches sited between the rivers Stour and Colne and down towards the Blackwater, such as Lawford, Great Bentley and Goldhanger.

Pudding stone is an unworkable natural concrete with pebbles showing; it is coloured in shades of russet and is sometimes used in the rubble walls, adding interest to the texture, as at Fryerning or Danbury. Kentish rag-stone is also found, transported from the quarries near Maidstone; it was used in the west tower at South Weald and St Andrew's, Ashingdon, and other churches towards the Thames. Mention should be made of flush-work, that beautiful East Anglian form of decoration consisting of knapped flint and stone, which combine to form patterns, on a level 'flush' surface. It is used with good effect in the porches at Ardleigh and Chelmsford cathedral, or in the embattled tower at Earls Colne, displaying the de Vere's mullet or star.

Norman

There are a surprisingly large number of **Norman (romanesque)** churches in Essex. Perhaps the Norman kings enjoined their newly rich followers to provide or rebuild a church for each settlement or parish; at any rate they were very active in church construction. Most of these buildings have a simple nave and chancel plan, suitable for their small congregations. Stondon Massey and South Shoebury are good examples, with a north and south doorway; the south one was usually more elaborate. Sometimes there is an apsidal east end, as at Copford and the two Braxteds; a rare exception is Langford, with an apse at the west. Copford had a tunnel-vaulted nave, now unfortunately destroyed – a rarity in England though common in France. Because of the small congregations, aisles were unusual; but some naves were very wide, as at Great Waltham and High Easter. The larger Norman church was cruciform with central crossing tower and this plan can be seen at Fyfield, Mount Bures and Boreham, all with central towers. There are a number of good Norman towers at the west end of their churches, particularly at Felsted, Stambourne, Finchingfield and Corringham. That at Great Tey is massive and was originally central. Round towers should also be mentioned here. Compared with Suffolk, where forty-one round towers still exist, Essex has but six surviving. They were built during the period of the Danish invasions, no doubt partly for defensive purposes or for storing valuables, although Bardfield Saling is as late as the fourteenth century. Some doorways have decorated columns as at South Ockendon; Copford has two kinds of capitals, cushion and acanthus scroll; North Ockendon has a stilted arch. More elaborate are those at High Ongar, Margaret Roding, Great Canfield with rare carving, and at Castle Hedingham. There are some fine romanesque chancel arches, such as Hadleigh or Great Hallingbury. South Shoebury has an unusual window head.

The Early English Style (Gothic)

The Norman style evolved gradually into the **Early English** style **(Gothic)** with its lancet windows and pointed arches about the end of the twelfth century, and it lasted for a century or so. The great work of this period is at Waltham Abbey, in the eastern portions started by Henry II and finished in 1242, now completely destroyed. Other examples in Essex are on a small scale; it seems as though there was a lull in church building activities after the enthusiasm of the previous era. Typical work in this style can be seen at Berden with its stiff-leafed capitals, and at Great Sampford and Newport. The chancel of Good Easter is interesting, with wall arcading; Mountnessing has interesting carved capitals; and Wethersfield a sturdy tower. The north arcade at Stisted, with circular piers and foliage capitals, is another example of this period. A fine arcade survives from the priory in the north wall of Little Dunmow, with four major and four minor shafts with alternate keeling. Maldon has a triangular tower which is unique.

The Decorated Style (Gothic)

Essex possesses some good examples of the **Decorated** style **(Gothic)** which followed during the reigns of Edward I, II and III, a style with flowing lines and ogee arches. At Lawford the chancel has elaborate tracery and foliage carvings, and at Tilty there is a fine east window in the chapel which survives from the former Cistercian monastery. Other good examples of this fourteenth century work may be seen in the south chapel at Waltham Abbey and at Little Dunmow, which has beautiful tracery to its four south windows, and at North Weald with its south chapel. The south aisle of All Saints, Maldon, should not be missed.

The quatrefoil section is used a good deal in the piers to arcades, with elaborations on the theme at Blackmore, Danbury and Henham. The nave piers at Thaxted are quatrefoil, with their shafts in the four corners, dating from the mid-fourteenth century; the two central arches have quadrant mouldings.

Quatrefoil windows may be seen in the clerestories of Little Sampford and Sible Hedingham, and in the porches of Great Bardfield and Stebbing. In these two churches are two remarkable stone screens of the fourteenth century; they are very beautiful and fill the chancel arch with their flowing tracery like one similar at Trondheim Cathedral in Norway. Great Sampford probably had a stone screen as well, but the connection between these screens is obscure. A rare example of fourteenth century work, although much restored, is the round church of the Knights Hospitallers at Little Maplestead, the last of the five round churches built in England.

The Perpendicular Style

Essex is less well represented in what is called the **Perpendicular** style of **late Gothic** architecture. This lasted roughly from Richard II's reign to mid-Tudor times, when parts of England prospered through the wool trade, and large churches were built in Norfolk and Suffolk. Only four churches need be mentioned which are comparable with those of adjacent counties: Saffron Walden, Dedham, Chelmsford and Thaxred, which was begun in the previous century by the de Clare family and their descendants.

Through its royal connections Thaxted was the richest of these churches, but Saffron Walden, begun in 1450, is the longest, nearly 200 ft. Dedham, built a little later (c.1500), lies close to the Suffolk border and takes on the characteristic of the neighbouring county. There are a number of fine towers and spires. Thaxted has an interesting spire, built probably by one of the famous Mortimer family; it is 181 ft high, and its construction is interesting. The tower at Dedham has a north-south passage-way beneath. Other good examples can be seen at Brightlingsea (100 ft high) or Canewdon (74 ft high). Sometimes the buttresses of these towers are connected diagonally, as at Great Dunmow, Bocking or Chelmsford. Many fine towers were built when brick became a fashionable material, as at Theydon Garnon, Ingatestone, Fryerning, Rayne and Rochford. In fact the use of brick in churches during Tudor times is a noteworthy characteristic of Essex churches. There are not only brick towers, of which about 30 were built, but also brick porches with stepped gables (Pebmarsh, Feering, Sandon), brick clerestories (Great Baddow), brick windows and tracery, brick arcades, even brick fonts (Chignal St Nicholas) and churches entirely of brick (Theydon Mount). The colour always seems pleasing and the skill of the brick-layers is evident in their diaper work, using dark blue or black headers to form a pattern, as at Sandon and Nazeing (west tower).

Window tracery is not outstanding, but the use of flushwork in panels to form a decorative pattern, produced some spectacular results as in the south porch at Chelmsford and Ardleigh.

Architectural elements in medieval churches

There are beautiful **porches** at Saffron Walden, which has a fan vault; at Thaxted, with a room above; and at Dedham, where the base of the tower acts as a porch. The fan vaults to the Littlebury porches were never completed. Thaxted and Saffron Walden have fine interiors; the piers to the arcades become more slender and elongated, the arches wider and the piers reduced. Chelmsford has slim piers with four shafts attached; and an octagonal pier with concave sides is also found at Prittlewell and Terling. The timber work in Essex is particularly noteworthy. Porches were seldom built before the fourteenth century, when it became customary for part of the baptism and marriage ceremonies to take place in them, as well as the announcement and discussion of parish matters. Some in Essex are very beautiful and resemble small houses, complete in themselves. Both Frating and Aldham have good examples of fourteenth century work, also to be found at White Notley; that at Radwinter was much restored in the nineteenth century. Benfleet has a very fine fifteenth century porch. Good Tudor work is found in Runwell's two porches, and also at Bulphan. Doddinghurst has an unusually long porch of about 1530.

Essex has some splendid timber **towers and belfries**, of an exceptionally high standard of craftmanship throughout several centuries. The belfries are in the south part of Essex; perhaps the oak trees grew more robustly there in gravelly soil and the trees were large enough to cut into required dimensions. Examples may be seen at Stock, Hanningfield, Margaretting, Blackmore and Navestock. Experts date Navestock's belfry as early as 1193, and claim that it was free-standing with an octagonal ground plan. The other belfries are later, and extend westward of the nave of the church with aisles round; they are designed as portal-frames, and are stabilised by shores, arch bracing and saltire bracing. At Blackmore the belfry rises like a pagoda; it is built against the Norman west wall and door of the priory church. Bulphan has lost its original spire, but follows the pattern of aisles round north, west and south. These belfries are an almost unique feature of Essex churches.

There are few remarkable timber **roofs** of the fourteenth century or later compared with those found in Suffolk and Norfolk. Portions of some roofs in Essex churches are of great antiquity, such as that in the chancel at Chipping Ongar, where the nine rafter couples at the east end seem contemporary with the building of the chancel (Norman, c.1080). The nave roof at Hadstock may be very old, pre-Norman; somewhat surprisingly, the Saxon builders may have known the methods of southern European roof construction. Many churches have the tie-beam type of roof, with king post and four struts. The ambitious type of double hammer beam roof may be seen at Castle Hedingham; there are only four examples in the county, the others being at Great Bromley, Sturmer and Gestingthorpe. The latter was wrought by a local carpenter, Thomas Loveday, who died in 1535; he may also have worked at Castle Hedingham. At Tendring there are about six examples of single hammer beam roofs, and a very early single truss linked to elaborate door surrounds, of the fourteenth century.

Post medieval churches

Only a few churches were built during the later Tudor and early Jacobean periods, as replacements for existing churches. Woodham Walter has one of red Elizabethan brick; Theydon Mount was built a little later by the Smith family of nearby Hill Hall, a charming small brick church. There were of course alterations and additions to buildings, often in brick, such as the chapels at Ingatestone and the north chapel at Stapleford Abbots, with its arched windows.

The Georgian period has not a great deal to offer. At Ingrave there is an interesting church of 1735, built in the manner of Hawksmoor; and at Mistley only the towers at each end survive of Robert Adams' unusual and unorthodox design. There are some good towers of this period at Toppesfield, Bradwell and Terling. The interior of Lambourne has a classical appearance, and should not be missed; Debden has some excellent eighteenth century Gothick work. John Johnson restored the 'cathedral' at Chelmsford in 1801 after its partial collapse, and there is an interesting Gothick church of 1838 at East Donyland in white brick.

The growth of population in Victorian times, the coming of the railway, and the expansion of London and other towns all stimulated church building in Essex. All styles of architecture were attempted and some are worth studying. There is a neo-Norman design of 1846 at St John's, Loughton, and others by Gilbert Scott at Halstead and St Nicholas, Colchester; also noteworthy are the work of Burges at Waltham Abbey on the infilling of the east end; Lee's big church at Brentwood; and Bodley and Garner's fine new church in Epping in 1889. There was great Victorian activity in church restoration with varying results; but at least the buildings were saved from decay after the neglect of the previous century. The Art Nouveau style is represented by Great Warley (1904) and St Thomas, Upshire; and modern churches may be seen in the new towns of Harlow and Basildon.

Furnishings

Church furnishings can only be dealt with briefly. So many were damaged or destroyed in Tudor and Puritan times that few **screens** are left which bear comparison with those in adjacent counties. The older ones have columns with shaft-rings, as at Magdalen Laver and Corringham. Later in date and richer are those at Finchingfield, Castle Hedingham and Henham; in their day they would have been gilded and coloured. The stone screens at Great Bardfield and Stebbing are famous.

Fonts make an interesting study, and there are so many good Norman examples that one wonders if they were produced in quantity at some specific centre. Often the bowl is square and the sides decorated with blank arcades, fleur de lis or sun and moon. Those at Fyfield, Moreton and Fryerning are typical. The thirteenth century is less well represented, but Springfield font has good stiff-leaf foliage carving and Newport gabled arches; that at Roydon has men at the corners wearing interesting hats. The later octagonal fonts, with quatrefoil decoration and shields inset, are quite common. There is a rare fifteenth century wooden font at Marks Tey. Sadly most of the fine font covers were destroyed; they are found only at Takeley, Thaxted, Littlebury and a few other places.

Pulpits were not constructed in early times, as the parish priest seldom preached; but there are some good Elizabethan and later examples. Great Baddow's is a notable Jacobean design and the fifteenth century pulpit at Sandon stands on a trumpet base. There are some good eighteenth century examples, such as at Theydon Garnon with a tester, and at Thaxted.

There are some fine old **lecterns** of the fifteenth century, as at Hadstock, Newport and Ridgewell; and quite a lot of **chests** or coffers, some dug-out, others iron-bound. The chest at Newport, which acted as a portable altar, has early oil paintings on the wooden lid inside, which lifts to form a reredos.

Of the few surviving **wall paintings** a spectacular twelfth century cycle at Copford church should not be missed, despite Victorian restoration. There is a beautiful Virgin and Child of the thirteenth century, centrally placed behind the altar at Great Canfield. At Fairstead the stories of the Passion are depicted over the chancel arch; and there are other good examples at Lambourne and Little Easton, and a Doom at Waltham Abbey.

Medieval **stained glass** has been dreadfully damaged through the centuries and little survives in Essex. The church at Rivenhall contains some twelfth and thirteenth century French glass intoduced in the last century. There are fourteenth century saints at Newport, at Thaxted beautiful fragments have been carefully re-assembled in the north chapel, and there are some later windows elsewhere. Good glass may be seen at Great Bardfield, Sheering, Margaretting and Stambourne. Messing has well known seventeenth century glass by van Linge in the chancel. Among the many examples of Victorian stained glass, Kempe did some good work in a number of churches including Epping and Thaxted. Burne-Jones designed glass for Waltham Abbey's new east wall.

The **brasses** and **church monuments** of the county deserve a book to themselves. Briefly, there is a fine early brass of 1323 to Sir William

Fitzralph in Pebmarsh church; figures at Bowers Gifford of the same century; unusual figures in a cross at Wimbish (partly damaged); and others at Chrishall and Harlow. At Wivenhoe lies the Countess of Oxford in her heraldic cloak; and a late brass at Chigwell depicts the bishop who founded the parish school. There are many more. Interesting carved oak effigies of about 1250 are found at Danbury and at Little Baddow. Often these depict knights, who lie cross-legged; Thorpe-le-Soken contains one, as does Elmstead. There are many alabaster monuments and splendid tombs. A fifteenth century monument to the Fitzwalters at Little Dunmow is of high quality, and the Earls of Sussex lie serenely at Boreham. Among the many splendid tombs worth visiting are those of the Smiths at Theydon Mount, the Petres at Ingatestone and Lord Rich at Felsted. Fine carving and lettering of the Renaissance, Georgian and Victorian periods may be seen on the monuments in so many churches; the tomb slabs and stones should also be noted. Families such as the Plantagenets, Bourchiers, de Veres and Nevilles are all commemorated among the wealth of tomb sculpture to be found in Essex churches.

Hatchments often hang on the walls of Essex churches, and make an interesting subject for study. These lozenge-shaped shields of canvas, stretched on a wooden frame and painted with the coat of arms of local dignitaries on their death, were hung outside the house of the deceased during the period of mourning and then transferred to the church. This custom was introduced in the seventeenth century, and much can be learnt about the local families from the heraldic devices shown thereon. There are good examples at Chigwell, Orsett, Theydon Mount, and in many other churches.

Royal Arms are sometimes found in churches. Henry VIII proclaimed himself Supreme Head of the Church of England in 1534, and at one time nearly all churches possessed a set of Royal Arms. Those prior to 1649 rarely survive, most of them having been removed during the Commonwealth period; but a well-known carving at Waltham Abbey bears the Tudor arms, and there is another of Elizabeth I's time at Middleton. Theydon Bois contains a painting with the Stuart arms, and Messing has a carved achievement of Charles I. Following Charles II's restoration in 1660, the royal arms were again displayed and there are examples of this period at Finchingfield, Great Baddow and so on. Unfortunately many of these colourful Royal Arms were lost during nineteenth century restorations.

In recent years the Church of England has been faced with the problem of maintaining so many historic and architecturally interesting churches; Essex has proved no exception to this rule. Through rising building costs, a shifting population and declining congregations, a number of churches have had to be declared redundant and put to other uses; a few have been demolished. A list of parish churches is included here which are no longer used for worship and have been adapted for other purposes.

GAZETTEER

Abberton, St Andrew: This church, which lies close to the south Essex reservoir, was restored in 1884 but dates from the fourteenth century. The west tower is of Tudor brick with its dark diaper pattern and contains one bell.

Abridge, Holy Trinity: The church is a simple brick building of the late nineteenth century.

Aldham, St Margaret: This rather picturesque Victorian church was built by Hakewill in 1855. It stands a mile away from its predecessor, but much of the old material was incorporated in the rebuilding. The timberwork of the porch, with ogee tracery and barge boards, is good and dates from the fourteenth century. The medieval doors also survive with iron work. Morant, the historian of Essex, was rector here in the eighteenth century, and the church contains his gravestone.

Alphamstone: This church, which has no known dedication, overlooks the Stour valley; it was much restored by the Victorian architect, Sir Arthur Blomfield. The nave is plastered externally; the chancel is built of Tudor brick, and flintwork of a nineteenth-century restoration. Most of the nave is early thirteenth century. It has a blocked Norman window and plain north doorway; the windows are thirteenth, fourteenth and fifteenth century. The wooden belfry contains three Tudor bells. In the chancel there is a good triple sedilia, framed in with the piscina, with cusped arches on detached shafts; note too the low side windows. The south arcade of three bays with octagonal piers dates from the fourteenth century. The square Norman font, of the Purbeck type, has blank arcading on each side.

Alresford, St Peter: This is a small lonely church. It was built around 1300 by Aufrey de Staunton, who is commemorated by a stone in the chancel; perhaps he rebuilt an earlier church on this site. The building has Roman bricks in the quoins at the west end of the nave and there has been much restoration. The timber belfry, with a shingled spire, contains one bell. Inside, a west gallery has twisted eighteenth-century balusters and there is a window by William Morris at the east end.

Althorne, St Andrew: The church is early Tudor. Inside, an interesting brass to William Ayklott (1508) declares that he 'paide for the workmanship of the walls of this churche'. The flint nave has battlements; the chancel, of Tudor brick, has a Victorian east window. The Perpendicular tower is built of flint and rag stone and has battlements which are trellis patterned in ashlar. Over the west door runs an inscription in Latin requesting prayers for the souls of John Wilson and John Hill, who presumably paid for the building of the tower. The octagonal font, also of the Perpendicular period, has carved panels depicting amongst other things the baptism of a king and the martyrdom of St Andrew.

Arkesden, St Mary: The church is set in a pretty village. It is built of flint rubble. The chancel and nave date from about 1250, but there was much restoration in 1855 when the west tower was built. The foundations of a circular Norman tower were then discovered. Roof, clerestory and chancel arch are of this restoration. Inside, the south arcade has medieval circular columns, and the north aisle was rebuilt in the sixteenth century by a rich fishmonger. The font has a square Norman bowl on a clunch pedestal of the thirteenth century, with pointed openings to each side. The monuments are good. An effigy of a fifteenth-century priest lies in the north wall of the chancel, in a low recess. There is a large sixteenth-century monument to Richard Cutte and his family, who lived at Horham Hall, near Thaxted. There is a good monument to John Withers (1692) attributed to Edward Pearce (Great Canfield has a similar work); and a brass to a fifteenth-century knight, Richard Fox.

Ardleigh, St Mary: This is a large flint church with a lofty west tower of c.1500 with diagonal buttresses. The rest of the church was extensively rebuilt by Butterfield in 1885, leaving little unrestored, except for the nave's west bay and the very handsome south porch of c.1500. It is built of flint and stone, and is a good example of East Anglian flush-work. The diagonal buttresses have stone panels with traceried heads to each stage and are finished with octagonal shafts supporting seated beasts. The archway is two-centred; the label is stopped with crowned lions on foliated brackets and the spandrels are carved with figures of St George and the Dragon. Above the arch are three niches with buttressed jambs and elaborately traceried and crocketed canopies. In each side wall is a window of three cinquefoiled lights. Inside, the surviving base of the fifteenth-century chancel screen has richly carved panels. The south door of 1460 is good, with rich tracery.

Ashdon, All Saints: The parish name derives from the Saxon Ash tree hill, and there may well have been a Saxon church here, built of flint. The present building stands in a picturesque churchyard; its plan is irregular, and the plinths below the piers suggest an early date. The chancel is thirteenth century, though the sedilia and piscina are fourteenth century insertions. The nave was rebuilt with three-bay arcades, aisles and clerestory, early in the fifteenth century; its octofoil clerestory windows are rather unusual. The fine Tyrrel chapel, south of the chancel, is dated about 1320; it is taller than the chancel itself, with good reticulated tracery around its east window, and is separated from the chancel by a two-bay arcade, whose fourteenth century column is circular and the arches moulded. The tower was added to the original structure about 1365; its walls are about 4 ft thick. Both north and south porches are fifteenth century. Inside, there is a fine early sixteenth century tomb chest in the chancel to Thomas Tyrrel of Warley (Essex) and Ashdon Place, now known as Waltons. There are remains of good medieval glass in the south aisle window, with angels and interesting armorial shields. The roof, mostly fourteenth century, is also noteworthy.

Asheldham, St Lawrence: The church is built on the site of an ancient British settlement, where the land rises above the marshes. It is mostly fourteenth century, although the very thick walls suggest an earlier date. The west tower is built of yellow septaria, some flint and odd Roman bricks. Nave and chancel have some cusped lancet windows and ogee detail. The piscina and sedilia in the chancel are a notable feature; they are grouped with the window and south doorway. The church was restored in 1867.

Ashen, St Augustine of Canterbury: This is a small church, with a thirteenth century nave of flint rubble. A west tower with buttresses and battlements was added early in the fifteenth century; it has a brick stair turret, with battlements on a Tudor corbel table. The three bells date from before the Reformation. The south porch shelters an ancient door with thirteenth century ironwork. The chancel is Victorian. Inside a carving reads 'This hath bin the churching, the mearring [marrying] stoole and so it shall be still 1620'. There is a brass to a knight (1440), a monument to Luce Tullakorne (1610), and marble monuments of 1721 and 1752.

Ashingdon, St Andrew: This was once the parish of Assundune, where Canute defeated the Saxons led by Edmund Ironside. It is recorded that, four years later in 1020, he built a church of stone and lime to commemorate his victory. As the first priest he appointed his chaplain Stigand, who later became Archbishop of Canterbury. Perhaps some materials of the existing small church suvive from those days; it is built of flint rubble, Tudor brick and Roman brick, and Kentish rag-stone which was added later. The present nave and chancel and also the small west tower would seem to be early fourteenth century. The brick east wall of the chancel is Tudor, and the brick south window to the nave is eighteenth century. The medieval roof trusses are good.

Aveley, St Michael: The church is built of roughly coursed flint and rag-stone, with some Roman bricks. The nave is early twelfth century. Its south aisle was added c.1160, and the north aisle c.1220. The chancel was rebuilt in the mid-thirteenth century, and the north chapel and west tower were added at the same time. In the fifteenth century the north porch was added and the upper part of the tower rebuilt. Although it was restored in 1886, the church retains a strong element of Norman and Early English work, with its north and south arcades of both periods. The square Norman font is of Purbeck stone, with arcaded ornament on the sides. The Flemish brass of 1370 to Ralph de Knevynton, an effigy in armour under an elaborate canopy, is noteworthy. The screen is fifteenth century, and the pulpit with its tester dates from 1620.

Great Baddow, St Mary: The church catches the eye with its west tower, built of flint rubble and capped with a lead spire, which contrasts with the rose-red Tudor brick clerestory. There was a Saxon and later a Norman church here, but only fragments of the latter remain. The original nave walls were pierced with three-bay arcades of the thirteenth century. The north arcade is older, with one circular and otherwise octagonal piers; its west head corbel is worth studying. The south arcade has circular piers and double-chamfered arches. The interesting south doorway was re-sited, and windows of the Decorated period were later inserted, which have been renewed a good deal. The tower was also built or rebuilt in the fourteenth century, with angle buttresses which do not run full height.

When brick was becoming a fashionable building material in early Tudor times, the fine brick clerestory was added, with its battlements on a trefoil corbel frieze and its pinnacles, and diaper work. North and south chancel chapels were also added, and later the brick south porch. The chancel dormers were built in the nineteenth century, probably together with the vestry.

Of interest is the great pulpit (1639) carved with the churchwarden's initials. It is the best of its kind in the county, with a beautiful tester, long back panel and elaborate carving. There is a notable brass to Jane Lewkenor (1614); and in the south aisle, a fine eighteenth century monument by Cheere to the Gwyns and Mrs Antrim. The eight hatchments and the royal coat of arms of 1660 are good.

Little Baddow, St Mary the Virgin: This church is set on the north edge of the village. There is a Norman doorway in the north wall; but the church was evidently widened in the fourteenth century, when the west tower was built and windows were inserted. The walls are of rubble with some Roman tiles. Inside on the south wall, linked with the piscina, are two recesses of the Decorated period, in which beautifully carved fourteenth century oak effigies of a man and woman lie on tomb chests. In the chancel is a resplendent monument to Sir Henry Mildmay (1639), who lived at Graces in the parish, and who fought in the Irish wars (see Mildmay family at Chelmsford). Below him kneel his two wives. There is some fourteenth century stained glass in the east window, and a wall painting of St Christopher.

Great Bardfield, St Mary: This is a parish church of much interest, set on the south fringe of the village which was perhaps moved after the devastating effects of the Black Death of 1349; this would seem to have been fairly common in Essex.

The west tower is early thirteenth century, built of flint without buttresses and with lancet windows. The rest of the church is fourteenth century, when it was probably rebuilt by Edmund Mortimer to commemorate his wife, Philippa, daughter of Lionel, Duke of Clarence, and heiress of the Clare estates through her mother, Elizabeth de Burgh (see Thaxted) who owned much property in this area.

The arcades of four bays have piers with four polygonal shafts and slim circular shafts in the diagonals. The windows are unusual because although dating from the fourteenth century, they are straight-headed; some have been renewed. The south porch has a quatrefoil window either side (cf. Stebbing porch), as well as a two-light window. The great glory of the church is its stone chancel screen, comparable with the beautiful one in Stebbing church but later in date – this one is about 1377; on each side are carved heads said to be of Edward III (who died that year) and Philippa, his queen. The screen is tripartite, the two shafts running up into the arch, heralding the Perpendicular style. The rich cusping and crocketting and carved medieval figures are worth studying, although the central rood figures are a reconstruction of 1892 by Bodley. The screen seems to have links with that in Trondheim Cathedral, Norway, as well as that at Stebbing and there may have been a similar one at Great Sampford; a stone screen is to be found at Bramford, Suffolk, dating from the early fourteenth century, but it is not as elaborate. The other carved head stops in the nave should be noticed, and also the carved oak door in the south porch which is fourteenth century, with remains of much fine carving. On either side of the doorway are the weather-worn heads of a king and queen, perhaps Edward III and Philippa again.

The carved organ case of c.1840 is reputed to be by Pugin, and its Gothic style fits very well in the chancel which has elaborately carved tie beams. There is also a very good brass to Alienor Bendlowes (1584) set on a tomb-chest/sedilia on the south side; she was the wife of William Bendlowes, Sergeant-at-Law to Queen Elizabeth I and lived at Place House in the High Street.

Though most of the stained glass is Victorian or later, the fragments of late fourteenth century glass in the north aisle are remarkable, especially the Mortimer shields in the west window, depicting the coats of arms of Edmund Mortimer and his wife, Philippa. (There is also a window in Thaxted church with the Mortimer shield borne by a knight in armour.) Note St Lawrence with his grid-iron, and St Stephen in a window further east; and a Crucifixion, also medieval fragments.

Little Bardfield, St Katharine: Sited next to Little Bardfield Hall, this church has a fine Saxon tower and nave. The tower, built about 1050 of flint and pebble rubble with some Roman tiles, is in five recessed stages with round-headed windows in the third, fourth and fifth stage; none of the Saxon windows has any dressing to jambs or cills. There are two Saxon windows in the nave, the one beside the south porch being double splayed. In typical Saxon fashion there are no true right angles in the setting out of tower and nave. The chancel is fourteenth century but much restored. In the Victorian organ chamber is a fine organ of c.1700 with its carved case from a Cambridge college and said to be by Renatus Harris. The nave roof with its king posts is probably fourteenth century.

Bardfield Saling, St Peter and St Paul: This small church, which is picturesque in its rural detachment, is built entirely of flint. Its round tower is one of the six surviving in Essex, of a later construction than the others; it seems to date from the fourteenth century, as does the rest of the building. There are good windows of the Decorated period and inside the piers to the south arcade are quatrefoil with keeled shafts in the diagonals; they look handsome (cf. Shalford). There is a screen of the same period with ogee arches and quatrefoils. The pulpit is a fine example of the Tudor style with arches in perspective carved on it. The chancel was reduced to its small size in Victorian times.

Barling, All Saints: The benefice of this church was presented to the dean and chapter of St Paul's by Edward the Confessor. It is a small stone Norman building with a south doorway of the same period; the massive west tower was added in the fifteenth century with its diagonal buttresses with a frieze of flint and stone chequer work above the west window, and ogee-headed niches. The north aisle is about the same date with octagonal arcade piers. The old rood stairs can still be seen. The font is the octagonal Perpendicular kind, and there is a panelled oak pulpit with sounding board. Also noteworthy are two carved alabaster figures of fifteenth century priests.

Barnston: The church, well sited close to Barnston Hall, has a Norman name with three Norman windows and south doorway, its columns having scalloped capitals. The chancel is Early English and the double piscina deserves attention with its intersecting round arches (like those of Jesus College, Cambridge (c.1220), St John's College and the tower gateway at Bury St Edmunds). The shafts have capitals carved with stiff-leaf foliage which run behind as a decorative frieze. The little belfry has an eighteenth century cupola.

Basildon, Holy Cross: This small church, on its hill, is built of rag-stone, rubble and brick. The nave is fourteenth century, the unbuttressed west tower dates from about 1500, and the chancel was rebuilt in brick in 1597. The church was much repaired in 1702 when the weather vane was added. The timber-framed south porch is good mid-fifteenth century work; and on the spandrel of the roof truss are carved a bear with ragged staff and a dragon.

Beaumont cum Maze: The church of Maze (meaning Marsh) has long since been demolished and its materials used to rebuild St Leonard's, the existing church, which is of Norman origin but was rebuilt to Hakewill's designs in 1854. It has a nave, chancel and an open stone bell turret at the west, like a pyramid, with angels north and south.

High Beech, Holy Innocents: This church stands in the heart of Epping Forest; it was built in 1873 by Sir Arthur Blomfield of grey stone. It has a north-west tower, transepts, apse and good Victorian stained glass.

Belchamp St Paul, St Andrew: The village is named 'St Paul' because Athelstan granted it to St Paul's Cathedral in 990 AD. The church was rebuilt in the fifteenth century, with nave, chancel and west tower with diagonal buttresses and battlements; it was restored in Victorian times. Both nave and chancel roof are Tudor and of much interest. The chancel stalls which are the only misericord seats in Essex other than those at Castle Hedingham. There are Tudor brasses to the Golding family and tablets recording the Pembertons, vicars of the parish.

Belchamp Walter, St Mary: The church has a thirteenth century chancel, a fourteenth century nave with windows of intersecting tracery and cusping, a fifteenth century timber south porch with good barge boards and diagonal mullions and a west tower of the same century with diagonal buttresses, battlements, stair turret and a tall west window of three lights. The nave contains an interesting wall painting of the Virgin and Child dating from the fourteenth century, a circular Norman font and an ornate fourteenth century recess decorated with foliage and shields but without its tomb chest or effigy. There is also a good monument of 1720 to Sir John Raymond with cherubs and pilasters, signed by Robert Taylor.

North Benfleet, All Saints: This small church stands near the site of the old moated hall. It has a Norman window in the nave's west wall, and a Tudor brick window of two lights with panel tracery. The tower is of 1703, but the timber construction of the belfry with braces and trellis strutting is Tudor. The font is thirteenth century, with six pointed arches to each side. Outside the old porch is a tombstone of 1836 to John Cole, a soldier at Waterloo, with an interesting inscription.

South Benfleet, St Mary: The church is imposing. There is a Norman doorway in the west wall of the nave, which has quite large Norman windows above, blocked when the church was subsequently enlarged. The west tower with its small spire is fourteenth century. The nave was given a clerestory and aisles in the Perpendicular style, also the chancel. The south porch is particularly good, with impressive carpentry work of the fifteenth century; it has a single hammer-beam roof, beautiful tracery to the eight lights each side, and cusped barge boarding. This is one of the finest porches in Essex. The nave was heightened in 1902. The west organ gallery and chancel screen of 1931 were both designed by Sir Charles Nicholson.

Bentley Common, St Paul: A Victorian church of 1878 by E.C.Lee, who also designed St Thomas', Brentwood. Set in a trim churchyard amongst trees, it is built of flint with stone dressings for the most part in Victorian Early English style. It has chancel, nave, south aisle and a tower placed unexpectedly on the north-east with broach spire, shingled, and a good staircase turret.

Great Bentley, St Mary the Virgin: The church, near the large village green, dates from about 1130, its walls built of coursed pudding stone laid herring-bone fashion with some septaria. There are Norman doorways north and south, the latter with scalloped capitals and lintel decorated with rosettes/sunflowers. The east end of the chancel was restored in the nineteenth century when the chancel arch was built but it contains two pretty niches of the fourteenth century with ogee heads and leafy spandrels. The west tower is also fourteenth century, with diagonal buttresses, doorway, and three-light window. The font is octagonal with trefoil and shields; and there are some medieval tiles in the chancel, with patterns depicting animals.

Little Bentley, St Mary the Virgin: The nave is Norman, and the chancel thirteenth century with stepped east lancet windows; the north aisle dates from the Perpendicular period but was much renewed with brick in Tudor times, when a south porch was built. The west tower is fifteenth century and looks well with its mixed stone, flint and brick; it was later heightened in brick and given battlements. The hammer-beam roof to the nave is very fine though sadly the angels have been beheaded. There is a brass of 1490 to Sir William Pyrton and his family; his arms are also on the octagonal font.

Berden, St Nicholas: The church is cruciform and two blocked Norman windows at the west end of the nave show its origins; but the transepts and chancel are thirteenth century of varying dates, and the west tower is a fifteenth century addition. Particularly interesting are the internal thirteenth century shafts to some of the windows, and the stiff-leaf carved enrichments to capitals and friezes of about 1260. The church was restored in Victorian times, and the east window is part of this work although it is in the Early English style. The organ of 1780 is believed to have belonged to Samuel Wesley, the church musician.

Berechurch, St Michael and All Angels: The west tower, built in red brick during early Tudor times, has diagonal buttresses and battlements. Of much interest is the north chapel built by the Audley family, who rose to fame in Henry VIII's reign and went from Colchester to establish themselves at Audley End; it has a splendid early sixteenth century hammer-beam roof, some of whose timbers are richly decorated with foliage motifs, and a fine monument to Sir Henry Audley, as a figure in armour with his children kneeling. There are also monuments to Sir Robert Smyth (1802) and to Mrs Charlotte White (1845). The south door with portions of linen fold panelling and tracery deserves inspection.

West Bergholt, St Mary: The church stands near the red brick hall. Nave, chancel and south aisle are mostly fourteenth century, with windows of the Decorated style; inside is an arcade of octagonal piers with double-chamfered arches. A small west gallery is supported on Tuscan columns. The west belfry, which stands on heavy tie beams, may be fifteenth century.

Billericay, St Mary Magdalene: The church stands in the High Street, with its good red brick fifteenth century tower on the pavement; the tower has buttresses that set back; the chamfered angles continue up and form a side of the polygonal pinnacles; a trefoil arch corbel frieze carries the stepped battlements and there is a good two-light west window with brick tracery. The remaining brick west front is in the same style but of a later date. The rest of the church is pleasant Georgian with shallow apses at the east end and on the north side of the aisle. Inside, galleries supported on slender cast iron columns run round three sides of the nave. Worth noticing are the eighteenth century communion rails, the font with its cherub heads and the carved royal arms of George I on the west gallery, and the stained glass (1880) in the two east windows.

Birch, St Mary: This is a Victorian church of 1850 by Teulon, in the Decorated style; it has a tall west steeple with a bell of 1737. The two parishes of Great and Little Birch are united, and the old church has been abandoned.

Birchanger, St Mary the Virgin: This small church, formerly possessed of a round tower, is built of flint, with a Norman nave and chancel added a century later; but it was much restored in Victorian times and a north aisle added by Sir Arthur Blomfield. No doubt at the same time the north Norman doorway was re-set as the west doorway when perhaps the round tower was demolished. Both Norman doorways are good, but the south one particularly so, for as well as its decoration of saltire crosses and unusual foliage or fleurs-de-lis along the extrados of the arch, it has a figure carved on its tympanum, a lamb with four rather long legs – the only figure carving of this kind in Essex.

Birdbrook, St Augustine of Canterbury: Set in a pleasant village, the small church is of Norman origin – there is herring-bone masonry in the north walls and a blocked Norman window. The nave was lengthened in the thirteenth century and also the chancel. There are two groups of three lancet windows of this period; at the east end with hood moulds and blank quatrefoils above and between, and in the west wall. Note the tablet recording that 'Martha Blewitt had nine husbands before her death in 1681' and Robert Hogan who had seven wives. There are also a number of monuments of the eighteenth and nineteenth century, including that of Thomas Walford, an historian who lived nearby. The nave roof is of considerable interest.

Blackmore, St Lawrence: This was originally the church of the priory for which the Bishop of London gave his authority in 1155. It was to have 12 canons and a prior of the Augustinian order. The west end of the nave remains Norman, with a west doorway, originally outside, that has three orders of columns and two Norman windows above with a circular window over. The first bays on each side are also Norman, with their upper windows. East of them, the north aisle has quatrefoil piers and moulded arches, while the south aisle has octagonal sixteenth century brick piers – this is because the priory was dissolved in 1525 by Henry VIII and granted in 1540 to John Smyth, one of the king's auditors, who converted the building into a parish church.

Henry himself used to visit Blackmore to see Elizabeth Tailbois, his mistress, at 'Jericho Priory' next door; and here his illegitimate son, the Duke of Richmond, was born in 1519. All traces of the rest of the priory have vanished; the doorway to the cloisters is at the east end of the south aisle, but is now blocked.

The striking feature of the church is the sixteenth century west tower built of oak and pagoda-like in its shape. It is in three stages, and is a most elaborate piece of carpentry, the largest post being 22 in x 19 in.; it is crowned by a shingled broach spire; internally, it possesses ten posts, making a nave and two aisles. Its construction is worth studying.

South of the altar on a tomb chest lie the two alabaster effigies of Thomas Smyth and his wife (1594) who rebuilt the east end of the nave after the priory was demolished; there are also good floor slabs to other Smyths with armorial bearings and fine lettering.

Bobbingworth, St Germain: The church stands pleasantly in the centre of the scatterd village, but was mostly rebuilt in different stages during the last century. The north-west tower of brick was built in 1841 and resembles that at High Ongar (1858); the chancel is of similar date (1840), and the nave was refaced in Victorian times. The pulpit has early seventeenth century decoration. The fifteenth century bowl of the font was found in the churchyard of Little Parndon and eventually returned here to its original position.

Timber tower at Blackmore

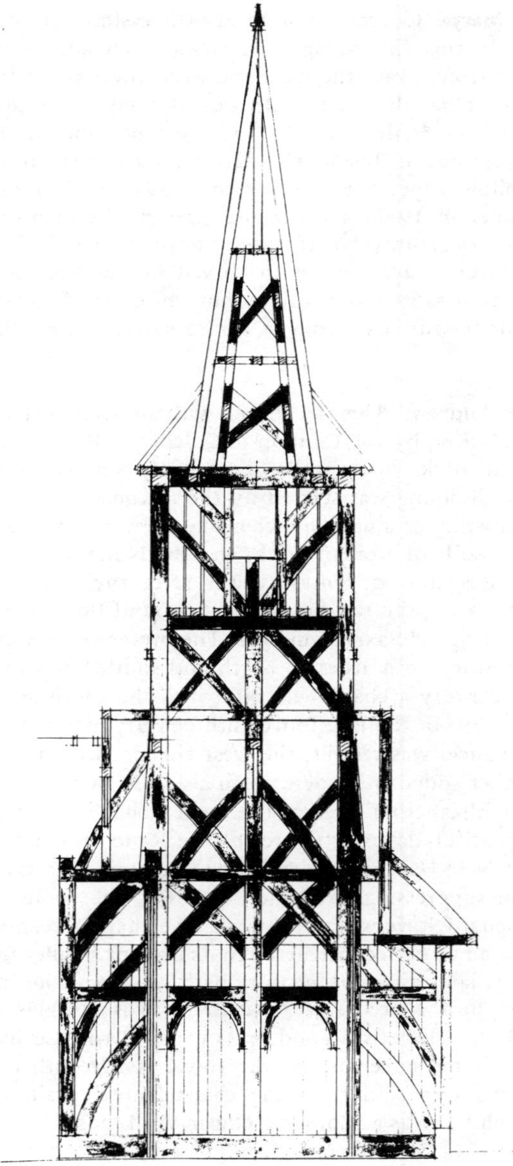

Blackmore: E-W section of fifteenth-century timber belfry. Drawn by John Hough after a drawing by Leonard Edwards.

Bocking, St Mary: Courtaulds showed little taste when they built their factory beside this fine village church. The chancel, mostly of flint rubble, dates from 1340; the nave and west tower are of the next century. The tower has diagonal buttresses of unusual design, and a stair turret as well as battlements. In 1520 a handsome south porch and clerestory were added. Inside, the nave piers are of the four shafts with diagonal hollow type; the fine screen is 1910 with additions by Sir Ninian Comper in 1950. The stained glass is Victorian or after, some given by the Courtaulds. Worth careful inspection is the beautiful early sixteenth century nave roof with carved bosses and spandrels. Also good are some brasses and a wall monument of 1624 to Gresell Moore. The south door with its scrolls is a rare survival from the thirteenth century.

Boreham, St Andrew: This is a church with an irregular plan and a long history. Sited close by the London to Colchester Roman road and with many Roman bricks in its walls, it probably stands on the site of a Roman villa. Building was started by the Saxons in the early eleventh century, consisting of a nave and chancel; the west tower arch was their chancel arch, built of Roman brick, and the Normans then turned the existing chancel into a central tower after their fashion, adding a chancel to the east; the windows on the ground floor of the tower are probably the original Saxon windows. The present nave was built in the thirteenth century with aisles to north and south 5 ft 9 in. wide. Later in the same century a chapel was built into the south aisle – this was restored in 1909. In the late fourteenth century many alterations were made; the chancel was rebuilt, the west chancel arch inserted, a south porch of timber added and a new north aisle 13 ft wide.

In Queen Elizabeth I's reign, the Sussex chapel was built to house the three beautiful alabaster figures of the Radcliffes (Earls of Sussex) who lived at New Hall nearby, which had been given to them by Queen Elizabeth for suppressing a rebellion in 1569. The white alabaster was carved by Richard Stevens of Southwark. The chapel became dilapidated in 1860 and had to be reconstructed in its present smaller form.

The font is late thirteenth century with its unusual hexagonal shape, but the tiles in the arches are Victorian, as is the glass in the west window (1880). There is a good brass of 1573 to Alse Byng, and the upper part of the screen under the tower is fifteenth century. Also worth noticing is a squint on the chancel north wall; was there an anchorite's cell there as at Chipping Ongar and Lindsell?

Borley, dedication unknown: Some fine old yews in the churchyard lead up to a Tudor porch of brick. The church has a chancel and west tower with slender diagonal buttresses and battlements. The nave could be Norman with its thick walling. Inside is a canopied tomb with six columns and recumbent effigies to Sir Edward Waldegrave, who was an official at Mary Tudor's court and was later inprisoned by Elizabeth for his Roman leanings; he died in the Tower. The Waldegrave family also lived at Navestock. In the chancel is a monument of 1598 to Magdala Southcote. Also note a floor slab to Humphrey Burrough (1757) a rector here and uncle of the painter Gainsborough who lived at Sudbury.

Bowers Gifford, St Margaret: The church is small and isolated; the ragstone west tower has shingled spire and one large buttress at the south-west corner, its wooden super-structure carried internally on four posts with trellis strutting. Inside is a fine brass of a 6 ft tall figure, supposedly Sir John Gifford (1348); though incomplete, the details of the armour and costume are of much interest. The chancel screen of 1926 is by Sir Charles Nicholson.

Boxted, St Peter: The church has a Norman nave and north tower of pudding stone, finished during the sixteenth century in Tudor brick and given diagonal buttresses and battlements. The nave walls were cut through in the fourteenth century to make north and south arcades, the piers being the full thickness of the walls. The chancel arch is Norman with plain imposts and roll moulding. Over it are two fourteenth century windows. The small clerestory windows have been supplemented by dormer windows, making the interior a little unusual. At the west end is a gallery of 1836 on cast iron columns. There is a monument carved with an angel and a skeleton to Elizabeth, wife of Nathaniel Bacon (1628); and another to Sir Richard Blackmore (1729), who was physician to William III and Queen Anne, and also a poet and school master; together with a long Latin epitaph to his wife Mary.

Bradfield, St Lawrence: The church is mostly thirteenth century. There is dog-tooth decoration on the piscina in the chancel, and there are lancet windows (renewed) in the nave. The top of the tower was rebuilt in brick and given corbel tables. The fourteenth century bell inside has the inscription 'I am cock (Koc) of this flock wit Gloria tibi Domine'. The transepts are nineteenth century and the outside has been cement rendered. Inside is a font of the thirteenth century and there is a brass to Joane Risbye (1598). The pulpit has some carving on it, probably seventeenth century.

Bradwell near Coggeshall, Holy Trinity: The walls of the church, in a pretty rural setting, are a pleasant mixture of flint, pudding stone and Roman brick dressings. Nave and chancel have a number of Norman windows, and north and south doorways, but there are some good windows of the Decorated period added in and the east window of later date. The south porch is fourteenth century with tracery of the period at the side but seventeenth century balusters have been inserted below, which is unusual. Inside is a good fifteenth century screen and some very interesting wall paintings in red and pink dating from the early fourteenth century; together with the belfry, which could date from the original building of the church and whose saltire bracing and notched lap-joints should be noted, these make the church of considerable interest. Behind the altar is a fine monument to the Maxey family of 1592, two arched recesses flanked by black columns.

Bradwell on sea, St Peter-on-the-Wall: This must be the church founded by St Cedd* in AD 654, in which case it is the oldest church in Essex, and one of the oldest in England, standing on a lonely site where the Blackwater runs into the North Sea. This church is built almost entirely of re-used Roman materials, ashlar, septaria and brick, and stands astride the former west wall of the great Roman fort of Othona. This fort is known to have been 520 ft long, we do not know its width as the east walls have been destroyed by the sea. The walls were 12 ft thick and constructed to guard against sea pirates. There were similar forts in Kent and Sussex; and one such fort, Burgh Castle in Norfolk, still survives.

St Peter's originally consisted of apse, nave and west porch and possibly porticus or side chambers on the north and south sides. A tower was subsequently added above the porch but apse and tower were destroyed. The apse projected about 17 ft to the east of the present east wall and its side walls rose about 21 ft high. The nave measures 49½ ft x 21½ ft, has walls 2½ ft thick and stands 24 ft high. In the east wall are Roman brick springers and responds of two arches, the arrangement indicating three arches as at St Pancras, Canterbury or Reculver, Kent. The north and south walls were apparently divided into bays by tabled buttresses. At the east end of the south wall are remains of an original doorway which may have opened into a porticus. The four windows, two on each side, have original jambs and splays; all are set high in the wall. In the west wall is an original doorway, and above it an original window with a round head of Roman brick and jambs partly of brick and stone. Flanking this doorway are traces of the junc-

* See introduction p. 2

Bradwell-on-Sea

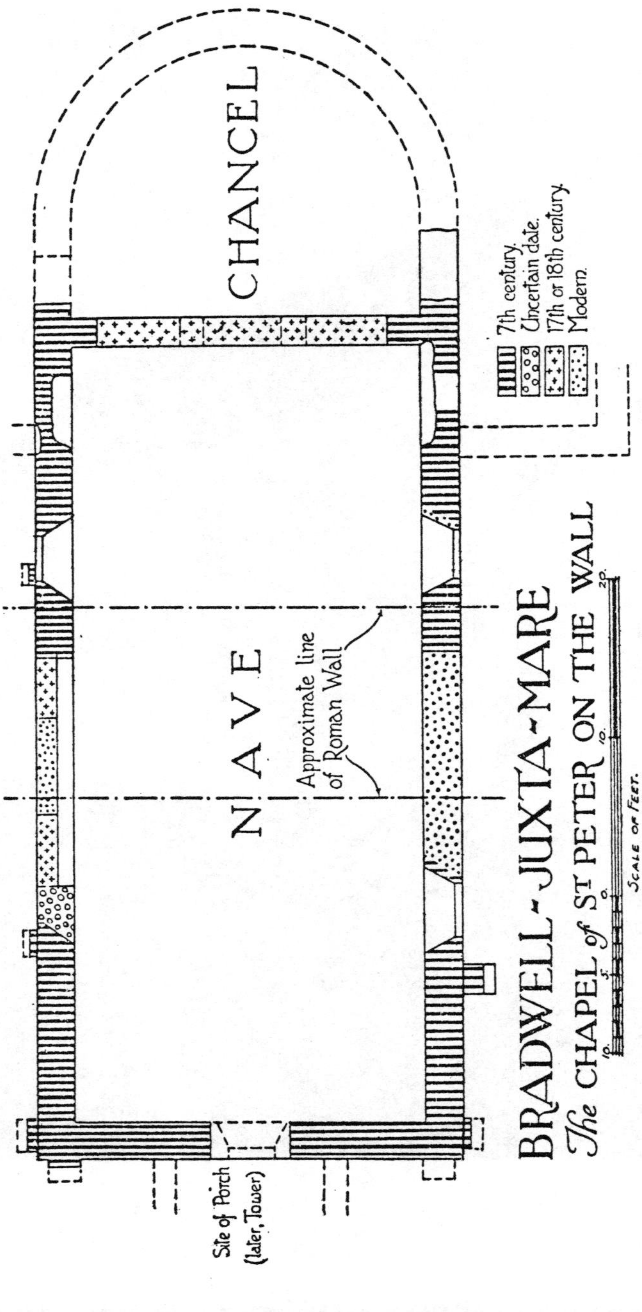

Plan of Bradwell

tion of the walls of the former porch, the foundations of which have been discovered; there is no evidence that this porch was contemporary with the church, and it may have been added later.

Architecturally it may be said that this church is a member of the Kentish group of early churches with apse, north and south porticus and west porch, but unlike these it has the Northumbrian characteristic, due doubtless to Cedd, of a relatively long and high nave.

When the Saxon settlement round the Roman fort was eventually abandoned, owing probably to the encroachment of the sea, St Cedd's church became a barn and a village grew up further to the west; a new church was built in medieval times in the village and dedicated to **St Thomas**; the nave and chancel are fourteenth century, although much renewed in Victorian times by Chancellor; it was given a west tower of brick in 1743 with arched windows and battlements. The east end of the nave had a Tudor brick gable rising from a trefoil and corbel frieze. The font is fourteenth century and there is a brass of 1526 to Margaret Wyott.

Braintree, St Michael the Archangel: The church was very much renewed in Victorian times yet the west tower with shingled spire dates from the thirteenth century; inside, the nave arcades, with circular and octagonal piers alternating, are also of the thirteenth century. The arches have quadrant hollow mouldings. The roofs in the nave and the chapels are worth noticing. A sixteenth century external washbasin was for pilgrims to wash their feet. There is an inscription outside to Dr Collins, the rector's son, who was physician to Peter the Great, Tzar of Russia.

Great Braxted, All Saints: In the beautiful setting of the park with its trees and lake, this church is basically Norman and once had an apsidal chancel. There are Norman windows in the nave and chancel, but in the thirteenth century the latter was altered and given lancet windows, and a west tower was built. The south porch, with its king-post roof, is fifteenth century and the timber additions to the tower are probably the Victorian work of E. Geldart, rector of Little Braxted. The north transept has a timber roof of 1761, built at the expense of the Du Cane family of Braxted Park, and there is stained glass of 1844 above their vault.

Little Braxted, St Nicholas: This is a small Norman church, whose chancel has an apse and a small original window, with thirteenth century lancet windows elsewhere. The north aisle is a Victorian addition, as is the half-timbered west gable; and perhaps the belfry was renewed during this period. The scissor-braced roof to the apse has a rare semicircular collar, possibly thirteenth century; and the nave roof is also noteworthy. The brass to William Roberts (1518) deserves attention; he was auditor to Henry VII. The rector here in late Victorian times, Ernest Geldart, painted the walls; his work can be seen in a number of Essex churches – Ardleigh, Rawreth, Stanford-le-Hope and Tolleshunts D'Arcy and Major.

Brentwood, St Thomas: A big church of 1882, built to cope with Brentwood's Victorian expansion and designed by E.C. Lee, who also designed the church at Bentley Common nearby. It has flint walls and a rather elaborate tall west steeple, with four small spires, one at each corner; the buttresses are mostly rounded, as is the stair turrent. The interior, in the Victorian Early English style, is symmetrical but impressive.

The little medieval **St Thomas Becket chapel** in the High Street, founded by an abbot of St Osyth, is a well kept ruin.

Brightlingsea, All Saints: Situated away from the small town, this is a fine church in its proud East Anglian style. The thirteenth century church – chancel, east half of the nave and aisles – was greatly enlarged in the prosperous days of the later fifteenth century. The tower, 94 ft high, was finished about 1500; it has beautiful flint and flushwork, its base being decorated with shields in quatrefoils, diagonal buttresses, much embellished with niches that once contained figures of saints, pierced and decorated battlements, and crocketted pinnacles. The nave was subsequently lengthened by two bays to join the tower; a south vestry was built, the north chapel lengthened, the north aisle reconstructed and finally the south porch with its flushwork base and battlements was added. Unfortunately the clerestory fell in 1814 and was never reinstated.

Inside, the church contains many niches, and in the north chapel there are monuments to the Beriffe family who prospered as merchants in Brightlingsea in the fifteenth and sixteenth centuries; the earliest, to John Beryf, dates from 1496. There is also a grandiose monument to Nicholas Magers, a rich London merchant, erected in 1779 and signed by N. Read.

Great Bromley, St George: This is a beautiful church containing much of interest. The fine west tower is fifteenth century, with a frieze of quatrefoils at its base; its buttresses start square, become octagonal and end as pinnacles between which are stepped battlements. It has a five-light west window and three-light bell openings. The south porch, also fifteenth century, has fine flushwork panelling, and a niche below the parapet and over the south doorway which is elaborately carved. The clerestory, also embellished with flushwork, has seven windows to each side but these do not correspond with the bays of the arcades below, one of which is earlier (fourteenth century), having octagonal piers; the capitals of these are carved with leaves or, in one case, with figures or grotesque beasts. Over the nave is a splendid double hammer-beam roof of about 1500; compare those at Castle Hedingham, Gestingthorpe and Sturmer. Some of the original colouring is still visible on the more easterly trusses. Also good is the north aisle roof and the north and south doors, with elaborate tracery. There is a handsome brass of 1432 to a priest called William Bischopton; he stands under an arch and gable crocketted and pinnacled.

Little Bromley, St Mary the Virgin: This church was built using much pudding stone; its nave is Norman with small west and south windows, and the chancel is thirteenth century with an east window of three lights and north and south lancet windows. In the fifteenth century the tower was given a red brick top, diagonal buttresses, and a three-light west window which is now obscured internally by a Victorian organ; and a south porch was built with timber framing. The octagonal font has fifteenth century carvings of the Evangelists, agreeably rustic.

Broomfield, St Mary: Standing peacefully away from the main road, this church is noteworthy for its round tower (one of the six remaining in Essex). It is built of coursed flint and some pudding stone, and incorporates many Roman bricks. The tower is only a little higher than the ridge of the roof of the nave (the shingled spire is a later addition); it is Norman with some round headed windows, with jambs and heads made of Roman brick. The nave and chancel are also eleventh century; the chancel was lengthened in the fifteenth century. The north aisle and south porch are Victorian additions. Inside there is a late twelfth century font, with a square bowl having shafts on each angle and three shallow pointed arches to each face. There are some good eighteenth century tombstones in the churchyard.

Broxted, St Mary: The church stands on the hillside, looking across to the Saxon church at Chickney. It has a thirteenth century nave and chancel, with lancet windows at the east end. The north aisle is fifteenth century, as is the belfry; and there are two Tudor brick windows in the south wall of the nave and a late Tudor pulpit with arabesque ornament. Also worth noticing are an ogee-headed fourteenth century niche, and an inscription to Thomas Bush, who bequeathed his fortune to his relations in the eighteenth century in a most judicious fashion.

Bulmer, St Andrew: The chancel and north aisle here are fourteenth century. The west tower is fifteenth century with diagonal buttresses, battlements, and flint and stone chequer work at the base. Inside, the long chancel has an arcade along the sanctuary wall, the sedilia and piscina having cusped arches on detached shafts; and there is a fine early sixteenth century roof with arched braces to the collars. The piers to the north arcade are octagonal with double chamfered arches. The nave roof is good nineteenth century work. The carvings on the fifteenth century font are worth noticing, especially the face of a man among the vines.

Bulphan, St Mary: Situated on the flat land towards the river Thames, the village derives its name ('Phan') from 'fen'. The church has suffered from restoration but retains interesting features. The west tower, though clad with Victorian tiles, is an example of Essex timber framing; it stands on oak posts with an aisle each side, and there are cross beams diagonal framing and cross braces. The south porch of about c.1500 is good timber work, with elaborate barge boards and tracery; and of the same period inside is the screen with each of the two side openings under one arch and cusped tracery. It may have come from Barking Abbey, which was demolished by Henry VIII.

Helions Bumpstead, St Andrew: The church was much altered in 1812 when the west tower was built. This is of red brick, with pointed windows and battlements. The walls of the south aisle were rebuilt at the same time. The chancel is thirteenth century; the piers of the south aisle are octagonal fourteenth century, with double chamfered arches over. The old brick floors inside are pleasing. There is an octagonal font with quatrefoils on the bowl of the Perpendicular type; and also a monument to Captain Tallakarne, who died in Buckingham's unfortunate expedition against Cardinal Richelieu at La Rochelle in 1627; it resembles that to Luce Tallakarne (1610) in Ashen church not far away.

Steeple Bumpstead, St Mary: The west tower and chancel of the church are Norman; the upper portion of the tower was rebuilt in red brick during Tudor times, as were the clerestory, tops of the aisles and the south porch. There was much restoration in Victorian days. The north and south arcades to the aisles seem fourteenth century, with semi-polygonal shafts to the nave and half-round shafts to the arches. Nave and chancel roofs have king posts on tie beams, and the south aisle roof is good, as is the south door. There is a fine monument of 1717 by Thomas Stayner to Sir Henry Bendysh, who reclines on a cushion, his infant son close by. Another, dated 1740, is to Sir John and Lady Bendyshe, it has an oval medallion, an obelisk and a cherub and is by Joseph Pickford. Edith Cavell sometimes worshipped in this church.

Mount Bures, St John: This church, which was much rebuilt in 1875, stands close to the Norman castle, the mound of which is still visible, and is basically Norman. It has nave, chancel, transepts and crossing tower; and there are Roman bricks in the quoins. The south porch is fifteenth century; the doorway has decorated spandrels in which can be seen the Sackville arms, the family who once owned the castle.

Burnham-on-Crouch, St Mary: Standing away from the town, this church with its west tower seems mainly fourteenth century. Its nave and chancel are of nine bays without division; the north windows and tower west window with its reticulated tracery are of this period, but the south windows with three lights are Perpendicular in style. The north porch, with a stepped gable, is good Tudor brick. The south porch is embattled and there are medieval stone shields with coats of arms. Inside, the vaulted plaster ceiling is lightened by Victorian dormer windows; the piers to the north arcade are octagonal, while those to the south arcade are fourteenth century quatrefoil with fillets. The font is a square bowl of Purbeck marble on five supports, of the Norman type.

Great Burstead, St Mary Magdalene: There was a Saxon church here; and tradition has it that Saebehrt, King of the East Saxons in the early seventh century, and the first of his line to embrace Christianity, is buried in the churchyard – perhaps close to the old yew tree south of the church which shelters so many beautiful eighteenth century tombstones. The nave is Norman – one window is still visible in the north wall. The chancel, south aisle and the two porches (an unusual feature) were added in the fourteenth and fifteenth centuries, as well as the stone west tower. The north doorway has head corbels of a king and queen, and angels in the spandrels depicting the Annunciation. The arcade to the south aisle has octagonal piers, and double-chamfered arches, and there is a composite pier to the chancel arcade. The king-post roof trusses to nave and chancel with some embattled tie-beams are good fifteenth century work. In the south aisle are well carved fifteenth century pews, and the elegant eighteenth century wall monuments are worth noticing. The chest from the reign of Henry I is of the dug-out type, bound with iron. The handsome stained glass east windows belong to the present century.

Little Burstead, St Mary the Virgin: This small church lies south of the village with fine views over the Thames valley; it has a Norman nave and a shingled spire on the white weather board belfry. The chancel, which has some pudding stone in the walls, is sixteenth century and has some good brickwork of the period, especially the two south windows and three-light east window with brick tracery. The nave and chancel roofs are both good work of the fifteenth century when the roof was raised; and the belfry is a fine example of the free-standing timber variety, dating from the early fifteenth century. It stands on six posts, all elaborately braced.

Buttsbury, St Mary: The village, which was once larger than its neighbour Stock, has quite vanished – due perhaps to the Black Death, as at Beauchamp Roding – leaving this small church in solitude. The nave with aisles is of only two bays, with piers of late Perpendicular character, but the effect is pleasing; and there are good east windows to each aisle of the fourteenth century. The bricks on the floor were made in the Stock potteries; the king post roof is worth noticing, and there are north and south doors which are of great antiquity; indeed, the north door is possibly Anglo-Saxon. There is a weatherboard belfry to the west, on a brick base.

Canewdon, St Nicholas: The name Canewdon probably derives from Canute's dun (hill), for he defeated Edmund Ironside here in 1016 and then later became a Christian, founding three churches, Canewdon, Hockley and Ashingdon. The existing church is mainly fifteenth century with some fourteenth century work, and it may derive from an earlier church. The west tower is big, 75 ft high of grey rag-stone, with very thick walls, strongly buttressed; it is a prominent landmark and was built in the time of Henry V, possibly by him. Over the west doorway, heraldic shields bear the quartered arms of England and France; other shields bear the Bohun escutcheon (Henry V's mother was a de Bohun) and those of the Fitzalan and Warren families. Inside, the octagonal piers of the north arcade are fourteenth century, and the medieval king post roof of the nave is good. The fine pulpit (and possibly the organ) was introduced by an eighteenth century vicar, George Walker, who was also Canon Residentiary of St Paul's Cathedral.

Great Canfield, St Mary: The church has a delightful setting, just west of the moat and earthworks (cf. Chipping Ongar) which are the remains of a castle owned by Aubrey de Vere, who founded Hatfield Broad Oak priory; the priory was patron of this church. It is Norman with a fifteenth century spire and belfry and south porch. Built about 1150 of

Facing page: Great Canfield, south doorway

flint, it contains several items of particular interest. The Norman doorways are characteristically placed to the north and south, but the south one is embellished with unusual carvings on the capitals. There is a face on each capital, the east one has scrolls flowing from the mouth, the west one has two birds (doves?) feeding from the mouth (of Christ?). The abaci have a broken chevron pattern and the western reveal has fylfots carved on it; fylfots or swastikas are an early Christian form of the Cross. Could this be a Danish influence?

Inside is a beautiful Norman chancel arch with above it, a circular opening as at Blackmore and, flanked by small Norman windows, there is a Norman recess forming a reredos containing one of the best thirteenth century wall paintings in the country of the Virgin and Child seated, drawn in red and yellow with foliage designs of the stiff-leaf type and masonry lines on either side. This rare painting was discovered when the Wiseman monument of 1684 (now on the nave south wall) was moved from its original position in front of the niche; Wiseman was auditor to Henry VIII and benefited from the dissolution of the monasteries by taking over property in Canfield. There is a good brass to John Wiseman and his wife (1558). Another rare item in the church is a stone Saxon grave slab carved in strange fashion, used as the abacus on the south respond of the chancel arch.

Little Canfield, All Saints: Although the church originally had a Norman nave and fourteenth century chancel, it was nearly all rebuilt in early Victorian times by the rector-architect C. L. Smith in his own style of 'Decorated' Gothic. He also added a north-west tower. The priest's doorway on the south chancel wall is indeed unusual.

Chadwell St Mary, St Mary: Tradition has it that St Cedd baptised his converts near here from a well during the seventh century. This church has a Norman nave, and over the north doorway the tympanum is decorated with rosettes and saltire crosses in the Norman way. The chancel is fourteenth century, and the west tower fifteenth century with diagonal buttresses and embattled parapet with chequerwork. Inside is a painting of the Discovery of Moses said to be by Carracci, and a fine carved seventeenth century chair.

Chappel: Situated on the banks of the river Colne, and so called because it was once a chapelry of Great Tey, this small church is fourteenth century, though parts of it could be older. The nave and chancel are in one with a belfry that has a small very pointed spire. The south door and porch date probably from the early seventeenth century.

Chelmsford, St Mary the Virgin: In Roman times, Chelmsford was a relatively unimportant settlement (colonia) named Caesaromagus which served as a staging post on the Roman road between London and Colchester, both places of great importance at this period. In late Saxon times there was a church here, and in the Domesday Survey of 1086 we learn that Bishop William of London held the manor; his residence was known as Bishop's Hall, and the bishops of London used it as a country residence from time to time in the period when the whole of Essex lay within their jurisdiction. The earlier bishops from London helped the town considerably; in the eleventh century bishop Maurice gave it a bridge over the river Can, and Bishop William of Ste-Mère-Eglise secured charters from King John for a weekly market and annual fair. These London bishops subsequently built themselves another house at Wickham Bishops. We hear of an ordination in the earlier church when Simon of Sudbury was bishop of London (he later became Archbishop of Canterbury); the service was held on St Barnabas Day in 1362. Rebuilding seems to have been undertaken by Bishop John Kemp in the Perpendicular style then fashionable. It was finished in 1424, as indicated by an inscription once to be seen on the south wall of the nave beneath the battlements. The chancel may have been finished earlier and the tower a little later.

By this time Chelmsford had become a prosperous medieval market town, and the church was designed in proportion to the town. The building only became a cathedral in 1913, and the first bishop was consecrated on February 24, 1914; but the church, although enlarged, in no way resembles a cathedral and remains basically a good fifteenth century parish church.

Considered in this way, it is a handsome building, with an impressive tower and south porch. The west tower was built perhaps to commemorate the wedding of William de Bourchier and Isabel de Vere when these two great Essex families were united in 1464; the de Vere mullet (a five pointed star) and the reef knot of the Bourchiers can be seen over the west door.

The tower, 90 ft high and in three stages, has set-back buttresses with chamfered angles between; the battlements have flushwork decoration and there are eight pinnacles. An open lantern which surmounts the tower was built in 1749 to replace a similar structure; it is crowned by a needle spire formerly sheathed in lead but now copper covered. At the foot of the battlements are some modern stone carvings by Huxley-Jones portraying symbols of the history of the church and county, e.g. a Mildmay lion and St Peter's keys.

The church, in particular the nave, has undergone several reconstructions. One took place in 1565 after a storm which destroyed the south and west windows; and in 1800 grave diggings close to the walls brought down the roof and a good deal of the fabric. John Johnson, who had designed the Shire Hall just across the churchyard and also the County Gaol, was in charge of this rebuilding, and the plaster ceiling in the nave may be compared with his plasterwork in the ballroom of the Shire Hall. Johnson also rebuilt the fifteenth century piers with their lozenge shape and mouldings characteristic of this period, on the south side he used Coade stone for the purpose. The clerestory windows were also renewed at this time.

The outer north aisle and transept were added in 1873; the chapter house vestries, and muniment room were built in 1926 to designs by Sir Charles Nicholson, and at the same time the fifteenth century chancel was lengthened by 18 ft, and Sir Arthur Blomfield's east window of 1875 re-set. The north chapel opens into the chancel with an unusual round arch which is divided into two pointed arches with the spandrels containing open tracery; the central pier has four shafts and hollows in the diagonals. The south porch, which greatly adds to the appearance of the cathedral from that side, was built in the mid-fifteenth century; it was restored in 1882 by Chancellor, and the upper room is now used as a library. It makes a handsome entrance to the nave with its flushwork decoration and battlements.

The interior of the church has been enriched by Essex friends of the American people to commemorate the war years of 1942-45, when the burdens of war were shared by the two nations. Inside the cathedral, some of the furnishings are modern, such as the elaborate bishop's throne of 1928 by Sir Charles Nicholson and the altar by Wykeham Chancellor; the stained glass is mostly Victorian or later; the five-light east window is 1878 by Clayton and Bell; an earlier window, which seems to have been mostly of plain glass, had been destroyed by a violent mob in 1641.

Particularly interesting are the monuments to the Mildmay family. Both are large; one dates from 1571 and is of unusual shape, to Thomas Mildmay, his wife Avice and their 13 children. Like so many Essex families, the Mildmays had grown rich on the acquisition of lands from the monasteries in Henry VIII's reign, receiving the manor of Moulsham and (perhaps in expiation of his misdeeds), founding the grammar school. Thomas had served Henry VIII; and his son, Walter, served Edward VI, Mary and Elizabeth founded Emmanuel College, Cambridge. In the same chapel is another large monument to Benjamin Mildmay (1736) and his wife, Frederica, daughter of the Duke of Schomberg – a surprisingly large marble urn flanked by Corinthian columns and cherubs; it is signed by James Lovell. Amongst other items of interest are the fine communion rails of 1675 with rich foliage carving, probably Dutch.

Great Chesterford, All Saints: Great Chesterford is on the river Cam, and the Romans had a settlement here. The church dates from the thirteenth century, although it has been very much restored. The piers to both north and south aisles seem to have been re-cut but there is an original lancet window in the chancel north wall. There is a fine sixteenth century oak roof to the south aisle. The fifteenth century west tower was rebuilt in 1792. The brasses inside are to be noted – one of an early sixteenth century female figure, and one of an infant son of Lord Howard (1600).

Little Chesterford, St Mary: The church is nicely grouped with the fine old manor house next to it. Nave and chancel are under one roof, and there is a Victorian bell turret on the west gable, built when the church was restored. The church is thirteenth century with windows of that period and of subsequent date. There is a plain fifteenth century screen inside and a monument (1728) to James Walsingham, a descendant of Sir Francis Walsingham, signed by Henry Cheere.

Chickney, St Mary the Virgin: Standing in rural isolation, this church is of great interest and charm. It had a Saxon nave and probably an apsidal chancel until alterations in the thirteenth century. Built of flint and pebble rubble, it retains two double-splayed pre-Conquest windows, in one of which are the original wooden jambs. Note how high up these windows are set. The church plan is remarkable for its haphazard Saxon layout, with no right angles, and the axes of chancel and tower deflect to the south. In the thirteenth century the chancel was extended and new windows inserted; the fourteenth century saw a west tower added, and a larger east window with north doorway and other windows introduced. There was probably a hermit's cell in the north wall of the chancel as at Lindsell and Chipping Ongar, since there is evidence of a blocked square aperture in the chancel.

The altar stone with its five incised crosses is of much interest and a rare survival from pre-Reformation days. Also to be noted is the late fourteenth century or very early fifteenth century font, with arms of Braybrook and Fitzwalter on the shields; the cover is early nineteenth century. There is a fine hatchment of the Cranmer family on the north wall of the nave.

Chigwell: brass of Archbishop Harsnett

Chignal Smealy, St Nicholas: The building is of much interest because it is one of the Essex brick churches dating from the early sixteenth century, with a north aisle added in 1847. It makes a pleasing picture; its west tower has diagonal buttresses, battlements, brick windows and good blue diaper work against the warm red brick. Inside, there is a two-bay brick arcade with octagonal pier, an octagonal *brick* font, brick niches on each side of the east window, brick piscinas and a fine arch to the tower. Note also the well-lettered floor slabs in the nave and chancel.

Chigwell, St Mary: The original church was Norman, comprising the present south aisle and lady chapel; and it is still entered by the fine south doorway with its scalloped capitals and other Norman decorations. In the fifteenth century the church was rebuilt, and given a north aisle and timber bell turret which are typical of many to be found in this part of Essex. In 1886 the north part of the church was rebuilt and enlarged to designs by Blomfield with decoration by Bodley; the old north aisle became the nave with a new chancel. The east window is by Kempe (1887). Note the fine late brass of 1631 to Samuel Harsnett, a vicar of Chigwell who later became archbishop of York and founded Chigwell School.

Chigwell Row, All Saints: A Victorian church of 1867 by Seddon, built in the thirteenth century style, of yellow stone, with a north-west tower and three-bay entrance porch. Inside the arcades have carved stiff-leaved capitals.

Childerditch, All Saints: A small Victorian church in the Early English style, comprising nave and chancel, built of Kentish rag-stone in 1869, and standing on the south slope of the hill with broad views to the Thames valley. The carved font is early Tudor.

Chrishall, Holy Trinity: This handsome church stands to the south of the village, with fine views to south and west. It is mostly fifteenth century, although the tower is in parts earlier and there has been some Victorian restoration. The building is of flint, complete with battlements (note the chequerwork on the tower battlements), north and south aisles and porches on both sides. Within, there is a fourteenth century stone effigy of a lady lying in a recess under an arch, and some brasses, among them a particularly fine one to Sir John de la Pole (c.1380) and his wife, Joan; they hold hands under a richly crocketted canopy.

Clacton-on-Sea, and Great & Little Clacton: The seaside resort grew with the coming of the railway. Its two churches are **St Paul's**, built in 1875 in the Early English style, and interesting as an example of the early use of artificial stone; and **St James**, built in 1913 by Temple Moore, externally in the Perpendicular style but with surprises inside.

Great Clacton is a place of antiquity and **St John the Baptist** is an impressive Norman church built of septaria, though overmuch restored in 1865 by Hakewill. There are doorways with two orders of columns to both north and south in the Norman fashion; the north side is more elaborate with decorated columns. The chancel is fourteenth century and the west tower of the fifteenth century, with diagonal buttresses and three-light west window. Perhaps it replaces a belfry, because the old tie-beams remain. A weatherboard upper storey was added later, as well as a nineteenth century parapet and roof. This church is particularly interesting because its nave was originally built with a stone vaulted roof, as at Copford – such vaulting being rare in England during Norman times although common enough in France.

Little Clacton. The church of **St James** stands in a pleasant churchyard; it is Norman but plastered outside. There is a Norman window in the chancel and Norman doorway to the nave. The belfry is an interesting example of fifteenth century timber construction, and is worth examining; it is built on four posts, with bracing and trellis strutting. Inside, the font is a square Norman Purbeck stone type, with blank arcading to each side. There is a robust medieval south porch.

Clavering, St Mary and St Clement: The visitor walks down a church lane with old houses each side to this very interesting church, built of flint rubble and all in the Perpendicular style of the late fourteenth and early fifteenth century. It lies just south of the castle which may predate the Norman Conquest. No doubt there were earlier churches here, for Edward the Confessor is supposed to have been present at the dedication of the church in the eleventh century; and inside is a thirteenth century font of Purbeck marble, and in the north aisle a knight's effigy of the same century. The outside is embattled, with a west tower that has angle buttresses, a south porch and aisles and clerestory with three-light windows. Inside, the piers to the north and south arcades are slim and elegant, and the arches are four centred. The roofs are original;

they are low-pitched, and have interesting head corbels as well as carved wooden angels below the rafters. The fifteenth century screen, with cusped and crocketted ogee heads, has figures of saints painted on the panels. The stairs to the old rood loft are still in existence. In the north aisles is some of the most beautiful stained glass in Essex which is well worth studying, particularly the east window depicting scenes from the life of St Catherine: they are fragments of fifteenth century glass. Also good are the wall monuments at the west end of the aisle, to Haynes Barlee and his wives. The early seventeenth century pulpit should be noted, as well as a monument of 1616 to the Rev John Smith in the chancel. There are good brasses and church chests from medieval times.

Great Coggeshall, St Peter ad Vincula: Although there was an earlier church here, the rich wool merchants of the town decided to rebuild in the early fifteenth century and created one of the largest churches in Essex, comparable with Chelmsford, Thaxted and Saffron Walden; it is 120 ft long excluding the tower and 62 ft wide. Badly damaged by a bomb in 1940, it has been carefully restored, the tower rebuilt completely and the eight bells re-hung. The plan (without the tower) forms a parallelogram. The tall piers of the arcades consist of four attached shafts with capitals and four subsidiary shafts; the arches over are four-centred. Clerestory and aisle windows have three lights, and the big renewed east window seven lights, all with panel tracery. There is a plinth outside at the east end with shields in quatrefoils and the crossed keys of St Peter. In the south porch is a good tierceron vault and the carved boss depicts a pelican feeding her young (also found at Thaxted). The font is Early English. Amongst interesting monuments are some brasses, those to John and Joan Paycocke of 1533 being noteworthy.

Little Coggeshall, St Nicholas: This church, although only a small rectangular building, is very interesting. It was originally the chapel without the walls (*capella extra muros*) of the Cistercian abbey founded by King Stephen. A few traces of the abbey remain in the house nearby, but the chapel (like Tilty) has survived and contains the earliest medieval brickwork in Essex and possibly England. These red bricks, about 2 in. thick are used as dressings round the simple lancet windows and elsewhere. They seem to date from about 1220, during the time of Abbot Benedict, and were possibly made at Tylkell, further north. The bricks beneath the doorway are shaped. The roof is also very interesting, comprising 25 rafter couples with collars and scissor braces; the secret notched lap-joint is used and the roof seems contemporary with the brickwork.

Colchester: Colchester possesses the remains of two important monastic foundations, St Botolph's Priory and St John's Abbey, and a number of churches, most of which are relatively uninteresting and some of which have now been adapted for secular use.

St Botolph's was the grandest of the churches. It was founded late in the eleventh century as the first house of Augustinian Canons in England and it must have been a magnificent priory. On its dissolution in 1536 by Henry VIII, the priory buildings were destroyed but the nave was retained as a parish church; during the Civil War when Colchester was besieged by Cromwell's troops for twelve weeks, the church was unfortunately wrecked by the bombardment and has been a ruin ever since. All that now remains is the west front and a nave of seven bays – transepts and east end are gone. Even so, what is left is impressive. The church was built of rubble plus a vast quantity of Roman bricks, in the walls as well as for dressings. The wide west front had two towers which lay outside the aisles, and between are three surviving doorways. The central one has four orders of columns, with decorated capitals and the arches with much zig-zag; above are two tiers of intersecting arches, and the remains of a round window – the re-use of Roman bricks is interesting. The nave, 27 ft wide, has massive circular piers 68 in. diameter but without proper capitals; they support the gallery, which has openings not divided and arches unmoulded on both sides. The aisles, relatively narrow, were groin-vaulted (as at Waltham Abbey originally). The wall surfaces would have been plastered and painted in Norman times, making the building less grim and severe perhaps. Winchester Cathedral is built in a similar severe style of early Norman work.

At about the same time as St Botoloph's, the **Abbey of St John** was founded for Benedictine monks by Eudo Dapifer, who was made governor of Colchester by William the Conqueror. Of this nothing remains except for the north gatehouse which dates from the fifteenth century, and has a splendid facade with its flushwork decoration of shafts and crocketted arches, angle turrets finished with pinnacles. The carriage way has a four centred arch, and a niche each side and one above; two-light upper windows and battlements complete the elevation. The facade to the abbey itself is much simpler but inside the gateway is a good lierne vault. This building was much restored in the last century.

The other churches are all parish churches in origin.
All Saints, opposite the Castle, is now a museum of natural history. It has a fine west tower of flint with diagonal buttresses of the fourteenth century, rebuilt in the sixteenth century. The rest of it was mostly rebuilt in Victorian times with stained glass of the same period.

St Botolph's, beside the great priory church, dates from 1838. It is a Victorian Norman design, fashionable at that time (cf. St John's, Loughton) in white brick with a heavy west tower, designed by Mason of Ipswich.

Holy Trinity, Trinity Street, is now a museum of social history. Most of the church was rebuilt in 1886, but the west wall of the nave is Saxon and the west tower is a very important example of mid-eleventh century Saxon work. The tower is 11½ ft square and in three stages. At its base is a small west doorway with a triangular head, built with Roman brick and illustrating eleventh century brick-laying. There is much Roman brick used throughout the tower, and the upper windows should be noted as examples of Saxon work together with the arch into the nave with its odd capitals. Traces of blank arcading can also be seen on the tower. At the east end of the chancel is a fourteenth century three-light window with flowing tracery.

St Giles has been a masonic hall since 1976. Close to St John's Abbey, it is a small church with a timber west tower of 1819. The nave interior is of the same date but the south porch is Tudor brickwork. Here lie the two Royalist leaders, Lucas and Lisle, shot by Cromwell's troops after the siege of Colchester during the Civil War.

St James the Greater, East Hill. The building is of interest because of its complicated history. The north-west angle of the nave is Norman, and the tower was probably added in the thirteenth century. The north and south arcades suggest four different periods of enlargement from the early fourteenth century onwards. The chancel, with north and south chapels (with good roofs) and vestry were rebuilt in 1500 and the west tower at about the same time; but the church was restored in the nineteenth century when the tower arch and north porch were rebuilt and the clerestory added. The work of the Perpendicular period is good and there are some brasses of 1569 and 1584 in the chancel worthy of note; also a wall monument of Arthur Winsley (1727) reclining and holding a book.

St John, Ipswich Road. A church of 1864 by Arthur Blomfield, mostly red brick with blue and yellow brick and stone dressings.

St Martin, West Stockwell Street, is now used for plays and concerts. The north aisle and tower date from Norman times, but the tower is a picturesque ruin. The chancel is fourteenth century; then the north chapel, and north and south arcades were built, and the north aisle widened, and finally the south aisle and north and south transepts. The fourteenth century arched roof truss across the chancel is very impressive with moulded wall posts and elaborate tracery.

St Mary at the Walls is now an arts centre. The west tower was built in the late fifteenth century, with diagonal buttresses and a frieze of shields at its base; it was damaged during the Civil War (as was the whole church) and the top part rebuilt in brick in 1729; the rest of the church was rebuilt in Victorian times by Sir Arthur Blomfield.

St Mary Magdalene, Magdalene Street. Built of flint in 1853, designed by F. Barnes.

St Michael, Mile End. 1854, by Hakewill.

St Peter, North Hill. The church was damaged in 1692 by an earthquake and was mostly rebuilt. Then, in 1758, the central tower was removed, the north and south arcades were extended, and a west tower built in red brick with white quoins and battlements. So the church is largely eighteenth century; although the thirteenth century door in the south doorway should be noted with its ironwork ascribed to Thomas of Leighton Buzzard, who made the beautiful grille for Queen Eleanor's tomb in Westminster Abbey. There are a number of interesting monuments in the church and about thirty brasses worthy of notice.

St Helen's Chapel. Now a museum store, it is a late thirteenth century building incorporating older work, and has late thirteenth century windows of one pointed light on its north wall.

Earls Colne, St Andrew: The parish takes its name from the River Colne and the de Vere family, Earls of Oxford. The church was mostly rebuilt in the Victorian era. The west tower, however, is good; built in 1534 with diagonal buttresses and three-light openings, its battlements are decorated in flushwork with the mullet (star) of the de Veres and their coat of arms; there is a gilded ironwork crown and weather-vane above. The south aisle is fourteenth century, the arcade having octagonal piers. Monuments to Richard Harlakendon (1602) and John Wale (1761) with carvings by Roubiliac.

Colne Engaine, St Andrew: The lower portion of the church's west tower is fourteenth century, but the upper part is built of Tudor brick. The de Vere mullet (star) can be seen in the east face, and there are battlements on a corbel frieze and pinnacles. The south porch with stepped battlements is also of brick. The nave is Norman, with much re-use of Roman brick. The church was restored in 1873.

Wakes Colne, All Saints: This small church has a nave and chancel and belfry. There are Norman windows and Norman north and south doorways in the nave, the north one having scalloped capitals and a roll moulding. The chancel walls are very thick, so there may have been a crossing tower at one time. There are windows of the fourteenth century and also a Tudor brick window in the north and south walls of the chancel. A timber belfry was built in the fifteenth century; and between its posts a screen of 1920 has been erected as a war memorial. The font is octagonal late twelfth century, with three blank arches to each side.

White Colne, St Andrew: The church was much restored in 1869 by C. Moxon, leaving little of interest, although there are Roman bricks in the quoins. The east window of 1884 is by Ward and Hughes. The hexagonal pulpit dates from the seventeenth century, with three finely carved panels depicting St James the Great with a staff, St Augustine of Hippo with mitre and crozier, and the Virgin. The Norman family of Le Blanc gave the parish its name of 'White'.

Copford: This church was dedicated after its 'restoration' in 1880 to St Michael and All Angels because its original dedication had been forgotten. It is a place of rare delights and should not be missed, chiefly on account of its remarkable wall paintings which were probably done in the middle of the twelfth century, shortly after the church was built.

The manor of Copford belonged to the Bishops of London and under their patronage the church was built in about 1130. In addition to the wall paintings, the building is of considerable architectural interest, belonging (in its original form) to a group of aisleless apsidal churches, of which 115 have been recorded in Great Britain. These are fairly widely distributed, but many occur in the eastern counties where building stone is scarce; Essex possesses 15 examples. Copford is an uncommon type because the dividing wall and arch serves only to separate the apse from the rest of the building; thus chancel and nave form an undivided rectangle, and no doubt a screen would have provided the necessary division. Eight of these churches had priests' chambers over. Copford is a rare example of a vaulted parish church, one of the very few in England. The other recorded examples are Great Clacton and Chepstow Priory in Monmouthshire; and the chapel in the Tower of London. Only the last survives with its tunnel vaulting; in the others it has been dismantled, which is a great loss, although similar vaulting is found in France.

Here at Copford, the apse retains its semi-spherical vault; in the nave only the springing of the vault has survived because the church was enlarged on its south side and the vaulting removed. Its original form can be traced from what remains; the upper windows of the nave joined the tunnel-vault with cross vaults of their own. The windows are shafted outside and in; the south side of the nave would have matched the present north side. Above was the priest's attic, lit by the two small round openings in the west wall and approached by a doorway (now

Wall paintings in apse at Copford

blocked) which was cut through the upper part of the second buttress in the north wall.

The other Norman doorways are still in existence; the main one on the north side has two orders of columns, and the arch has roll mouldings. The outside walls are buttressed in Norman fashion, with broad flat pilaster buttresses which can still be seen. A surprisingly large number of Roman bricks are evident in the church's construction, together with septaria and rubble.

Around 1190, the church was enlarged on the south side with a small transept or side chapel – the arch is pointed in the Transitional style, and the responds have angle shafts. About a century later, this transept was itself enlarged, forming a south aisle to the church. The arch immediately west of the first was built of early medieval brick. It should be compared with the brick at Little Coggeshall which perhaps came from the same kiln, since the two places are not very far apart; they furnish proof of an early knowledge of brick-making for the medieval period. The nave roof seems characteristically late thirteenth century, which corresponds with the date of the alterations, and removal of the vault. The bell-turret was a later improvement; standing on two great oak posts with arched braces and transom, it dates from the fifteenth century, as does the screen. The lower west window of two lights is a fourteenth century replacement of the Norman window, and in its head is some medieval glass showing the arms of the Tey family.

No doubt the wall paintings were covered by whitewash during the Reformation. According to Wright's *History of Essex*, they were discovered in 1690 when the church was being repaired; workmen preparing the walls for whitewashing found 'very good paintings of the Crucifixion, St Peter's mother-in-law lying sick of a fever, of Mary Magdalen and other subjects'. The paintings were washed over again, but in 1871, the whitewash in the apse was scraped off and the designs brought to light. The following year, Mr Daniel Bell 'restored these paintings, adding and supplying what was necessary'. When the nave was repaired in 1880, other paintings were discovered, and although an elaborate dado border was restored with some freedom, the pictures above were left in their original condition.

In the twelfth century, these richly painted walls and vault must have produced a display of colour as brilliant as that of an illuminated manuscript. The length of the nave with windows placed uniformly on both sides would have been emphasized by its tunnel vaulted roof. The difficulty confronting the antiquarian is the restoration work, which falsifies the originals. The restored painting in the apse gives a general idea of its former composition and of the original colour scheme, but it diverges from the original in certain details. The style of its execution is Victorian rather than twelfth century; for instance, the crown in the restored painting was probably added without original authority, and some of the colouring has been altered. This apse vault was painted with a 'Paradise' or 'coelum' – a Christ in Majesty occupied the central position within an aureole of rainbow colours. The top of the aureole was supported by two large flying angels, and underneath two angels on thrones, one with an open, the other with a closed book; the base of the aureole was upheld by two smaller angels on the vault above the east window. Over the side windows were two more angels. The adjacent parts of the walls were profusely decorated with Romanesque patterns. The buildings of the Heavenly Jerusalem appeared on the ground between the angels. On the splays of the east window were the remains of two figures, now restored as St Michael and St Gabriel, but which probably depicted other characters originally. Between the windows under canopies were ten standing figures representing Apostles, drastically altered in restoration. On the soffit of the arch in front of the apse were depicted the signs of the Zodiac in a series of medallions. The *Virgo* is in a nimbus, representing Mary. The painting on the spandrels and on the walls above the arch is modern – post 1872.

The workmanship of the original paintings was consistently of the first order with a highly accomplished technique, and employing a range of colours similar to those of mid-twelfth century miniatures. The image of Our Lord in Majesty was taken up by artists in the early fourth century. During the fifth century it became customary to depict religious subjects on the walls of churches, either in paint or in mosaic. The vision of Christ in Glory was a favourite subject, which usually decorated the apse and its arch – the most sacred part of the building, symbolising the Courts of Heaven. The Copford 'Paradise' resembles these early representations, reminding us that Christian art of the west and eastern churches possessed a unity of style and image. Until the thirteenth century, church art was largely under monastic control, preventing any intrinsic development; it followed prescribed lines and there was no scope for individual imagination. The art of the western church was largely based on motifs derived from Byzantium. These motifs were disseminated by means of illuminated manuscripts which conveyed artistic tradition between the scattered monasteries. In western art during the later Romanesque period, modes of representation became rather stereotyped and the same layout is often encountered, namely the figure of Christ in Majesty, seated within an aureole, supported by angels and accompanied by the Apostles. Christ is almost invariably depicted with a beard, and he often holds a book in the left hand and blesses with the right. Two further important examples of this theme dating from the twelfth century survive in England; the earliest is in the apse of St Gabriel's Chapel in the crypt of Canterbury, similar to the Copford paintings and preceding it by about 20 years; fortunately it is well preserved. The second is at Kempley, Gloucestershire, of a later date (1160) and a little different. Lesser examples also survive. Originally the ceiling of the choir at Canterbury was also painted with a 'Heaven' and this may have been the example for Copford, together with the work in the crypt – the same workmen may have been employed.

Numerous representations of Christ in Majesty also exist in Romanesque sculptures, such as those on the tympana of doorways. The signs of the Zodiac were another favourite theme in medieval art, often appearing in the pages of psalter manuscripts; their symbolism acquired further significance because they could be associated with the Twelve Apostles. A number of arch soffits on the Continent are decorated thus; and the famous twelfth century doorways at Kilpeck, Herefordshire, and Barfreston, Kent, bear carvings of the Zodiac.

Most of the paintings in the body of Copford church occurred on the vaulted roof which was taken down in the fourteenth century; hence the paintings on the nave walls formed part of a co-ordinated scheme. The representation of David and the Lion on one of the springers on the north side suggests that there were Old Testament subjects on the nave's vaulting; and the presence of a king at the east end of the south wall further suggests that a series of kings and prophets were depicted.

It is difficult to account for the subject of the painting above the organ arch, where an angel bears upward a heart in a napkin to another angel emerging from heaven to receive it. It has few parallels; flying angels with napkins are found in Romanesque art, but seldom afterwards, when European art had developed away from Byzantine influence.

The Miracle of the Raising of Jairus' daughter on the nave's north wall is also an unusual subject. The miracles of Christ were often depicted in early Christian times, but this particular one was rarely chosen for illustration, whereas others like the Raising of Lazarus were quite common. The painting here is the best surviving original work in the church, and must be regarded as one of the most important examples of its period in this country. The composition is divided into two; in the left hand compartment, a curtain hangs from an arch and a girl lies on a couch covered by a dark red coverlet; beside her stands a woman, wearing a veiled head-dress; she rests her head on her right hand in sorrow. In the other compartment, Jairus stands at the doorway entreating Christ, who occupies the central position of this half.

Christ has a yellow nimbus with a black cross, and he blesses with his right hand; behind him is an Apostle, also with a nimbus, his left hand raised in astonishment at the miracle being wrought. Bands of blue and green form the background. The style of the painting is Byzantine, but the dramatic treatment of the figure of Jairus departs somewhat from tradition. The details of the costumes, which are twelfth century, lend additional interest.

At the sides of the nave windows and the chancel east window were a series of figures, depicting Virtues trampling on Vices – the so-called St Michael and St Gabriel were perhaps originally mailed figures representing Virtues. In twelfth century wall paintings and sculptures, Virtues are often represented as individual armed figures trampling on monsters, symbolizing the Vices. In this form they often decorate window splays. At Cloverley (Shropshire) a painting 50 ft long survives, in which fourteen knights triumph over the Vices.

A fourth century poem entitled *Psychomachia* (Battle of the Soul) was a common source of inspiration to medieval craftsmen; it described the armies of Virtues and Vices confronting one another, when seven champions from each side come forth and engage in single combat; the Virtues celebrate their victory by erecting a Temple like the New Jerusalem. This poem probably inspired the subjects on the west wall of the nave – Faith and Charity enthroned in the Temple of Virtue after defeating Vice. This subject is also found carved on fonts (Southrop in Gloucestershire) and appears on the chapter-house doorway at Salisbury (1280).

The notorious Bishop Bonner who burned so many Protestants during Queen Mary's reign is supposed to have been buried by the altar – he was Bishop of London and the last bishop to own the manor of Copford.

Corringham, St Mary: The west tower is one of the finest and most impressive Norman towers in Essex, without buttresses, and with two tiers of blank arcading below the parapet. The centre one on each side of the top row is pierced to form a bell-opening and has a colonette. The windows are very small. The tower arch into the nave is also small, with plain imposts with a strange face on the keystone. The nave may be partly pre-Conquest but the north aisle, the north chancel chapel and the chancel are fourteenth century. The east window is part of Gilbert Scott's Victorian resotration. In the north aisle is a screen of the early fourteenth century; the main screen is modern. There is a brass to the medieval priest Richard Beltoun.

Creeksea, All Saints: This church was built in 1878 by F. Chancellor, who also designed churches at Ford End, Steeple and who rebuilt Pleshey. He achieved unusual surface effects in his use of stone, flint, brick and tiles (cf. Steeple). The font, dating from the fifteenth century, is from the previous church here; and so is a brass of 1631 to Sir Arthur Harris, with a long inscription.

Cressing, All Saints: The small church without aisles has Norman work in the nave – zig-zag work over the north doorway; the thirteenth century chancel has two lancet windows, and there are fourteenth and fifteenth century windows as well. The nave roof is unusual with its arched braces to the collars and is worth studying. The west belfry is built upon two portal frames, and would seem to be early Tudor. There is a monument of 1607 to Anne Smith, of the little girl at prayer and the baby in swaddling clothes.

Danbury, St John the Baptist: The church stands in a former Danish encampment on a hill 365 ft high (hence the name – originally Daningbury). Built of flint and some pudding stone, it is mostly fourteenth century, although part of the north aisle is c.1300. It is a wide church with north and south three-bay nave arcades of quatrefoil piers, and double hollow chamfer arches. The west tower has diagonal buttresses and a shingled spire. In the arch to the nave is a gallery of c.1600. The south aisle and chancel chapel are a Victorian re-building by Gilbert Scott, but the north aisle retains its original fourteenth century roof. Of particular interest are the three oak effigies of recumbent knights of the family of St Clere who came over with William the Conqueror and were local landowners; each lies in a different position, two in the north aisle and one in the south aisle. They are late thirteenth or early fourteenth century work. Note also the four carved benches with poppy heads and heraldic beasts of the fifteenth century.

Debden, St Mary and All Saints: In Domesday Book the parish name is written as Depeduna, i.e. deep valley. The church was built about 1220 and has fine arcades with circular piers, two of which are decorated with stiff-leaved foliage. Originally it had a central steeple in the Norman cathedral tradition, but this fell in 1698. The Chiswell family, rich publishers, came to Debden Hall in 1715; they eventually rebuilt the house to designs of Henry Holland and re-fashioned the church. It was incorporated into the beautiful landscaping of the park, perhaps laid out by Repton, with a lake, waterfall and bridge below, and given an eighteenth century Gothick look. A chapel in white brick was added at the east end with a ribbed plaster vault and pendants, and battlements and pinnacles were added to the church.

Inside a beautiful font in artificial Coade stone, designed by Richard Holland, was installed and in the chapel a tomb chest to R. M. T. Chiswell (1797). There is some good heraldic eighteenth century glass in a south window, and other wall monuments worth noting. Debden Hall was demolished in 1936, but the church still forms part of this very good example of eighteenth century landscaping.

Dedham, St Mary the Virgin: Prosperity came to this attractive town on the River Stour in the reign of Edward III, when Flemish weavers established their industry here. Thanks to the cloth trade, Dedham remained a flourishing centre until the seventeenth century, when its fortunes declined, and a petition for help in their reduced circumstances was sent to the king in 1642 by the inhabitants. Two families, rich from the cloth industry, the Webbes and the Gardons, set about rebuilding their church in 1492. It was constructed all in one piece and, it seems, without interruption. The building stands along the main street, and has a symmetrical plan, with west tower, long nave and long chancel, and porches to north and south. Its length is about 170 ft (compare Thaxted's 183 ft); it is more a Suffolk than Essex church in style.

The tower, 131 ft high, with a peal of eight bells, is built of knapped flint, and has polygonal turrets at the corners as buttresses, with stone dressings rising above the battlements to end in tapering pinnacles. It has a large four-light west window and three-light bell openings; the battlements are decorated with flushwork. At the tower's base blank shields and the Maria monogram with crown over are used as a decorative motif, set in cusped panels of flint inlay.

The passage running north and south beneath the tower is unusual; its vault panelled with tracery, quatrefoils, portcullis and roses, which are Tudor emblems; also worth noticing are the Webbe family initials, trade mark and busts in period costume. The building is a fine composition, standing well in a flat landscape, but apart from the tower, most of the church is externally covered in plaster which hides the flint rubble.

The aisles have three-light windows; the higher two-centred arch windows in the chancel also have three lights, but there are five lights at the east end. The north aisle and porch are more elaborately decorated, perhaps to commemorate the Webbe family; externally the base has flushwork decoration and there are battlemented parapets. The north porch has similar decorations and buttresses with flushwork; its doorway has lions couchant, and spandrels decorated with tracery and niches each side of the upper window. The carved doors are of the same period (fifteenth century) and cut horizontally across about 3 ft from

Dedham

the top. The upper part was fixed so that galleries could be erected in Puritan days; for Dedham was the centre for famous preachers in those times, the most famous of whom was John Rogers – 'Roaring Rogers' – who would fill the church to capacity, so eager were people to hear his sermons and listen to the great man. He is buried in the churchyard, and a carved bust of him can be seen in a niche in the chancel wearing his skull cap and ruff. He died in 1636.

Other well-known Puritans and theologians connected with Dedham were Matthew Newcomen and William Burkett, whose *Commentary on the New Testament* was published in 1700 and became a well-known work. Tablets to their memory are also in the chancel. It is worth noting that an early settlement in Massachusetts was called Dedham.

In the south porch the original fourteenth century doorway is reset. The interior of the church is spacious and uncluttered, with six-bay arcades to the nave, the piers rising with their shafts and shallow diagonal hollows which run up and round the arches. The clerestory windows with four-centred arches are two to each bay, and the flat pitched roof above is carried on shafts rising from these piers, as well as from the centre of the arches.

The chancel is without side chapels, and is roofed in low-pitched fashion similar to the nave. There are six angels on corbels, carved by Aileen Kent and fixed in 1960. The five-light east window has glass by Kempe of 1902; he also did the north and south windows in the chancel five years later. The original glass was destroyed during the Reformation. In the north aisle is the monument to Thomas Webbe, the rich merchant and co-founder of the rebuilt church, erected by his son John. It is a rather conventional monument, much enriched with quatrefoils. The font is made up of a base which formed part of the original octagonal piers of the fourteenth century church; and a bowl – also octagonal – which derives from another source. The oak cover is made from the timber of the *Royal George*, which sank in 1782 off Portsmouth; it was fashioned by a local craftsman.

Dengie, St James: The church has a chancel and nave with bell-turret. Its walls, built in the fourteenth century, are of flint, septaria, Roman bricks and also yellow bricks thought to date from the fourteenth century. This is interesting, as bricks from this period are rare in medieval buildings in Essex (cf. the chapel of St Nicholas, Little Coggeshall, with brickwork of about 1225, and Copford). Inside is a brass of 1520 to a mother and her children.

Doddinghurst, All Saints: The church is situated in a village untidily overdeveloped. It is built of flint and was very much restored in

Victorian times. The belfry is interesting, with vertical boarding and shingled spire, standing on six posts with arched braces and trellis strutting. Also of interest is the late medieval porch, unusually long, with ten openings to each side. The thirteenth century south doorway is good Early English, with nice dog-tooth ornament. The nave roof is fifteenth century with king posts and four-way struts; it is a rare example of a roof having alternate double and single collars.

East Donyland, St Lawrence: The old church was replaced in 1837 by this very unusual octagonal structure, built of white brick 'in imitation of the chapter house at York Minster' with groups of stepped lancet windows and two entrances, and a slated roof. Inside there is an interesting monument of 1613 to Elizabeth Marshall, she is seated with an obelisk to each side; below are a daughter and babies in cradles. There is a long inscription attributed to the parson of that time, Gilbert Longe.

Dovercourt, All Saints: The church, pebble-dashed outside, consists of nave, chancel, and a west tower which is of the Perpendicular style, with diagonal buttresses and battlements. The nave is Norman with a blocked window on the north side. The chancel is fourteenth century and the church contains some good window tracery of that period. Also noteworthy is the nave roof of the mid-fourteenth century with its king posts, and the seventeenth century rood beam at the chancel division. The octagonal font dates from the fourteenth century, and the tower window was given by a German to commemorate the unfortunate Walcheren expedition of 1809 when the Germans were our allies. There is a fifteenth century brass of a man in a fur-trimmed gown.

Downham, St Margaret: The substantial west tower is fifteenth century and is built of red brick with diaper patterns, and has diagonal buttresses and battlements. The rest of the church was rebuilt in 1871, the nave of Kentish rag-stone and chancel of flint with conglomerate stone. The south porch has fifteenth century timber work, and there are some interesting monuments under the tower.

Great Dunmow, St Mary: This is a big parish church, built of flint and rubble, but much restored; it lies outside the town, north of the Roman road of Stane Street, by a ford over the Chelmer. The church is early fourteenth century, with windows of the period including a large east window; these have been mostly renewed. The handsome west tower is fifteenth century with chamfered angle buttresses (cf. Thaxted); the chamfers are carried up to form the square turrets, set diagonally at each corner. The south porch is of two storeys, embattled and with a stair turret. There are niches on each side of its doorway, and inside its upper floor extends into the aisle as a balcony, making a charming feature. The south door is c.1280, and the four-bay nave arcades are fifteenth century, the piers having four shafts and four hollows. There are good monuments to William Beaumont (1718) by C. Horsnaile, and Sir George Beaumont (1815) by Rossi, and also a few pieces of medieval glass.

Little Dunmow, St Mary: This church is all that remains of an Augustinian priory founded in 1104 by Lady Juga, the sister of Ralph Baynard, a follower of William the Conqueror. Although a small religious house, the priory was an impressive building and the present church formed its south chancel (or Lady chapel). The existing north wall arcade was that of the south chancel; there are five bays of beautiful piers dating from about 1220, each consisting of four major and four minor shafts, keeled alternately; the capitals and rich mouldings to the arches are worthy of note. The mid-fourteenth century east window and four south windows are very good examples of the Decorated style of tracery and very beautiful; each window has a different design, and two of the five have four-centred arches. The arcading on the walls inside includes charming figures of animals and leaf carving. The alabaster effigies of Walter Fitzwalter and his wife (1432) are particularly good of their kind; an earlier Fitzwalter attempted to enforce King John's observance of Magna Carta and the Fitzwalter family held this manor for ten generations. The other figure on a tomb chest is of an unknown woman. The fine wall monument in the chancel is of Sir James Halley (1753) by Thomas Adye. The Dunmow Flitch chair, partly thirteenth century, is kept in the chancel.

Dunton, St Mary: The church, which stands in a neglected churchyard, was rebuilt in 1873, and has a red brick chancel and nave, by Bartlett. The timbers of the original tower were preserved in the fabric, and the spire is shingled.

Good Easter, St Andrew: The parish is named 'Good' perhaps because Lady Godiva in Canute's reign gave her estate to the monastery of Ely; 'Easter' is derived from the Saxon 'Eowestre' meaning sheepfold. This flint church was originally probably Norman and was rebuilt about 1200. A south aisle was added soon after and later widened in the fourteenth century, and a south porch was added in the fifteenth century. The wooden tower and spire were built in 1885 after a bad fire when the whole church was restored. The arcading on the chancel north and south walls is notable, and dates from 1240, but a little hard to explain.

Little Dunmow, from Wright's *Essex*

The two blank half arches on the east wall of the nave no doubt flanked a narrower chancel arch which was then widened to its present size. The south arcade is about 1300 and the south porch has a good fifteenth century doorway.

High Easter, St Mary: The parish is called 'High' because it is the more important of the two Easters. There is a good approach to this interesting church, which is largely Norman. The building is of flint, with a considerable number of Roman tiles forming the quoins or set in herring-bone pattern to form horizontal bands. The church was enlarged in the fourteenth century, and (after building delays) it was given a north aisle and larger chancel arch. In the mid-fifteenth century a fine flint tower was erected and a north vestry added. In the sixteenth century, the nave walls were raised to form a handsome brick clerestory; a new elaborate flat-pitched roof was made to replace the early steep-pitched one, and a brick south porch was added. In 1865 general restoration took place and the window tracery was renewed. It all adds up to a very fine church, but particularly worth noting are the splendid roof to the nave with its brick clerestory and the imposing tower. The octagonal font, and parclose screens at the east end of the north aisle, of about 1420, should not be missed.

Easthorpe, St Edmund: This small church, with nave and chancel under one roof, dates from Norman times, when it had an apse, the beginnings of which can be seen outside on the south side. The chancel was rebuilt in the thirteenth century, but Norman windows are still visible in the nave. In the chancel is a good sedilia with pointed trefoil arches on shafts; and there are three lancet windows, stepped, with dog-tooth decoration inside. More windows were inserted later in the fourteenth century. There is some thirteenth century painting of figures on the splay of a south window and some sixteenth century stained glass of Christ preaching.

Great Easton, St John and St Giles: This church stands on a hill not far from the earthworks of the ancient castle. The building has a Norman nave with a good south doorway, having one order of columns; the variation in thickness of the nave walls suggests that there may once have been a central tower. There are a number of Roman tiles in the quoins and walls; the chancel is thirteenth century Early English with its lancet windows. Painted on the reredos panels are the twelve apostles. The belfry at the west end is nineteenth century.

Little Easton, St Mary: The church is set in pretty surroundings and is built of flint. It has a west tower with battlements and diagonal buttresses. The nave is evidently Norman, since the remains of two windows are just visible on the north wall; the north chapel is Victorian, but the rest is fifteenth century. Inside there is much of interest. There are fine wall paintings in the nave: a seated prophet on the north wall of about 1175 and the Passion of Christ on the south wall (fifteenth century). There are two tomb chests in the chancel to the Bourchiers, who eventually became Earls of Essex – on the north side, that of Lady Eleanor de Louvain, sole heiress of the manor of Little Easton, who married William Bourchier in 1365; and on the south side an elaborate tomb chest (1483) to Henry Bourchier, 1st Earl of Essex, and his wife Isabel Plantagenet, who was aunt to Edward IV. Inside the Bourchier Chapel are some magnificent monuments to the Maynard family who were granted the estate in 1590; and in the pseudo-Norman windows some very good glass now attributed to a London glazier, Baptista Sutton, in six panels portraying scenes from the life of Christ (1638). The wrought iron gate and railings were once at Easton Lodge.

Eastwood, St Lawrence and All Saints: Although now close to Southend's airport, the church is Norman. Three windows of the period can be seen above the north arcade, which was built in the fourteenth century. The chancel is thirteenth century with lancet windows, as also

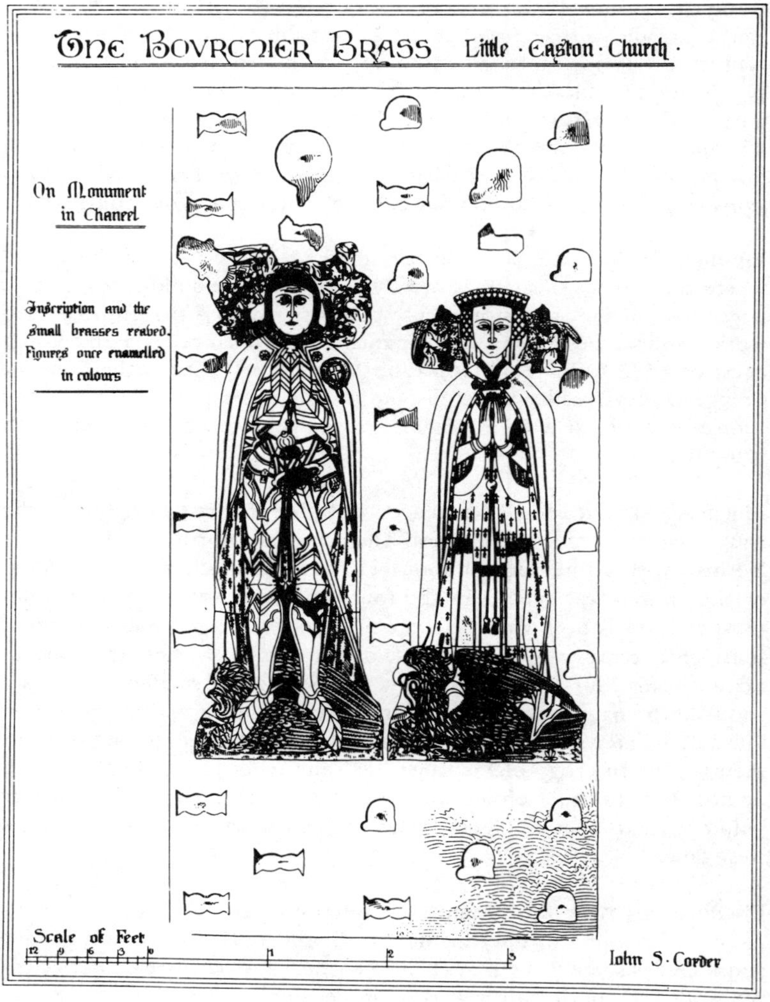

Little Easton: brass of the Bourchiers, 1483

the west tower with its weatherboarded upper portion and spire; the south arcade with octagonal piers probably dates from the same century. In Tudor times, a brick porch was added to the south side and two plastered gables and a timber-framed priest's room were built in the north aisle. Not to be missed are the Norman north and south doors, one made of three oak planks and both with the ironwork of the period; on one of the straps is the legend '*Pax regat intrantes eadem regat egredientes*' (Peace be upon your coming in and upon your going out).

Elmdon, St Nicholas: The church stands in the centre of the village where three roads meet. It is mostly a Victorian re-building on quite a large scale in flint and stone; only the west tower is fifteenth century work with buttresses and battlements. In the chancel is a fine tomb chest of 1585 to Sir Thomas Meade (who was a Justice of the Court of Common Pleas) with quatrefoils and shields and a coat of arms in the centre of the back wall; the brasses of the same century are also worth studying.

Elmstead, St Ann and St Lawrence: With the Hall as its neighbour, the church contains much of interest. The nave has a north doorway that is Norman with a fine door of about 1180 (cf. Castle Hedingham). Most of the church was rebuilt in the fourteenth century; the tower is unfinished, and is no higher than the nave roof. In the chancel are good fourteenth century sedilia and piscina; the cusped arches rest on well-carved heads, but the east window has been made smaller. There is a good south chapel, its arcade having a quatrefoil pier; and there are two low side windows containing old fourteenth century glass, and beneath them an oaken effigy of Sir Roger de Tany who died in 1301. Also to be noted are the quatrefoil squint near the chancel arch, the two decker pulpit with its sounding board, and the box pews in the nave with its west gallery.

Elsenham, St Mary the Virgin: This interesting church lies to the south of the village, in a nice setting next to Elsenham Hall. It is built of flint and includes some Roman brick. The chancel and nave are early twelfth century. The south doorway is a fine example of Norman work, the columns carved in zig-zag, the capitals decorated with symbols and the tympanum with stars and saltire crosses. On the inside, a stone coffin lid acts as the tympanum with the cross of St John and Jerusalem incised, together with saltire crosses. Of the same date are the deeply splayed Norman windows, and the chancel arch with its fine decorations of star and chevron. Also notable is the squint to the north of the arch made so that worshippers could see the celebration of Mass. In the south wall of the chancel is a double piscina – a rare feature, dating probably from the early thirteenth century, with its stiff-leafed capital and dog-tooth ornament. The south porch is sixteenth century and the tower fifteenth century, without buttresses but with walls 5 ft thick at the base. The two brasses in the chancel of the early seventeenth century are also worthy of note.

Epping, St John the Baptist: When the present church was built in 1889 to replace the old free chapel, and designed by Bodley & Garner in fourteenth century Gothic style, Epping at last acquired a fine parish church of its own; the old parish church was at Epping Upland. The tower at the north-east corner, which is separated from the main body of the church, was added in 1908; it is 96 ft high, and may be seen from the High Street. On it are eight carved figures of saints. Inside the elaborate tryptich reredos is by Bodley & Hare and the rood screen by Bodley. There is also some good stained glass by Kempe.

Epping Upland, All Saints: Epping's original parish church has a pebble dash exterior, but a fine brick tower of the late sixteenth century with diagonal buttresses and battlements. There are a number of good brick towers in this area, such as those at North Weald and Theydon Garnon. Inside, the nave and chancel seem almost one. The lancet windows, though restored, seem thirteenth century as does the nave piscina. The brick arch from the nave into the tower is good. There are monuments to the Conyers family who lived at Copped Hall nearby, and a brass to Thomas Palmer (1621).

Fairstead, St Mary: This is an interesting church in a pretty rural setting. During its restoration in 1890, a series of wall paintings were discovered beneath the whitewash. The nave is Norman with some original windows, and a plain chancel arch and a south doorway may still be seen. The tower seems early thirteenth century with a north doorway; much Roman brick is used in it. A little later the chancel was extended, with its three-stepped lancet windows at the east end. Inside the church are a sedilia and piscina, contemporary with the chancel; a niche at the north-east corner of the nave with a ribbed soffit of c.1500; some good bench ends with linen-fold carving thereon; and a fine old dug-out type chest of about c.1300. But much the most exciting features are the wall paintings, particularly those over the chancel arch. Dating probably from the mid-thirteenth century, and restored in 1936 by Professor Tristram, these depict scenes from the life of Christ. They are in tiers, and though some are faded, one can distinguish, at the top, Christ riding into Jerusalem and, below, the Last Supper, and then Christ being mocked and brought before Pilate. On the other walls can be seen red consecration crosses, and also faded paintings, possibly of a later date. The north porch is fifteenth century.

North Fambridge: The parish, which lies on the flats of the Crouch estuary, probably takes its name from an earlier bridge over the fen. Here stands an eighteenth century brick church with arched windows and a bell turret. The west end was pebble-dashed and half-timbered in late Victorian times.

South Fambridge, All Saints: The church has a nave and chancel with bell-cote; it was built in 1846 of yellow brick, with lancet windows.

Farnham, St Mary the Virgin: The church was built in 1859 by Joseph Clarke; it has a gold mosaic reredos of 1885 and a medieval glass figure of St Basil. It stands beside the wooded park of Hassobury.

Faulkbourne, St Germanus: Churches dedicated to this saint are rare. This small church on the edge of the park is mostly Norman, as may be seen from the north, south and west windows, and also the unusual south doorway which has semi-polygonal columns with capitals bearing rough crosses, and rather similar bases. The brick porch and vestry are nineteenth century. Monuments include a figure of a thirteenth century knight wearing a flat topped helmet and carrying a shield; there are several good ones to the Bullock family who lived in the Hall nearby, especially the seated figure of Hannah Bullock (1759) in front of a black obelisk, by Scheemakers.

Feering, All Saints: This is a good village church with some fine Tudor brickwork. The chancel and north aisle are fourteenth century, with windows of that period; and the piers to the north arcade are square with four demi-shafts (those of Witham nearby of the same period are similar). The west tower is fifteenth century. Nave and porch are Tudor, with beautiful brickwork, in which dark diaper-work contrasts with the red background; the porch has battlements on a corbel table, pinnacles, good vaulting and boss. The nave roof with alternate braced collars and tie beams is noteworthy. Some stained glass with tabernacle work of the fourteenth century may be seen, and there is a canopied recess in the north wall with an ogee head. There is also a fine Constable painting of the risen Christ in the north aisle, and a Nottingham alabaster of the Virgin and Child c.1400. The pulpit has seventeenth century Flemish carvings of the Crucifixion.

Felsted, Holy Cross: The approach to the church is picturesque, and leads under the arch formed by the original school-house of Lord Rich's foundation, where some of Oliver Cromwell's sons were taught. The west tower of flint is the oldest part of the church, dating from about 1120; it is unbuttressed and capped by an eighteenth century octagonal lantern. There is a good west door with three orders, of typically Norman design; and a fine arch into the nave with a Norman doorway over, which led perhaps on to the original roof. The four-bay arcades to the nave are of different periods. The south one with two-centred arches is late Norman; it is transitional and therefore unusual. The north arcade dates from about a century later, when the north aisle was built. The south doorway is worth noting as an example of good Early English work; the porch itself is fifteenth century. The chancel was much restored in Victorian times, although the altar tomb of fourteenth century on the north wall is good. In the south chapel, built in the sixteenth century, stands the well-known monument to the notorious and unscrupulous Lord Rich (1568) and his son (1581); it was probably erected about 1621 and carved either by the celebrated Epiphanius Evesham or by his pupil Isaac James. The font bowl is Norman, square and much worn – it was said to have been recovered from the bed of the River Chelmer, where it was perhaps thrown by the Puritans, who disliked fonts.

Finchingfield, St John the Baptist: The church is well sited on its hill, and gazes down serenely at this exceptionally pretty village. The approach, up Church Hill and through the fifteenth century gatehouse of the Guildhouse of the Holy Trinity (formerly the village school), is very picturesque. Historical evidence suggests that there was a Saxon church here of some kind. The base of the tower may have provided a stronghold and a shrine; inside it, the blank arcading suggests that altars may have stood here formerly – it is very unusual and otherwise difficult to account for.

The outside of the west tower, originally without buttresses, is Norman; it has a west doorway of three orders of columns, and the capitals are scalloped and the arches decorated with zig-zag. Unfortunately the tympanum has vanished, although there are corbel heads, somewhat defaced, at the head of the inner jambs. A buttress was added in the nineteenth century to strengthen the tower. The historian Wright tells us that 'the lofty leaded spire was blown down in 1702 by the extraordinary high wind', and replaced by the elegant eighteenth century cupola which we now see. The present one is actually a copy of the original.

The church is a good example of an Essex parish church of medium size; built of flint rubble, like so many others, it contains something of most periods. Apart from the west tower, which is Norman and possibly pre-Norman, it consists of nave, north and south aisles, chancel and north and south chapels and south porch. The nave, doubtless of Norman origin, was rebuilt in the thirteenth century; work of this period may be seen in the chancel arch and the south arcade of the nave, where there are five bays with octagonal piers and double-chamfered arches. Also thirteenth century are the two north bays of the chancel arcade.

A north aisle was added just before the Black Death in 1349; here the piers are elaborate, with four major and four minor shafts, all with fillets. Work was stopped by the arrival of the plague, during which many villagers died. When work was eventually resumed at the west end of the aisle, architectural style had changed and the pier – like that of the south chancel chapel – is characteristic of the Perpendicular period. The window tracery, which dates mostly from the later fourteenth century, is a good design of its period. Both chancel and nave have a clerestory; the latter was added in the fifteenth century as is often the case, and that in the chancel dates from about 1370. The brick battlements to the nave are a Tudor addition.

The south porch is a copy of the original and was built in 1865 when the church was much restored; it shelters the remarkable fourteenth century south door, on which may still be seen fine tracery and carvings, such as the Crucifixion, a pelican 'in piety' piercing her breast, a dove (symbol of the Holy Spirit), and perhaps the figure of St John the Baptist, to whom the church is dedicated.

Inside, the most striking feature is the elaborate screen, one of the best in Essex and possibly the work of one Leacock who worked for the de Vere family at Castle Hedingham in the fifteenth century. The ogee heads are crocketted and there is elaborate panel tracery above. It was much damaged in Puritan times but has recently been carefully restored. The south aisle screen, with interesting carvings of figures, is older and dates from the fourteenth century. The north aisle screen is Victorian, designed by Geldart, the parson at Little Braxted. The nave and chancel roofs are dated 1561; the Kempe chapel in the north chancel also has a fine roof with king posts.

The medieval font is octagonal, with shields set within quatrefoils. There are a number of interesting monuments in the church; in particular that to Sir John Berners and his wife of 1523, which stands close to the organ in the south chapel. It comprises a tomb chest decorated with quatrefoils and on top, a Purbeck marble slab with two finely incised brasses. Opposite, in the north chapel, is a tomb to Robert Kempe, and there are other memorials to the Kempes, who rebuilt Spains Hall in

Elizabethan times and were a great family in the neighbourhood.

There is another good eighteenth century monument to Thomas Marriott, a bust against a medallion by W. Tyler, a pupil of Roubiliac, and also to Anne Marriott, from the early nineteenth century by R. Westmacott, in Greek style. Westmacott was famous in his day and had studied under Canova. The church is well-known also for its peal of eight bells, which were re-cast in 1781.

Fingringhoe, St Andrew or St Ouen: Here is a church of charm and interest, in a pretty setting near the Roman River Colne. The nave is Norman; the west tower, south aisle and chancel are fourteenth century. The tower has bands of flint and stone; at its base there is stone and flint chequerwork, and at its top a parapet instead of battlements, although there are battlements to the south aisle. Inside, the nave roof is unusual, with round arches to the collars and grotesque faces carved on them. Also important are the medieval paintings portraying the Virgin, Christ as a Man of Sorrows, St Michael and St Christopher. The south door is good fourteenth century traceried work, and there is a brass to John Alleyn (1600) and a good sculptured figure of George Frere (1655).

Fobbing, St Michael: The church, with its tall rag-stone west tower, overlooks the Thames. There is a Saxon window in the north wall of the nave and a lancet window in the chancel; but the church is mostly fourteenth century work, and the tower, with diagonal buttresses and stair turret, dates from the fifteenth century. The south aisle is as wide as the nave, and has octagonal piers; it is fourteenth century, as is the chancel and its chapel. The timber south porch dates from 1551, but both north and south doors are probably thirteenth century, as is the font of Purbeck marble, octagonal with shallow blank trefoil arcades. The chancel chapel contains a fine medieval effigy, although it is headless. There is an inscription in Norman-French on the chancel wall to Thomas de Craweden (fourteenth century).

Ford End, St John the Evangelist: This is a red brick Victorian church of 1871 by Chancellor (who rebuilt Pleshey church and also restored Great Waltham nearby a year or two earlier). It has a nave and south aisle, with a tower placed oddly at the east end of this aisle. There is a south porch of unusual design and a chancel with polygonal apse, so the church possesses original features. On the tower (itself of unusual design) stand the figures of the four Evangelists at the corners. Inside the wall surfaces are red brick, and there are round columns to the five-bay south arcade.

Fordham, All Saints: Built of flint with some Roman brick, this church is mostly fourteenth century. There are bands of bricks in the aisle walls. The west tower with diagonal buttresses was repaired in brick in 1796 when it lost its wooden spire. The outside walls of aisles and the windows were rebuilt in late medieval times, but the octagonal piers of the south arcade are fourteenth century. There is a monument to John Pulley, a rector's son, who became a naval captain and died in 1715; and also a carving in low relief of men-of-war.

Foulness, St Mary the Virgin: Built in 1850 by William Hambley, in the Early English style fashionable at the time, this church comprises a nave with aisles, chancel, and tower with spire.

Foxearth, St Peter and St Paul: The church was very much restored in 1885, and an elaborate west tower built in 1862 with bell openings of grouped lancet windows each side. The chancel, however, is fourteenth century; the east window has flowing tracery of the period, and the north arcade has octagonal piers and double-chamfered arches. Both nave and chancel roofs are of considerable interest and are possibly fourteenth century too, the chancel having a single hammerbeam type; its gilding is probably from the Victorian restoration. The dado of the screen is original, but the figures of saints have been much restored.

Frating: This small church is without a known dedication. It has a Norman window in the nave, with a surround of Roman brick, and windows of the Decorated period. The chancel windows are late thirteenth century. The west tower has diagonal buttresses, a three-light west window and battlements with brick and flint panelling. The south porch is a good example of fourteenth century carpentry. Inside stands an altar tomb of 1603 to Thomas Bendish.

Frinton-on-Sea: All that is left of the old village in this late Victorian seaside resort is the church, Old St Mary's. The building is small, with its fourteenth century nave and Tudor red brick porch; the chancel is a Victorian addition, and the west extension was made in the present century. To be noted are the early William Morris / Burne-Jones stained glass panels in the east window. The new St Mary's dates from 1928; it was designed by Sir Charles Nicholson, and is built of flint with bands of brick. The interior is not in accord with the exterior in the Perpendicular style; it has a Renaissance atmosphere, with painted ceilings.

Fryerning, St Mary: The parish name derives from Friars Ing (Ing being pasture). The church is set in pleasant countryside; it has a Norman nave constructed of Essex pudding stone together with a considerable number of Roman bricks; the building stands not far from the old Roman London to Colchester road. There are Norman windows in the nave, and a plain Norman doorway to north and south in the usual style. The west tower is a very good example of early sixteenth century brickwork; it is well-proportioned, with blue brick diaper work, and has stepped battlements on an arched corbel frieze and brick pinnacles at the corners (cf. Ingatestone). Inside, note the square font, dating from about 1200, with interesting carving of leaves (cf. other early fonts at Fyfield and Moreton). There is a brass (palimpsest) of 1460 in the vestry. The east window is by Willement.

Fyfield, St Nicholas: This church lies just east of the River Roding. The exterior looks a little dismal with its cement rendering. The building has an unusual Norman plan with the tower centrally placed. Tower and nave are still basically Norman, and the fabric incorporates much Roman brick, which may be seen in the tower staircase and belfry. The round headed windows are now blocked. The tower was partly rebuilt in 1853, and has a weatherboarded top with a shingled octagonal spire. The north arcade to the nave has thirteenth century circular piers, while the south arcade with its octagonal columns is a little later in date. The chancel is fourteenth century; an arch, visible from below the east window outside, suggests there was once a crypt below, where perhaps holy relics were kept. Inside, the east window has a charming surround of fleuron motifs and of beasts of the chase, with cowled heads in the arch. There is a sedilia with marble shafts, cusped arches, head stops and the three balls (symbols of St Nicholas) may be seen, also piscina and credence. The square font is Norman, with arcading on two sides and fleur-de-lis and leaves on the others. In the north aisle is a stoup and at its east end a fifteenth century niche, placed diagonally: no doubt it once held a statue of the Virgin Mary.

Galleywood, St Michael and All Angels: This church was built in 1873 by St Aubyn, like that at Widford, also given by Mr Pryor of Hylands at Writtle. The building is of yellow brick and red brick dressings, and has a stone spire, 127 ft high, much crocketted at the base in the Decorated style.

Gestingthorpe, St Mary: Overlooking farmland, this church contains work of the Norman period and of subsequent centuries. The fine west tower of brick with diaper work was built in Henry VII's reign, at about the same time as the elaborate double hammerbeam roof. These are uncommon in Essex; and this one is particularly good, with its varied tracery panels and pendants. The names 'Peter Baynard and Marget hys wyf', and 'Thomas Loveda and Alys hys wyf' are inscribed on the roof. Thomas Loveday constructed the hammerbeam roof at Castle Hedingham nearby, so he presumably worked on or gave this splendid one to Gestingthorpe. Other interesting features of the church are the fourteenth century windows, particularly the reticulated tracery of the east window; the screen with crocketted ogee arches, a north window in the nave containing stained glass of the Virgin Mary; an alabaster monument of 1626 to John Sparrow; and a good late fourteenth century font with symbols of the Evangelists on it. Captain Oates, of Scott's Antarctic expedition, is commemorated on a brass plate.

Goldhanger, St Peter: The church is set in a pleasant village near the Blackwater estuary. Its walls incorporate Roman bricks, as well as flint and septaria. The building was much restored in mid-Victorian times, but the original Norman windows may be seen in the north wall of nave and chancel. The south aisle dates from the fourteenth century, and the west tower, which is of stone with diagonal buttresses, from the fifteenth century. Inside, the south arcade is nineteenth century, as is most of the stained glass. There is a good altar tomb in the south chapel to Thomas Heigham and his wives (1531). The nave roof with its fourteenth century kingposts and traceried spandrels is noteworthy.

Gosfield, St Katharine: The church stands at the edge of the park, and dates mostly from the fifteenth and sixteenth centuries. The west tower, which is buttressed diagonally, was built in 1435 by the Rolf family who lived nearby at the Hall. The later parts are built in warm red brick. There are handsome windows, the east window having an embattled transome. In the eighteenth century the Knight family built a square room just west of the north chapel in order to house the squire's pew, from which the altar could be viewed. It has a beautiful plaster ceiling; and contains a large impressive monument carved by Rysbrack, with white marble figures on each side of an urn, to John Knight and his wife (1733). In the north chapel are tomb chests to Sir Hugh Rich (1554), a son of the Lord Rich who helped Henry VIII despoil the monasteries; and to Sir John Wentworth (1567), who built or rebuilt Gosfield Hall. The nave roof of about 1435 is of considerable interest.

Greensted-juxta-Ongar, St Andrew: No-one interested in old churches should miss this remarkable relic of Saxon times, the oldest wooden church in the world. It is now assumed to date from about 845 AD, a time when the kingdom of Essex was probably under the control of

Facing page: Greensted juxta Ongar

Greensted, from Suckling's *Essex*

Wessex, which had risen to power under Ecgberht, just before the wave of Danish invasions.

Perhaps the building owes its survival to its position, sheltered in the great forest of Waltham, which once stretched east of London almost to Chelmsford. The marauding Danes who killed St Osyth and St Edmund in 870 AD, for instance, would have had difficulty in finding this small remote shrine, lying about 2½ miles east of the old Roman road from Woodford to Dunmow. There is thought to have been an earlier church here, constructed of wood in about 650 AD; but this may have been a pagan shrine, later converted to Christian worship after St Cedd had re-introduced the faith during the seventh century. This was not uncommon in the early days of the church, and it is probable that Cedd and his missionaries came here.

The nave is 29 ft long and 17 ft wide, and is built of oak logs; there are 29 logs in the north wall, 23 in the south wall, two corner logs and five taken from the former west gable. The largest is about 18 in. diameter, and most of the trees used were less than 100 years old; the use of smaller sections of timber made transport and handling easier. The logs were cut in half and set vertically with the flat surface inwards; each log was then grooved at its sides for fillets, inserted to exclude draughts; and the top part of the logs were cut into a thin tongue which was let into a plate. On the inner face of the uprights are a number of triangular cuts, with a burr on one side produced by the angle of an adze; these cuts were the key for the plaster which covered the interior. The west end was carried up as high as the ridge of the roof and the logs were jointed with square butt joints, as if timbers of sufficient length were not available. An unexplained feature of the construction is that the logs on the north and south sides have pegs driven into their outer chamfer where they are reduced in size to meet the top plate. The south doorway still exists and there was formerly a north door 2 ft 5 in. in width. At the west end, two three-quarter logs are used as corner posts with a right angle rebate cut internally. There was also a wooden chancel. The building would have been thatched. Saxon churches were normally built of timber where it was available; this was the custom in Scandinavia, and the Saxons brought their methods of building with them. The Venerable Bede who died in 735 AD, writes that 'There was a time when there was not a stone church in all the land, but the custom was to build them all of wood. Finan, the second Bishop of Lindisfarne, built a church in that island AD 652 for a cathedral, which yet was not of stone, but of wood and covered with reeds.' At York the earliest cathedral was constructed of wood, and the abbey church of Aethelingey which Alfred the Great built was also wooden.

Greensted is the only preserved 'stave' church outside the Nordic countries, but remains of churches of this kind, dated about 1050, have been excavated at Lund in Sweden. Greensted can be classified as a 'palisade' building – its walls consisted of rough planks or trunks of oak trees, hewn into halves and sunk in a trench in the ground close together. In Norway hardly any of the surviving stave churches were constructed earlier than 1200 AD; many were built or extended in the thirteenth century. About 32 survive in Norway, and their constructional details vary considerably; in other European countries wooden churches have been replaced with buildings of stone. The Norwegian stave churches are richly adorned with carvings of dragons and such like, but they are of a later date than Greensted.

We learn from Dugdale's *Monasticon* that during the year 1013, the body of St Edmund rested at Greensted on its way to Bury St Edmunds for re-interment; according to a description written in 1300, the body of St Edmund was accommodated at 'Aungre' and a wooden chapel built in his name remained at the time of writing. In the thirteenth century, St Edmund was greatly venerated as the patron saint of England, although he was born at Nuremburg, Germany, in 840 AD. His father Alemund had promised Offa, the king of East Anglia, that his son should succeed Offa; and because of Offa's early death, this occurred sooner than expected. Edmund, aged only 15, was crowned king at

Bury St Edmunds on Christmas Day, 856. He was much loved for his piety and gentle disposition. At this time the Danes were ravaging the eastern coast, and in 869 they fought a desperate battle with the Saxons at Thetford. The Danes under their king Hinguar were victorious, and Edmund fled to Framlingham Castle, which was then besieged by the Danes. Edmund escaped, but was captured in the woods near Hoxne and offered half his kingdom back if he would renounce Christianity. On refusing to do so, he was bound to a tree and shot to death with arrows. It is said that this tree lived until 1840, when it fell down and an arrow head was found embedded in its bark. The saint was buried at Hellesdon in Norfolk; in 1010 his remains were taken to the church of St Gregory (now demolished) in London as a safer resting place because of continuing Danish raids. After three years his body was carried back to Suffolk and on the journey the cortège rested at Greensted which was in those days an acknowledged holy place. It seems odd that this church is dedicated to St Andrew, patron saint of Scotland, and not St Edmund. Perhaps the dedication has since been changed. The church at Greenstead near Colchester is also dedicated to St Andrew and possibly some confusion arose from this.

In Norman times the wooden chancel was taken down and the nave's east wall removed. A chancel of flint and rubble was built; this in turn was demolished except for the footings; and rebuilt in brick in about 1500. On the south side is an early sixteenth century brick priest's doorway, with moulded jambs and elliptical head, with a window to the west of it. The chancel arch dates from the same century, when the nave was probably re-roofed and provided with dormer windows, two on the north and one of the south side.

The west tower cannot be dated with any certainty; although it is probably seventeenth century. It is constructed of timber and is weatherboarded, painted white and topped with a shingled broach spire. One of the bells dates from the seventeenth century; and the smaller of them is perhaps a Sanctus bell of later date.

In 1848 the church required extensive repairs; the oak cill and the bottom of the logs were decayed. These were shortened and tenoned to new cills supported on a brick plinth. The plaster was removed from the inside walls and oak fillets fitted over the joints. The north doorway was blocked by the insertion of three new timbers, and the nave roof was replaced with the addition of three more dormers, making three on each side; a new window was put in the west gable and the spandrels of the new roof were carved by a local craftsman, James Barlow. These depict St Edmund's head being guarded by a wolf, together with his emblem of three crowns and other devices.

The east wall of the chancel was also rebuilt with a new window, with stone tracery in the Perpendicular style, and new windows were inserted in the north and south chancel walls. Buttresses were added to the chancel's east wall and the chancel arch. A new timber south porch was built, reputedly a copy of its predecessor, which was Tudor.

In 1892 the roof was again repaired, copying the former one, under the guidance of F. Chancellor. The octagonal piscina in the chancel is worthy of note; it probably dates from the twelfth century. Also of interest is the stoup for holy water near the old north door – this may be thirteenth century, as is a coffin lid of stone by the door in the churchyard. There is a small piece of fifteenth century stained glass in the quatrefoil window let into the tower, reputed to be the head of St Edmund. The rest of the coloured glass is Victorian or later.

Few people can fail to be impressed by this unique church, which together with Hadstock and Bradwell-juxta-mare is one of the oldest in Essex.

Hadleigh, St James the Less: This small church has changed little since Norman times; situated near Southend and new developments, it deserves a better setting. The boarded belfry to the west is fifteenth century; but nearly all the rest of the building is as the Normans left it in the mid-twelfth century, with its nave, chancel and an apse with flat pilaster buttresses outside and three round-headed windows. A few windows have been inserted elsewhere in later centuries. Round-headed arches, each with a squint, flank the small chancel arch, which is semicircular and of two plain orders. The wall painting on the nave north-east window splay must not be missed. It depicts St Thomas of Canterbury, made a saint by the Pope in 1174, and is inscribed 'Beate Thomas'. There are some other interesting paintings as well, dating probably from the thirteenth and fourteenth centuries. Parts of the font have good thirteenth century carvings.

Hadstock, St Botolph: This church, which is situated close to the Cambridgeshire border, is one of the oldest and most interesting in Essex. Recent excavations have revealed a wealth of information regarding its history, and it now seems possible that St Botolph may have been buried or indeed lived here, and that this was his religious centre. St Botolph was an East Anglian saint who died about 680 AD; he was abbot of Icanho, where he built a monastery on land donated by Ethelwold, King of East Anglia. His church was supposed to have been destroyed by Danish invaders, but little is known about him or the whereabouts of his monastery, and 'Icanho' has been identified both with Hadstock and with Iken in Suffolk.

As many as 64 churches were dedicated to him, and he was much

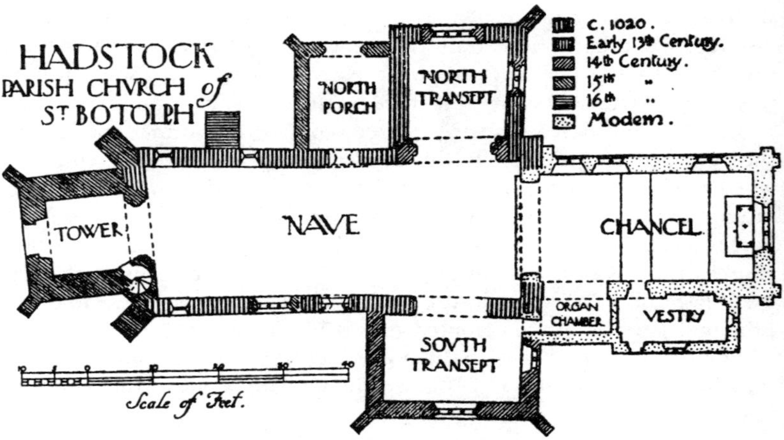

Plan of Hadstock

revered in olden times. In the *Liber Eliensis* (Book of Ely), Hadstock – which in earlier days was called Cadenho – is referred to as 'that place which was consecrated to religion long ago by the Holy Botolph, there at rest'. The latest findings show that there had been a Saxon church on this site since the seventh century; it was built of stone, with transepts, in plan not unlike Deerhurst, Gloucester, or Bradford-on-Avon in Wiltshire.

The remains of a grave of considerable importance and once containing a stone coffin, have been discovered in the south transept, set against the east wall. It is possible that this was the burial place of Botolph, whose remains were later removed for safe keeping to three other religious houses. If this were the case, then it would refute the theory, held by some historians, that this church is 'the minster of stone and lime' built by King Canute after his victory over the Saxons led by Edmund Ironside, at the battle of Assandun in 1016. Assandun is thought to correspond to Ashdon, Hadstock's neighbour just to the east, rather than Ashingdon in south-east Essex; but the correct site of this important battle has never been determined.

The building has a long and complicated history, involving much alteration and reconstruction. As it now exists, it has a tall narrow nave of late Anglo-Saxon date, originally lit by six small double-splayed windows, of which four survive intact. At the east end, there were transepts or porticus (as at St Peter's, Bradwell on Sea) opening off the nave; the one to the north is original but the south one is a medieval replacement. The chancel is a Victorian erection of 1884 by Butterfield; it replaced a small apse of 1790, which in turn replaced a larger medieval chancel. The west tower was built in the fifteenth century to replace a central crossing tower which had fallen, so it is thought, in the thirteenth century.

The first church was probably seventh century, consisting of nave, transepts and apsidal chancel; only the north and south walls of the nave of this building survive, together with the lowest courses of the north transept. The original main doorway may have been in the west wall – this was customary in earlier Saxon churches – and there may well have been a triple arch from the nave into the central space or choir. This church bears a greater ressemblance to the northern type of early Saxon church inspired by the Celtic missions – tall narrow rectangular cells with primitive transepts – than to the southern type inspired by St Augustine and whose form is that of a basilica with aisles. In the second phase of construction, the nave was shortened and the present west wall built, on the skew; at the same time, the main doorway was transferred to the north wall of the nave. The central part of the church was rebuilt and a timber tower erected.

There was a major reconstruction of the church in the late Saxon period, perhaps immediately before the Conquest. A central stone tower was built, the north doorway was moved further east, and apsidal chapels were probably added to the east sides of the transepts. The architecture which flanks the openings leading off the crossing and also the present north doorway belong to this phase. So do the double splayed windows and the north door itself, and the oak window frames, and possibly the five bays of the nave roof, whose low pitch seems Saxon-Romanesque, suggesting that Saxon kings had access to southern European knowledge of building construction. The west door in the present tower is very ancient and may be Saxon as well.

The details of the arches to the two transepts, as well as those of the north doorway, are very interesting because Saxon transepts are seldom found, and the capitals of the colonettes decorated with a palmette or leaf pattern are very rare; it is worth comparing these carvings with some at Sompting Church in Sussex representing foliage in triple strands and trefoils. This palmette motif at Hadstock suggests Scandinavian inspiration, as does the carving of broken chevrons and swastikas on the south doorway at Great Canfield in Essex, although the latter is a Norman church. The leaf pattern is repeated on the abacus and the band round the arch of the doorway, providing an example of late Saxon craftsmanship. The door itself is an object of remarkable interest, being constructed in the early eleventh century – it must be the oldest door in Essex together with the north door at Buttsbury of almost the same age; the details of their construction are worth studying. At Hadstock the ledges at the back of the door are three-quarter circle section and iron rivets are passed through them.

In the thirteenth century the central tower is thought to have collapsed; it was not rebuilt but replaced with a wooden bell-cote. The western archway of the crossing was demolished and the other three rebuilt to some extent. A decorated south doorway was inserted in the nave during this century. The south transept was rebuilt in the following (fourteenth) century and new windows replaced the openings in the north transept and a long chancel built on. In the fifteenth century the west tower was built with flint and stone chequerwork at its base and diagonal buttresses, and a tall arch opening into the nave. The screen to the south transept is also of this century, as is the north porch.

During the eighteenth century the chancel became ruinous and had to be demolished, much to the indignation of the Bishop of London, who wrote to expostulate to the rector. It was replaced by a small apse which was pulled down in its turn and replaced by a Victorian chancel, vestry and organ chamber, built on the foundations of its medieval predecessor. The square Norman font should not be missed.

Great Hallingbury, St Giles: The church was lavishly rebuilt in 1873 and considerably enlarged, with a north aisle by John Archer Houblon (the rich landowner of nearby Hallingbury Place, now demolished); the work was done with care and taste. The splendid Saxon chancel arch remains, built entirely of Roman brick – Stane Street lies just north of the village; and there is a Norman window in the south wall of the nave. The west tower is also original, dating from the fifteenth century, with a spire of 1873; and there is a good fourteenth century south doorway under the Victorian porch. Of interest is the piscina high up on the west wall of the chancel arch, evidently put there to serve an altar which was once situated in the rood loft.

Little Hallingbury, St Mary the Virgin: This small church, which stands just off the main road, is built of flint interspersed with some Roman bricks. The interesting south porch of the fourteenth century has unusual timber tracery of flattened ogee arches; it shelters a Norman doorway built of Roman bricks. Part of the chancel as well as the nave is Norman; it was lengthened in the thirteenth century. The lancet windows have since been renewed. The single hammerbeam chancel roof of the Perpendicular period is noteworthy. The western belfry of half timber work (seventeenth century) is crowned by a shingled spire.

Halstead: The town possesses three churches and a chapel. The medieval church of St Andrew stands up on the hill; the building is mostly fourteenth century, but it was much restored when the old west tower fell and was rebuilt in 1850. Porches and vestry are fifteenth century. Inside are fourteenth century arcades of six bays, the piers square with demi-shafts, the arches double-chamfered. The font is octagonal, in the Perpendicular style, and there are a late Victorian reredos by Blomfield and stained glass, mostly of the same period. Of great interest are the tombs of the Bourchier family who featured prominently in the history of the fourteenth and fifteenth centuries; they lived at Stanstead Hall not far away. There is a brass of Bartholomew Bourchier and his two wives of 1409; a tomb chest to John, Lord Bourchier and his wife of 1400; and several more tombs. The family produced a number of distinguished soldiers, scholars and ecclesiastics. John Bourchier, the second Lord Berners, made a famous translation of Froissart's *Chronicles*.

The other two churches are Victorian and designed by George Gilbert Scott.

Holy Trinity was built in 1843, in his Early English style; it is of flint, with lancet windows, and a big tower and spire at the south-west corner. Inside, the piers are circular or octagonal, and the capitals have thirteenth century style decorations; the Victorian stained glass is by Clutterbuck.

At **Greenstead Green**, stands the church of **St James** built two years later in the Decorated style, with a fine shingled spire.

Also to be noted is a late Victorian chapel at Fremlins Brewery, housing some very fine church fittings from a Wren church in London, All Hallows.

South Hanningfield, St Peter: The church stands in a beautiful setting with a view across Hanningfield reservoir; it is built of pebble rubble. The nave has a Norman window on the north wall and two other lengthened windows to north and south, as well as a fifteenth century south window. The brick chancel was built in the nineteenth century. The belfry, which is weatherboarded with shingled spire, stands on two portal frames, and though much restored, may date from the fourteenth century. Vine scrolls are painted on the south window jambs. The south door is also interesting.

West Hanningfield, St Mary and St Edward: The church is of considerable interest because it incorporates one of the Essex timber towers. This is of unusual shape, like a cross, and has a curious west window projecting above. It stands against part of the west wall of the south aisle, which is mid-fourteenth century, so the tower may date from the same period; it has arched braces in all directions, and on the upper floor arched braces like ribs meet in a boss which is carved with a grotesque face. The south porch is of structural interest as well; it is fifteenth century work, comparable with the porch at Horndon-on-the-Hill. The nave of the church is Norman; the chancel is Tudor. The brass to Isabel Clouville (1381) is an early example and there is an altar tomb to a later Clouville who lived nearby. The dug out iron-bound chest should also be noted.

Harlow (New Town), St Paul's: This church has slender concrete columns, clear glass, yellow brick and a mosaic east wall by John Piper, portraying figures against a dark background.

Harlow (Old Harlow), St Mary the Virgin: The old church was burnt down in 1708, and rebuilt. It was again rebuilt by Woodyer in 1878. The only indications of an original medieval church are its shape, a central tower, and the many interesting brasses now collected in the north transept.

Harlow Common, Potter Street, St Mary Magdalene: The building is a good example of a late Victorian Gothic church all in flint. Its chancel was built in 1888, the foundation stone being laid by Catherine Arkwright whose family were local landowners and benefactors to the church. The nave, of 1834, was rebuilt in 1893 and the tower in 1898. On its east face we see the carved head of William Gladstone who died in that year; on its south face that of the Rev Henry Elwell who did so much for the church and parish.

Harwich, St Nicholas: The church was built in 1821, for about £20,000; to a design by G. Thompson, and replaced a chapel-of-ease to the main church at Dovercourt. It is in the Church Commissioners' style of yellow brick, with castellated porches and west tower with spire. Inside, the nave has galleries and slender piers; the polygonal chancel is of equal height. The original octagonal font of the thirteenth century survives. There are monuments to the Cox family, who founded the bank of Cox's & King's which acted as paymaster to the Army.

Hatfield Broad Oak, St Mary the Virgin: Aubrey de Vere, the 1st Earl of Oxford who lived at Castle Hedingham, founded a Benedictine priory here in 1135, as a cell of the abbey of St Melanius at Rennes in Brittany. It would seem to have been a monastery of fair size; the present church formed the nave of the priory church, the original being nearly twice as long. There was a central tower, of which only the two western piers remain, with demi-shafts visible from outside; nothing to the east of this survives. The church is built of flint and rubble. The aisle windows on the north side are placed high up, because the cloisters lay on that side. All these ancillary buildings were swept away in 1534 during the Reformation. Parts of the walls were damaged when a quarrel arose between village and priory in 1378, and the nave and aisles were rebuilt, with the arcades of five bays as we see them now; the piers have four shaft and four hollow sections. The nave roof was replaced in 1843. Stone heads of the priory's medieval benefactors may be seen above the columns: to the north, these are John of Gaunt, the Duke of York, Richard II, and Eleanor Bohun of Pleshey Castle, the heiress who married the Duke of Gloucester; on the south, the Duke of Gloucester, uncle of Richard II, Sir John Barrington, Robert de Vere, ninth Earl of Oxford, and Robert de Braybrook, Bishop of London. From the fifteenth century date most of the windows; the south porch which has battlements, pinnacles and three-light side openings; the south turret to the old rood loft; the south chapel with its large window; and the big west tower with its angle buttresses and stair turret. In the chancel lies the recumbent effigy of Robert de Vere, third Earl of Oxford, who died in 1221; the monument is thought to date from 1271 and its white stone is much defaced, although the shield still has good carving on it, with diaper work, fleurs-de-lis and the de Vere five-pointed star. The chancel panelling and reredos are good early eighteenth century work, supposedly by John Woodward who was employed in the chapel of Trinity College, Cambridge; the seat at the west of the south aisle is by the same hand, and probably also the communion rails. The figure of a priest, which was once part of a hammer-beam roof truss 600 years ago, is used as a litany desk. Other items of interest are the fifteenth century screen in the north chapel; a beautiful eighteenth century brass candelabra in the nave; and a number of wall monuments, including one to Sir John Barrington of nearby Barrington Hall (1691), several to the Chamberlayne family from the eighteenth century, and one to Lady Ibbetson of Down Hall (1816) by Flaxman. Unusual in a church is the library, built to the east of the south chapel in 1708 by Sir Charles Barrington, which contains 300 rare books.

Hatfield Peverel, St Andrew: Ranulf de Peverel, who was granted the manor by William the Conqueror, married the beautiful Saxon Ingelrica, William's concubine. In atonement for her sins, she founded a college here for secular canons; her son William converted it into a Benedictine priory, which was dissolved in 1536. The present church is formed of the original priory church which was cruciform in plan, but of which only the nave and north aisle survive (cf. Hatfield Broad Oak). In the west wall is the original Norman doorway, with one order of columns and scalloped capitals. At the east end survives the west arch of the crossing, in which the chancel wall and east window are set. There is an original window on the north wall of the nave. The church was much restored in 1873, when the south aisle was added. The north arcade of octagonal piers and the screen are fifteenth century. The west window is late Victorian by Kempe, but there are fragments of fourteenth and fifteenth century stained glass in the north windows; and on a cill there is an interesting thirteenth century recumbent stone effigy.

Hawkwell, St Mary: This is a small church, with a nave and chancel of the fourteenth century. The west belfry with its broach spire is later, probably fifteenth century. It rests on four posts, and has arched braces suggesting Early Perpendicular work. The south door dates, no doubt, from the same century.

Castle Hedingham, St Nicholas: Set in a very pretty village, this is one of the best churches in Essex, both architecturally and also historically, because of its long association with the de Vere family who lived at the castle close by. Aubrey de Vere came over with William the Conqueror, and, like the Mandeville and de Clare family, was richly rewarded after the battle of Hastings with large areas of land in Essex. The de Vere headquarters were at Castle Hedingham and the castle was built in King Stephen's reign by Aubrey's son. Described by Macaulay as the most illustrious line of nobles that England has seen, the de Veres later became Earls of Oxford and the line continued until 1703 when the last Earl died. Throughout the middle ages they were probably the most powerful and influential family in Essex.

The church is a splendid example of late Norman work, although it was considerably altered by the 13th Earl of Oxford who fought for Henry VII at the Battle of Bosworth and died in 1512. The west tower of red brick is actually dated 1616 (the inscription reads 'R. Archer, the master builder of this stepell 1616') but must have been started much earlier; over its west window of five lights can be seen a frieze of shields depicting the badges of the 13th Earl who was Lord High Admiral and Great Chamberlain, amongst them the boar and star with five points, both emblems of the family. The tower is fine Tudor brick work with diagonal buttresses, stair turret, stepped battlements and pinnacles; the small cupola on top is eighteenth century. Also in Tudor brick are the south porch which replaced an earlier one, the battlements over the aisle walls and the clerestory; over the clerestory windows can be seen

Norman nave and chancel at Castle Hedingham

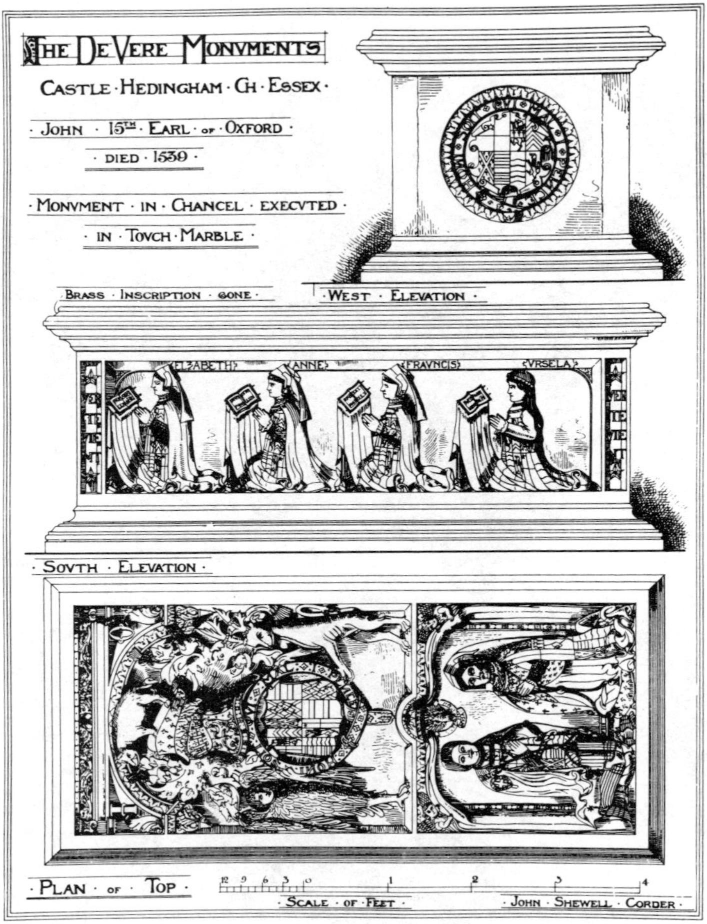

Castle Hedingham: de Vere tomb

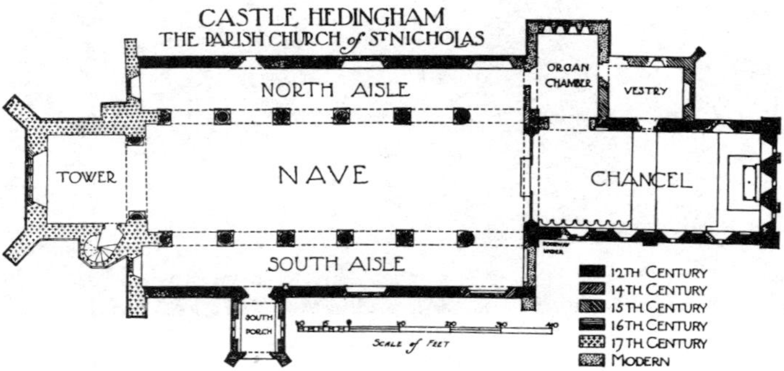

Plan of Castle Hedingham

the de Vere star (mullet) and boar alternately. On the outside only the chancel reveals the Norman origin of the church, especially the east elevation with its flat buttresses, string courses and fine wheel window with eight spokes like columns. During restoration in the last century, one of these spokes was found to have been made of wood. Norman wheel windows are rarely found in England; there is one at Peterborough. There is also a south (priests') doorway, the colonettes having thin volute capitals and the arches zig-zag decoration. The windows on the north, east and south sides are all shafted.

Internally, the church is very impressive as an example of an ambitious Norman church of about 1180, towards the end of Henry II's reign. The nave and aisles have six bays and the chancel is quite big. The piers of the arcades are alternately circular and octagonal, and the capitals are extremely good, being crocket-like leaves of the type found at the end of the Norman period; the motif is varied. The mouldings of the arches are complex and the north and south doorways to the nave are impressive, the capitals to the columns having volutes and water-leaf carving.

The chancel is equally fine with its wheel window above the three lancet windows which are shafted inside; an impressive arcade links these windows with round arches of varying widths. The chancel arch should be noticed, because it has the Norman zig-zag decoration and thin shafts but also a pointed arch, which must indicate that it belongs to the tail-end of the Norman style. The stepped sedilia and piscina are handsome additions to this fine chancel, but unfortunately they were considerably restored in Victorian times.

Over the nave is a splendid double hammerbeam roof of the early sixteenth century, replacing the Norman flat painted ceiling (which was probably similar to the one in Waltham Abbey, itself a copy). This was put up when the new brick clerestory was built, and is thought to be the work of a local craftsman, Thomas Loveday; he was responsible for the roof of Gestingthorpe church (also double hammerbeam) and for work at St John's College, Cambridge; he died in 1535. The carvings are rich, and include once again the star and boar of the de Veres. There are only four roofs of this kind in Essex.

The screen is particularly fine and dates from the early fifteenth century; it has ogee arches, cusped and crocketted and elaborate panel tracery above. There are few good screens in the county, though Finchingfield not far away can boast one.

Another rare feature of this church are the choir stalls with misericords below the seats; these are carved in a series of humorous medieval scenes such as a fox carrying away the priest whilst a wolf blows a trumpet. Also to be noted are the three doors in the Norman doorways, all of which are as old as the stonework; note their counter-rebated plank edges and their original iron strapwork.

The stoup in the south nave wall with its cushion shape and primitive lion head inverted may have come from an earlier church in Hedingham; and there is another stone built into the wall of the side chapel, carved as a head of a penitent that may be Saxon. Considering the cross in the churchyard whose carved column seems partly Saxon, partly Norman, there is reason to suppose that there was an earlier church here. This column was found in the cellar of the village inn and rescued in 1921. Originally it may have stood on Crouch (from *crux* = cross) Green in the village.

The de Vere family vault is under the chancel; the black marble tomb to the 15th Earl and his wife was moved in the nineteenth century to the north wall of the chancel, unfortunately obscuring the carvings of his four sons on the north side, which correspond to the carvings of the four daughters kneeling in prayer on the other side. On the lid kneels John, the 15th Earl, who died in 1539, and his wife Elizabeth. The work should be compared with the monument of 1544 to Lord Audley in Saffron Walden church, as it may be by the same craftsman, Cornelius Harman. Most of the de Vere family were buried in Earls Colne priory and several fine tombs of theirs have since been removed to Bures.

Sible Hedingham, St Peter: Following the Norman conquest, the parishes of Sible and Castle Hedingham were conveyed to the de Vere family, who retained them until 1625. The church is mid-fourteenth century, but the tower was restored in the sixteenth century and there was further restoration in the nineteenth century. There is a fine hammerbeam roof in the chancel, and the sixteenth century oak roof in the porch carried the Bourchier knot, and the mullet and two bears of the de Veres. The monument in the south aisle is the cenotaph of Sir John Hawkwood, who was born in 1320, the son of a tanner in Sible Hedingham. As a soldier he served under the Black Prince in France, was knighted at Poitiers and then went on to become Europe's most famous mercenary with his 'White Company'. In Italy his services were greatly in demand, and he led the Florentines to victory in the battle of Cascina in 1364; greatly honoured by them, he died there in 1394, having married the Duke of Milan's daughter. His tomb in Florence cathedral has a fresco, executed by Paolo Uccello, showing him in armour on horseback. Legend has it that his body was brought back by Richard II and interred in the south aisle of this church. His tomb chest is decorated with cusped panels, holding shields, and in the ogee arch hawks and other beasts are carved.

Hempstead, St Andrew: The church was consecrated in 1365 as a chapel of ease to the parish of Great Sampford. The handsome quatrefoil piers of the nave arcades are of this period; the fifteenth century chancel had its east end extended in Tudor brick and the brick north chapel was built over the Harvey vault in the seventeenth century. The whole church was restored in 1887, when the aisle walls and porch were rebuilt. After its collapse in 1882 the tower was finally rebuilt in 1933. Of great interest are the monuments to the Harvey family in the north chapel, and particularly the fine bust to the famous William Harvey, physician to Charles I and discoverer of the circulation of blood. Amongst others, there is one to Sir William Harvey (1719), an urn on a column set in a niche; and also two profiles by Roubiliac of 1758 to William Harvey and his wife.

Henham, St Mary the Virgin: This is a handsome church in a pretty village with many greens. The chancel is thirteenth century, as is the south doorway which is protected by the fifteenth century porch; the rest of the building is fourteenth century, although the brick battlements on the tower with its lead spire are a later addition. Inside are good arcades of the fourteenth century, both of four bays with quatrefoil piers. At the east end of the earlier south arcade are semi-octagonal responds, which belong to an older transept. The north and taller arcade has a fine carving on one of its capitals depicting the Virgin and Angels on either side. The old stairs to the rood loft are of interest; and there is a beautiful fifteenth century screen with ogee heads and tracery over. The hexagonal fifteenth century pulpit and the seventeenth century lectern are also noteworthy. In the chancel is an unusual monument to Samuel Feake (1790); against an obelisk is an urn on which is a good carving of an East Indiaman. The font is fifteenth century. The pammet floor gives a good finish to the church.

Great Henny, St Mary: The lower parts of the flint west tower are Norman. The diagonal buttresses and broach spire are later, probably fifteenth century. The nave and chancel which are not separated, are fourteenth century; the south porch of brick is Tudor, as is the brick window in the south side. Inside, the sedilia has cusped arches on shafts, and the nave roof is good Tudor work with its alternate tie-beams and arch-braces, collar-frames and carved wall-pieces. The east window has stained glass of 1860, and there is a brass of William Fyscher, with his wife and fifteen children in Tudor costume.

Heybridge, St Andrews: Built in the reign of Henry II, the church is almost wholly Norman; but because of flooding by the river Blackwater during the fifteenth century, the tower collapsed onto the nave and the church had to be restored by Sir Henry Bourchier and his wife Isobel Plantagenet. The fine tower was reduced to its present height, and the nave and chancel reconstructed. Some original Norman windows remain; parts of the clerestory are also visible, together with the Norman doorways and original south door complete with its ironwork. The east end and east window of the chancel were rebuilt at the same time, with the hammerbeam roof truss over. Inside, the stairs to the rood screen may be seen. There are a square font of Purbeck marble, a few pieces of thirteenth century stained glass (a female saint) in the north chancel window, and nearby a fine monument of 1638 to Thomas Freshwater and his wife.

Hockley, St Peter and St Paul: The church stands on a hill overlooking the Crouch valley, where Canute defeated Edmund Ironside in 1016. He founded the three churches of Hockley, Canewdon and Ashingdon. Although much restored by the Victorians, this building is thirteenth century. The west tower is most unusual; the lower part is square with walls of great thickness, and the upper part is octagonal, finishing with battlements and a shingled spire. The four-bay arcade between nave and north aisle is carried on circular piers, with stiff-leaf capitals and chamfered arches over. The thirteenth century font is unusually large and may have served for baptism by immersion. The nave roof, with its king posts and moulded capitals, is probably fourteenth century.

Great Holland, All Saints: The church was rebuilt in 1866 to designs of Sir Arthur Blomfield. It is in Early English style with circular piers and similar details. The original battlemented west tower remains, built in red Tudor brick with polygonal buttresses and stair turret, and four-light brick west window with panel tracery. Inside, there is a monument of 1812 to Henry Rice by Hinchcliff.

Great Horkesley, All Saints: The nave incorporates a little Norman work in the south-west quoins and west window; and the west tower is thirteenth century without buttresses and having small lancet windows, but the rest of the building is almost entirely Perpendicular work, the windows with three lights and panel tracery; the north arcade of three bays is fifteenth century, having piers consisting of four main shafts and four subsidiary shafts and the arches decorated with fleurons. The south porch is good work of the mid-fifteenth century; the side lights have cinquefoil tracery. The nave roof is important, with arched braces to the collars, likewise the chancel roof. The pulpit is Elizabethan, with arched panels.

Little Horkesley, St Peter and St Paul: The old church was destroyed by a bomb in 1940; a new church was built in 1957, but the beautiful oak effigies and brasses from the medieval church have survived and been reinstated. The three (surprisingly large) effigies of two men and a woman are said to represent members of the de Horkesley family, who were Lords of the Manor until 1322. The men are in thirteenth century mail and the younger one has his heart in his hands, indicating that only the heart was brought back for burial. These figures would originally have been painted and gilded. The remarkable brasses include two Swynborne knights – this family succeeded the Horkesleys – lying under a double canopy; the father has his monogram on his sword hilt (1391). In the chancel lies Dame Bridget Marney (1549) between her two husbands, Thomas Fyndorne and John Lord Marney (see Layer Marney); the heraldic detail of all three figures is most interesting.

East Horndon: Standing alone on a green hill and looking across the Southend–London road the church is built entirely of warm red brick. The west tower of the seventeenth century, though squat, is handsome, with heavy diagonal buttresses and stepped battlements between pinnacles and bell openings which consist of round-headed windows. Otherwise the church is sixteenth century; it has a small north and south transept with an adjacent south porch, and a chancel chapel on the other side. The inside of the church has charm, with a gallery in each transept, a two-bay arcade between chancel and its south chapel with moulded four centre arches. Both chancel and nave have good roofs. There is a square thirteenth century font, and interesting monuments to the Tyrell family who lived nearby at Herongate. Particularly good is the figure of Alice, wife of Sir John Tyrell (1422) incised on limestone; her figure presents vividly to us the fashions of the period of Agincourt. Note also a monument of 1766 to a later Sir John Tyrell, signed by Nollekens.

Horndon on the Hill, St Peter and St Paul: This is an interesting and attractive parish church, built of rag-stone and flint rubble. It is mostly thirteenth century, with handsome Early English arcades; the piers are octagonal and circular alternately, and the capitals have either crockets or flat stiff-leaf decorations, or are sometimes left undecorated. The clerestory windows were quatrefoil, but are now supplemented by dormer windows. The south doorway is good with its colonettes. The chancel was lengthened in the fifteenth century and there was other rebuilding. A south porch was added; and a fine timber belfry was erected inside the church which stands on four stout posts with cross beams braces and trellis strutting. The north and south beams are cantilevered

Little Horkesley: Swynborne brasses

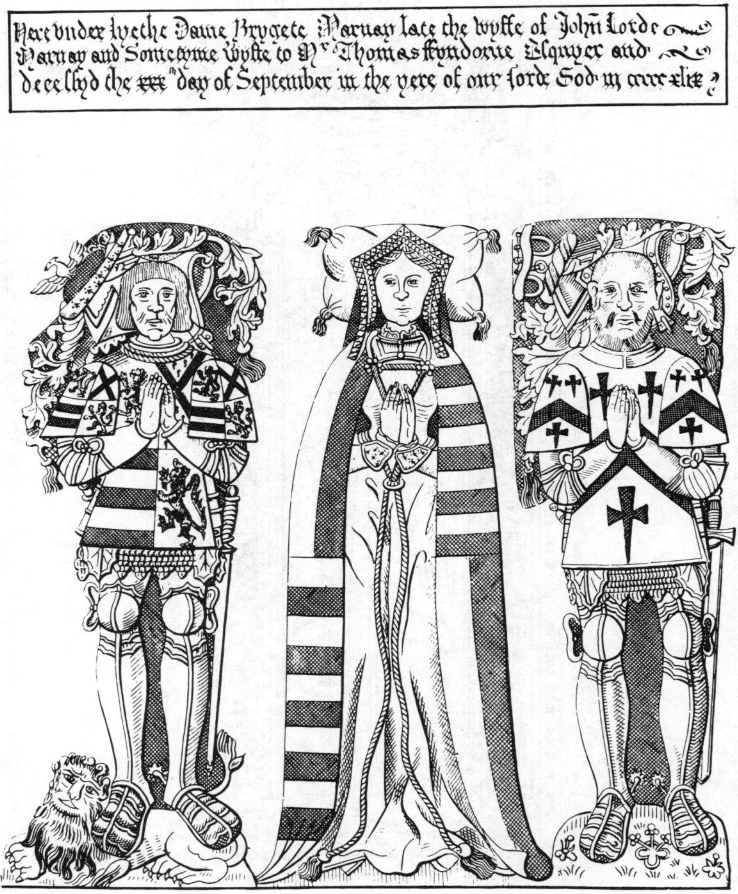

Little Horkesley: Marney brasses

East Horndon: incised tomb slab of Alice Tyrell

out to the east, and there is a broach spire on top. In the chancel stands a monument of 1634 to Daniel Caldwell and his wife; and the lectern of 1898 is an example of Art Nouveau.

Hutton, All Saints: The church still stands in a rural setting. The outside, entirely of flint, dates mostly from the Victorian rebuilding of 1873 by G.E. Street in his Gothic style. Inside, the nave arcades of quatrefoil piers, with moulded capitals and arches, are good fourteenth century work. Six posts with bracing and trellis strutting support the belfry and shingled spire, a fine example of Essex carpentry. The north porch is also original, although set on Victorian flint walls. The metalwork to pulpit and lectern is also Victorian. There is a brass of 1525 on the south chapel wall of a knight in armour and his wife.

Hythe, Colchester, St Leonard: The church was much restored after being damaged in the Essex earthquake of 1884, especially the west tower and south porch. The north aisle was built in the fourteenth century; the piers of the arcade have a quatrefoil section. The south arcade dates from the following century. The church has good roofs; the nave boasts a single hammerbeam without pendants, which is noteworthy. The font is octagonal, of the Perpendicular type, with shields in the quatrefoils. The parish was a medieval suburban one of Colchester.

Ingatestone, St Edmund and St Mary: The dedication to the Saxon saint suggests that there was a small wooden Saxon church here, all traces of which have vanished. As at Fryerning, the neighbouring parish, the nave is Norman and is built of pudding stone with some Roman brick. The tower, built about 1470 of local brick, is the striking feature of this church; it is tall, with angle buttresses, stepped battlements on a corbel frieze and pinnacles. The red brick is decorated with diaper work in black. The south chancel chapel is of sixteenth century brick, as is the three-bay arcade inside, with its octagonal piers and chamfered arches. The north chapel is early seventeenth century brickwork. The south arcade of three bays has piers of the Perpendicular style; and the nave roof is good, with octagonal king posts and four-way struts. The monuments to the Petre family are very good, especially the alabaster tomb chest to Sir William Petre and his wife (1572), recumbent effigies on a tomb decorated with shell-headed panels. In the south chapel lies Robert Petre (1593) and in the north chapel there is an elaborate composition to the 1st Lord Petre and his wife (1613). Also in the south chapel stands a fine bust in high relief to Captain John Troughton (1621), probably by the celebrated sculptor Epiphanius Evesham.

Ingrave, St Nicholas: This church was built in 1734 by Lord Petre, during a period when there was little ecclesiastical building in Essex. It is constructed entirely of brick. The architect is unknown, but his style resembles that of Hawksmoor. The bold west tower has octagonal turrets north and south; these rise above the parapet, which is carried on three arched corbels to each side. Doors and windows are round-headed with some circular windows to give variety. There are a white cornice and modillions to the nave and chancel eaves and a large stone inscription over the west door. The exterior is more successful than the interior, which is rather bleak. There are good brasses to Margaret Wake (1466) and to Sir Richard Fitzlewes (1528) with his four wives. There is also a good floor slab of 1787 to Charles Lucas, with fine lettering.

Inworth, All Saints: The west tower of red brick and the porch are Victorian work; but with the exception of the east end of the chancel, which is fourteenth century, the church dates from the late Saxon or Early Norman periods. It has several interesting features, such as the walls, which are built of pudding stone and flint, with some Roman brick, and its windows, splayed both inside and out. The low chancel arch has blank arches either side, where perhaps there were side altars, and there are squints each side of the chancel arch, possibly for lepers. Over the chancel arch are wall paintings depicting a bishop or saint by a tower, and a sailing boat, perhaps scenes from the life of St Nicholas. A south window incorporates fragments of medieval stained glass, and a screen of three bays dates from the fifteenth century.

Kelvedon, St Mary the Virgin: Norman work can be seen in the north-west angle of the nave; the nave and aisles are mostly thirteenth century, with fine arcades. Their circular piers have some good examples of stiff-leaf decoration; one pier only has four shafts with hollows between. The chancel, and the west tower with diagonal buttresses, battlements and a recessed spire, are of the fourteenth century. The chancel's east window is a Victorian insertion by Sir Arthur Blomfield. On the north side is some Tudor brick work, with a stepped gable and four-light window. The fifteenth century nave roof is very fine, with arched braces to the tie beams and traceried spandrels. The stained glass, mostly Victorian, includes a copy of a Rossetti picture of the Annunciation by Davis; and amongst the memorials to the Abdy family of Felix Hall nearby is one to Sir Thomas, of 1679.

Kelvedon Hatch, St Nicholas: The church was built of red brick in 1895, to a design by J.T.Newman. It has an unusual apse and dormer windows; it contains the fifteenth century font from the old church, which (although threatened with demolition) still stands in the grounds of Kelvedon Hall nearby.

Kirby-le-Soken, St Michael: The church, built of flint in the fourteenth and fifteenth centuries, was much restored in 1870. The west tower is big and impressive, with a quatrefoil frieze at the base, heavy diagonal buttresses, two-light bell openings and flint and stone chequered battlements.

Laindon, St Nicholas: This small church, which stands on a hill above new housing, contains notable timberwork. The west timber belfry is a typical Essex example. It is a complex structure, dating probably from the fourteenth century, with one tower rising within the other to carry the bells. The chancel roof is very fine, of seven cants and arched to the collars; the south porch, which has been rebuilt, has strange carvings in the spandrels depicting a dragon and a beast pierced by a cross. There is also an interesting two storied seventeenth century 'priest house' at the west end, built of timber. Nave and chancel are fourteenth century like the belfry; the font is thirteenth century, with blank pointed arches. There are two brasses of priests, one of 1480 and the other of 1510.

Lamarsh, Holy Innocents: The church has one of the six round towers of Essex, which is Norman. The roof and dormers are part of the 1865 restoration, also perhaps the lancet windows in the chancel. The nave and chancel, which are united, have fourteenth century windows; the south porch is built of red Tudor brick. The screen of ten bays separating nave and chancel is fifteenth century, and is decorated with traceried panels. The Beauchamp family received the manor of Lamarsh from King Stephen in 1140; they probably built the church at about that time, with the round tower for purposes of defence. The dedication to Holy Innocents is very rarely found in old churches. The stained glass in the east window dates from 1895.

Lambourne, St Mary and All Saints: Set amidst trees and looking out across the Roding valley, this church should not be missed by the connoisseur. It has a Norman nave and chancel, though the Norman doorways to north and south are now blocked. The north doorway is more elaborate, though the columns are missing; the tympanum has some interesting diaper work with stars and similar motifs carved in stone. A west doorway, dated 1726, leads one into the nave which has been remodelled as a Georgian interior of great charm. There is a fifteenth century roof, and a tie beam hidden beneath the plasterwork; the tie beam has a key pattern on its soffit, and the king post is covered with acanthus leaves. The chancel arch is segmental and coffered, and it rests on brackets in the correct Georgian style. Other features of interest are the reredos with Corinthian pilasters; numerous monuments to the Lockwood family, who lived at the nearby Hall, now demolished; a fourteenth century wall painting of St Christopher; and some very good panels of glass, made in Basel in the seventeenth century.

Langdon Hills: The pretty Tudor church of red brick, with a timber belfry, has become a house. Nearby, up the hill, stands the Victorian church of St Mary by William White (1876), built of rag-stone in the Early English style with a west tower and north aisle; it is now the parish church.

Langenhoe, St Mary (demolished): There was an earthquake in this part of Essex in 1884, and the old church was wrecked. A new one was built in 1886 using some of the old materials; but it was demolished when the parishes were amalgamated after the reservoir was created.

Langford, St Giles: The building was much restored in 1882; but it is of great interest as a rare English example of a Norman church with an apse at both ends. Here only the western apse survives with three small windows; the eastern apse (of which traces can be seen) was removed in late medieval times. The plain south doorway is also Norman. Churches with apses at each end derive their plan from the Roman basilicas, and are often found on the continent.

Langham, St Mary: Constable is said to have painted from the tower of this church; he was friendly with the rector here. The tower is thirteenth century, but was completed in Tudor brick, with pinnacles. The nave was already here in Norman times. The south aisle is fourteenth century; it has a six-bay arcade of octagonal piers, windows of the same period, and a recess in the south wall with three quaint heads. The chancel is also fourteenth century; its east window has reticulated tracery. There is a monument of 1853 to Margaret Maud and a cast-iron Victorian inscription in the porch urging drivers to rest their horses when going up Gun Hill on the main Ipswich–London road nearby.

Langley, St John the Evangelist: This church has a nave, chancel and unbuttressed west tower. The nave is Early English, and has a good south doorway. The chancel is built of Tudor red brick. The nave roof with its hammerbeam assembly is noteworthy. The church is much restored.

Latton, St Mary the Virgin: Now incorporated in Harlow New Town, this interesting old church manages to retain much of its rural flavour. It is built mainly of flint rubble, with nave, chancel and a west tower with diagonal buttresses. There are traces of Norman work in the south doorway, with a round-headed arch over the sixteenth century doorway and small Norman window close beside; Roman bricks are used as voussoirs. The north chapel is of brick, built in the later fifteenth century as are some windows in the nave south wall. The north side of the church was rebuilt in brick in the eighteenth century, but the south porch is a good sixteenth century example with brick walls and good timber work. Inside is a tomb chest to Peter Arderne, panelled with quatrefoils and shields, set between the north chapel and chancel. There are also a number of interesting brasses of the fifteenth and sixteenth century, including a good one to Francis Frankelin (1604). The north chapel has a wagon-vaulted ceiling and traces of wall paintings of the fifteenth century.

High Laver, All Saints: The church has a Norman nave, with many Roman bricks in the quoins, as at Magdalen Laver: there was probably a Roman villa at the Lavers. There is one Norman north window, an Early English chancel, and a fourteenth century tower with battlements and spire. The chancel arch is also fourteenth century. The font is octagonal, of the Perpendicular period. A brass to Edward Sulyard and his wife of c.1500 is of interest. The philosopher John Locke (1632-1704) is buried here and a wall tablet with wording composed by himself is on the south wall inside. He lived at nearby Otes, a country mansion, with his friends the Mashams – Mrs Masham was Queen Anne's great friend – but nothing now remains of the house. The Mashams are buried in the churchyard.

Little Laver, St Mary the Virgin: This church, standing next to the Grange, was rebuilt in 1872 with an apse in which are three windows with a slender arcade of alabaster (or marble) columns to each window. A good square font c.1200 (compare Moreton and Fyfield) which is decorated with fleur-de-lis, sun, moon, and whorl, roses, rosettes, was perhaps re-cut at the time of the rebuilding. The church has no tower or belfry, but Wright says it had a wooden central belfry and spire in 1842, so these disappeared in the rebuilding.

Magdalen Laver, St Mary Magdalen: The church lies in picturesque isolation, with a lake to its south. It stands close to the site of a Roman villa, and has Roman bricks in its quoins. The building is Norman in parts, with blocked windows of this period in south and west walls; it was much restored in 1875. There is an interesting wooden bell turret at the west end. A tie beam on wall pieces with arch braces carries the two east posts, which are probably fourteenth century. The tower aisles have pent roofs, and there is a pyramid roof on top. The screen is interesting, and probably dates from 1350; note also the painted reredos of The Ten Commandments (seventeenth century), and a beautiful tomb outside the south door to William Cole (1729), who was treasurer to St Thomas' Hospital and Sheriff of Essex. Did he give the reredos? There is a good west door and octagonal font, Perpendicular in style.

Lawford, St Mary: This church has a fourteenth century chancel with really beautiful examples of the Decorated style at its most exuberant; the carving may be compared with examples at Maldon and Little Dunmow, but this is especially lavish. The eight windows, four on each side, have varying tracery patterns, some of which are highly original. The east window itself has been renewed, and the reredos below is Victorian; but the rest of the work is medieval. The north and south windows, which are shafted, stand in pairs divided by a narrow blank arch with a tall gable over and buttresses on each side. There is carved foliage around the arches; owls and squirrels peer out from the leaves. In the north window arch are chains of little men playing instruments, wrestling, and so on. The piscina and sedilia have similar lavish decorations with the spandrels covered with angels playing harps. The whole effect is remarkable. The nave, porch and west tower are also fourteenth century, more restrained in style. The north arcade was built in 1826, while the chancel arch itself is Victorian, as is the glass in the east window. The font is Georgian, and there is a monument to Edward Waldegrave and his wife of 1584.

Layer Breton, St Mary: Built in 1923, this church is new and simple. It contains a good piece of Italian sculpture of the Virgin playing with Child, and a fragment of sixteenth century wood carving depicting Abraham and Isaac.

Layer de la Haye, St John the Baptist: The church now looks across the Abberton reservoir. Although building began in Norman times, it is mostly fourteenth century, with a west tower of Kentish rag-stone. The south arcade is nineteenth century, but the south porch with its verge boards and trenched collars is probably late fourteenth century work. In a recess of the chancel lies a marble tomb chest to Thomas Tey and his wife, without effigies or brasses (fifteenth century).

Layer Marney, St Mary the Virgin: The Marney family owned land in these parts since Henry II's reign. Henry VIII created the first Lord Marney in 1523; he died in 1523, and was succeeded by his son who became the second and last peer of the family. The church was rebuilt by the Marneys, no doubt at the same time as the great house close by, in the decades after 1500; it is constructed entirely of red brick with blue diaper work. The west tower, with its stone dressed diagonal buttresses, battlements and stair turret may be compared with other fine brick Tudor towers in Essex such as Fryerning, Rochford, Ingatestone and North Weald. The west window has three lights and the bell openings two lights. The south aisle, south porch and chancel porch have battlements. The windows all have four-centred arches and brick tracery, the east window having five lights and panel tracery at the top. A priest's chamber at the west of the north aisle has a chimney. The arcade piers have semi-octagonal shafts, and so does the tower arch; all are built in brick. Of great interest are the Marney tombs inside the church. The alabaster effigy of Sir William Marney (1414), on a tomb chest, is from the earlier church. His descendants, the first and second Lord Marney, lie on more elaborate tomb chests with canopies over; their effigies are beautifully carved in black Cornish marble (Catacusan). The terracotta panels and canopy are the work of craftsmen influenced or directed by Torrigiani whom Cardinal Wolsey had brought over from Italy to work for Henry VIII and himself. They should be compared with the tombs at Framlingham, in Suffolk, where lie buried the Duke of Richmond, Henry VIII's natural son, and the Duke of Norfolk. Terracotta is also used on the great gatehouse of the big house nearby.

Leigh-on-Sea, St Clement: This old parish church stands high, up steps from the village. The west tower with diagonal buttresses, three-light west window, and stair turret is fifteenth century, as is the north aisle. The south porch is of Tudor brick; the chancel is nineteenth century, and has a dramatic Crucifixion scene in the east window with fine colouring. There are various brasses, including one of 1453 to Richard Haddock, his wife and their many descendants; also a coloured bust to Robert Salmon (1617) who was Master of Trinity House, and described as 'the glory of it for 24 years'.

Great Leighs, St Mary: This is a church of much interest, set comfortably in the Ter valley. It has a round tower, one of six left in Essex (the seventh at Birchanger was demolished). The tower, built of flint, is of Saxon origin. It was altered by the Normans, who gave it a west doorway and flat buttresses. Its spire was rebuilt in 1882 and re-shingled in 1947. The nave is Norman, with Norman windows north and south, and a south doorway in which is set a fourteenth century door. The chancel dates from 1330; it has windows of the Decorated period and a fine east window with reticulated tracery. Inside, there is an interesting recess on the chancel north wall, with its arch cusped and gabled, and carved leaves in the spandrel. Opposite are sedilia and piscina with ogee heads; all are much restored, but seem to date from the early fourteenth century. In the nave is an octagonal font in the Perpendicular style; as well as some pews with good traceried ends (fifteenth century) and a nice gallery of George I's reign. There are a few pieces of medieval glass left in the windows.

Little Leighs, St John: This church lies off the main road in pleasant rural surroundings. It is built of flint, with the twelfth century nave of coursed, the thirteenth century chancel of uncoursed flintwork. There are Norman windows in the nave's north and south walls, and a weather-board belfry with shingled spire at the west end. The south doorway, with its door and scrolled hinges, is thirteenth century. Inside on the chancel north wall is a fourteenth century recess, with much cusped ogee arch and finial; it contains a finely carved wooden figure of a priest in his cope and alb. In the nave stands a good wall monument to Herman Olmins; there are an octagonal fourteenth century font, and some interesting pews with reeded ends. The chancel east wall was re-built in 1895.

Lexden, St Leonard: The nave of this church was built in 1821, at a time when Lexden was becoming a fashionable suburb of Colchester; the chancel was added in 1894. Inside is a fine monument of 1771 to Richard Hewitt, and some stained glass by Kempe of about 1900.

Lindsell: This small flint church stands in a pretty setting of trees, adjacent to Lindsell Hall, itself a fine old house. According to the records of Walden Abbey, a priest named Henry held office at this church in 1154. There is a good Norman arch from the nave into the chancel, which frames interesting fragments of medieval glass arranged in the east window. South of this arch is a squinch arch so that people in the south aisle could view the altar. The pier in the south arcade is quatrefoil and dates from the fourteenth century. The tower is unusually placed on the south-west corner but makes a pleasing composition. It is built of flint with sixteenth century brick buttresses and parapet. In the chancel north wall is a small opening, through which an anchorite (or hermit) could look from his cell outside. Anchorites were quite common in the Middle Ages, and there are examples of such openings at Chickney and Chipping Ongar. The font is good octagonal fifteenth century with quatrefoils and shields, and there is a brass to Thomas Fytche (1514) and his wife, six sons and five daughters.

Liston: There is a good west tower of red Tudor brick, with dark blue diaper work, diagonal buttresses and a three-light west window; stepped battlements stand on a trefoil corbel frieze and there is a high stair turret. Nave and chancel are Norman; there is a plain blocked north doorway. The chancel was widened in the thirteenth century and the windows have been renewed. A south chancel chapel was added in Victorian times, built of gauged flintwork. The chancel roof is good; the principals are panelled with figure carvings of the early sixteenth century. There is some good stained glass in the tracery of the north window, with small fifteenth century figures. Also of interest is a marble monument to Dr Clopton, and a tablet commemorating members of the Thornhill family killed at Cawnpore during the Indian Mutiny.

Littlebury, Holy Trinity: This interesting church was much restored in 1875 when the chancel was entirely rebuilt by Edward Barr. The west tower is fourteenth century, with windows typical of the period. The Norman nave dates from the late twelfth century. The south doorway is unusual, with differing capitals on its columns, one being late Norman in style, the other of the stiff-leaf type. The north arcade in the nave, with its circular piers, is also late Norman; the south arcade is later, and there must have once been a south transept. Both north and south porches are spacious sixteenth century additions, and unusually, contain traces of unfinished fan vaulting; perhaps the masons working at Saffron Walden began work here. Inside are some excellent brasses, with good details of medieval costume; a spectacular sixteenth century font case, with linen-fold panelling and pyramid canopy; and a fine north door with shears carved over the wicket door, indicating the local importance of the wool trade in those days.

Loughton: The two main churches were built in Victorian times to cope with suburban expansion.

St John the Baptist, Church Lane, was built in 1846 by Sydney Smirke. It is neo-Norman in style, and uses yellow brick with stone dressings, which were fashionable at the time. The architect copied the Norman plan of a central tower with transepts, nave and chancel.

St Mary the Virgin, High Street, was built in 1871 by T. H. Watson. It is in yellow and red brick, and has an east apse and aisles, whose circular piers have capitals carved with lush foliage.

St Nicholas, Rectory Lane, stands on the site of the old village church, which was rebuilt in 1877. The building is quite small, and contains some glass of the fifteenth century and interesting brasses. There is also an unusual shrine in the churchyard (1860) which supposedly resembles the shrine of Edward the Confessor.

Maldon: This picturesque old borough has three churches; much the most interesting of them is All Saints.

All Saints has two remarkable features – a triangular west tower of the thirteenth century and a very beautiful south aisle of the fourteenth century. The unusual shape of the tower was contrived in order to fit between the end of the old nave and the fish market once held in Silver Street; a shingled spire and three spirelets surmount it. The nave was rebuilt in 1728 of brick. The chancel and its chapels are fifteenth century; the south aisle, which was probably built by the D'Arcy family in 1330, contains some of the best decorative arcading in Essex, comparable with that in the Lady Chapel at Ely of similar date. Arcades on the south and west wall stand in two tiers with cinquefoil arches, with trails of roses decorating the jambs and voussoirs. The elaborate window tracery is said to be a copy of the original work. Below is a crypt, reached by a spiral staircase with vaulting; the piers of the arcade are quatrefoil with fillets made of Purbeck stone, and the arches are finely moulded. Also noteworthy are the Flemish stained glass figures of the four Evangelists; and in the chancel a monument of 1602 to Thomas Cammock, his two wives and twenty two children.

St Peter: Only the medieval flint west tower of this church survives; the rest was rebuilt in 1704 by Dr Plume in order to house a library.

St Mary the Virgin: Down the hill by the Blackwater stands the third church. It has a wide Norman nave (cf. Great Waltham) and the responds of the original chancel are still visible. The south aisle is all Victorian. A sturdy west tower dates from 1300; it was altered with brickwork in Charles I's reign, and given an octagon and spire in the eighteenth century.

Manuden, St Mary: This medieval church stands in the centre of a pretty village. It was largely rebuilt in 1863-67; only the fifteenth century north transept remains in its original state, and was for centuries the private chapel of the lords of the manor. Fortunately the beautiful early fifteenth century screen survives, with its dado panels and cusped and crocketted ogee arches, as well as the king post roof to the nave and north transept. Here lies the interesting monument to Sir William Waad, Lieutenant of the Tower of London at the time when Guy Fawkes and Sir Walter Raleigh were imprisoned there.

Great Maplestead, St Giles: This is an interesting old church, dating from Norman times, but much altered in the course of centuries, and especially by the Victorians. Its plan is unusual. Originally apse, sanctuary, choir, nave and west tower were Norman. An original round-headed window still exists in the apse, and there is Roman brick in the fabric. The chancel was rebuilt in the thirteenth century and a lancet window of this period may be seen. The nave was altered in the mid-fourteenth century, when the chancel arch was renewed and a south aisle built with octagonal piers to the arcade. The south transept, which is of the same century, was later enlarged in 1626 by the Deane family. The Norman tower, unbuttressed and built of flint, was repaired in red brick during the seventeenth century after being struck by lightning. The Victorians built the north transept and aisle to balance the south side. The two monuments to the Deane family, of nearby Dynes Hall, are noteworthy; in their chapel lies Sir John Deane (1625), clad in armour; at his feet lies the family crest (a muzzled bear), and on a shelf above kneel his wife and children. Opposite is the monument to Sir Daue Deane (1634). Standing over is the monument of Anne Deane, clad in widow's weeds; the fine carving is attributed to William Wright of Charing Cross. This elaborate monument stands on three columns. Also noteworthy is the font of about 1400, octagonal with shields enclosed in quatrefoils, and once elaborately coloured; the colouring was discovered in 1930 when the plaster was being removed.

Little Maplestead, St John the Baptist (the Round Church): This important church is unique in Essex. It is one of the five circular churches surviving in England; the others are at the Temple in London, at Ludlow Castle, and in Northampton and Cambridge. This, the latest of them, was built as a church of the Commandery of the Knights Hospitallers, probably on the pattern of the Church of the Holy Sepulchre in Jerusalem, which is circular.

The military orders of Knights Hospitallers (and Knights Templars) were bound by vows of poverty, chastity and obedience like other religious orders. Both were founded after the First Crusade in 1096.

Like the Templars, the Knights Hospitallers of the Order of St John of Jerusalem were pledged to devote their lives to the succour of sick and needy pilgrims or wounded crusaders. They followed the Augustinian Rule, took monastic vows and wore a black robe with a white cross on the left breast. None were admitted to the order unless of blameless character and noble birth. The knights possessed castles in Syria and priories in Western Europe, and their houses provided hospitals for sick and wounded crusaders. By 1240 the order had become very rich. Its churches (like those of the Templars) were planned with a circular nave

Little Maplestead, from Wallen

to the choir. The priory of St John in Clerkenwell, founded in 1150, formed its English headquarters; the head of the order, the Grand Prior, ranked as the first baron and took precedence over all the temporal peers of the realm.

Little Maplestead is their only church of importance which survives; it was built in about 1335, taking the place of an earlier structure which was probably round. Pope Clement V had dissolved the Order of Knights Templar in 1312 on the instigation of Philip, King of France, who coveted their wealth; eighteen of its English houses were made over to the Hospitallers and with this influx of wealth, the Hospitallers may well have rebuilt their church. It was built primarily for the use of the Knights, and not as a parish church, for the chancel formed the private chapel of the Knights to which the laity were not admitted.

A solid screen or pulpitum, with a central doorway, stood at the west end of the chancel, shutting it off from the circular portion; across the chord of the chancel apse was another screen, forming a vestry which was approached by a door just south of the present altar. Between these screens were the Knights' stalls; the circular nave was an adjunct to the preceptory whose use in the Hospitallers' time is uncertain. Probably it contained an altar for servants under the eastern arch, minor members of the order and the few parishioners of the area. By 1463, the Knights had ceased to reside at the priory, and the order drew a rent from the estate. In 1542 Henry VIII disposed of the manor and priory buildings to George Harper, but the church remained to serve the parish, the order itself having been dissolved in 1540.

In the years 1851-57 the church was drastically restored, and many of the old details were renewed or replaced under the direction of R.C. Carpenter. The walls were re-faced externally, the windows and buttresses renewed, dormer ventilators placed above the aisle roof, and the hexagonal belfry rebuilt. A new west porch took the place of the old one. The interior stonework was scraped or renewed; an altar was placed against the east wall of the apse and the ancient font moved to its present position. This restoration was probably necessary, but some of the character of the building was lost.

The chancel and apse are 35 ft long; the apse is windowless, but the windows on the side walls are reproductions of the original fourteenth century designs. There is no chancel arch and the junction with the round nave is unusual. The nave of six sides is only 10 ft in diameter, or 30 ft with its encircling aisles. The piers consist of three shafts, which are filleted and have V-shaped shafts to separate them. From the capitals of each pier spring arches, which rest on corbels on the aisle walls with their elaborate foliage carvings. These retain their fourteenth century design, but were probably 'renewed' during Carpenter's restor-

Little Maplestead, west doorway, from Wallen

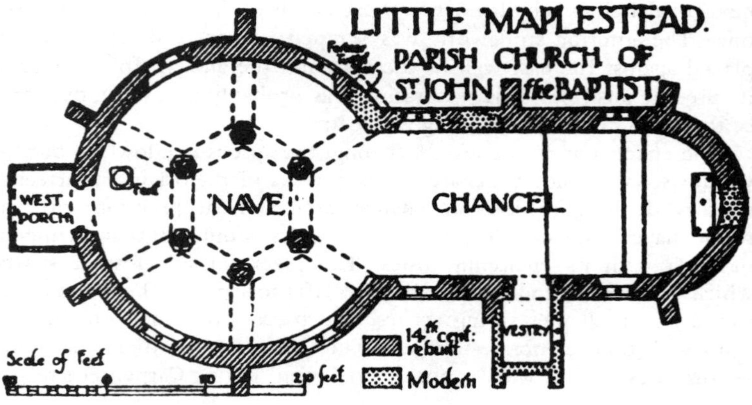

Plan of Little Maplestead

ration, as is recorded in his minute book. The circular aisle is lit by four windows, each of two lights, which are copies of the originals. In its general appearance, then, the church remains faithful to the original.

The west doorway seems to date from the fourteenth century. It has rectangular panels on its western face, containing quatrefoil flowers; the drip-stone is also carved with the three petalled flowers, and the whole doorway deserves study.

The belfry is no doubt a reproduction of the original design. The font is however the oldest feature of this very interesting church; it survived from the earlier church, and seems to date from the late eleventh century, with its crude Romanesque carvings and deep bowl for total immersion (as was the practice in early times).

Margaretting, St Margaret: The church has very interesting fifteenth century carpentry, particularly in its timber belfry (cf. Blackmore and Bulphan), designed as an extension to the nave. It is on ten posts, with arched braces north and south, as well as east and west; and there are the usual cross struts above. Outside, the tower is vertically weather-boarded, and on the north, south and west sides there is a hipped roof. Above the shingled bell tower is a shingled broach spire, which represents one of the final developments of timber belfry construction in the county. The nave roof, with an arch rising to the collar, is note-worthy (cf. Gosfield); and the north porch of timber is another example of good fifteenth century carpentry work. Inside, the fifteenth century piers to the south arcade have four shafts with hollows between, and four centred arches over. Of the same century, although somewhat restored, is the fine stained glass in the east window depicting the Tree of Jesse; a vine stem encircles the round panels and figures. Contemporary with the glass is a brass of a knight and his lady.

Mashbury: This small flint church is well grouped with the Hall and pond. The building is Norman; it has two windows of this period, and a plain doorway on the north side. There is a more elaborate Norman doorway on the south, with columns and decoration of the usual kind, which is sheltered by a Tudor brick porch. There are also fifteenth century improvements to the nave and chancel. On the west gable stands a pretty little nineteenth century bell turret. Inside, there is a seventeenth century pulpit. The windows contain some interesting fragments of medieval glass. Also worthy of note are the old doors and their ironwork.

Matching, St Mary the Virgin: The church stands in an idyllic setting; a lane leads past a lake, and up through oak and chestnut trees to the churchyard. There is a moated Hall to the south, and a marriage feast room to the west; the rectory lies on the north side. The church was much restored in 1875 by Blomfield, but the west tower is fifteenth century and some of the north and south aisle arcades are thirteenth century. There is a good Jacobean pulpit, and a well carved monument to Nicholas Ashton of 1716; also a brass of 1638 to John Ballett and his family. The stained glass is Victorian.

Mayland, St Barnabas: This church, which stands near Mundon Creek, was built in 1867 by the younger Hardwick. It has a nave and chancel with south porch, in the Early English style. The lancet windows are cusped, and there is a bellcote on the nave's eastern gable.

East Mersea, St Edmund King and Martyr: Baring Gould was a rector here in Victorian times, author of many books, including *Mehalah*, which is set in the village. The church has altered little since his day. It is nearly all fifteenth century, with a big west tower, built of stone with diagonal buttresses, battlements, stair turret and some flushwork at the base. The piers to the north arcade have four attached shafts, deeply undercut; the arches of the chancel and north chancel chapel are similar. Some windows were altered in the eighteenth century. The font is fifteenth century, with a modern cover; the pulpit and tester are seventeenth century.

West Mersea, St Peter and St Paul: The church stands on a Roman site in the old village. It has a very early Norman west tower; the upper parts with bell openings and battlements were added in the fourteenth century, as were the buttresses. The medieval nave was heightened in 1833, when its walls were painted with pretty cartouches; but the tower arch is plain early Norman, and the octagonal piers of the south arcade are fourteenth century. The octagonal font is thirteenth century and of Purbeck marble, with pointed arches to each side. There is a good sculptured lunette of Christ and Angels in the style of della Robbia – probably sixteenth century.

Messing, All Saints: A large and ugly brick tower was added to the west end of the church in 1840, together with a south transept; but parts of the nave and chancel are medieval, and some of the nave roof is very good. The chancel was enriched in Charles I's reign by the vicar Nehemiah Rogers, a friend of Archbishop Laud; it has elaborate panelling and stalls, which are decorated with rusticated oval frames and Jacobean ornament, all dating from 1634. Also remarkable is the beautiful stained glass in the east window, from the same period. This depicts the Acts of Mercy, with Faith, Hope and Charity in the upper windows, and is thought to be by van Linge, son of the famous glazier who worked at Cambridge.

Middleton, All Saints: This church lies close to the river Stour and the Suffolk border in a pleasant wooded setting. It has several unusual features, particularly its Norman architecture. The south doorway with its columns and zig-zag decoration is good Norman work, and the chancel arch is quite unusual; the polygonal inner shafts have a rare triangular form of Norman decoration, and the abacus which runs across to the north and south walls of the nave is elaborately carved. The nave also has interesting recesses on each side. In the chancel is a rare incised slab, commemorating the priest James Samson (1349); unfortunately the head has been removed. On the nave wall hangs a painting of the Annunciation in the style of Titian. Both the nave and chancel have well constructed roofs, and the south door is good Perpendicular work.

Mistley, St Mary: When Richard Rigby was altering Mistley Hall nearby in 1776, he called in Robert Adam to improve the new brick church, which was an oblong building put up in 1735. This he did by adding a tower at both ends, the base of the eastern one containing the chancel and altar. In the middle of each long side he built porticoed projections, to make internally segmental recesses screened by Ionic columns and fitted with galleries. It was an unusual church plan. Unfortunately the body of the church was demolished in 1870 and only the towers survive, made symmetrical by adding the Tuscan columns from the demolished porticoes. As a replacement, a Victorian Gothic church was erected on another site, designed by Wadmore and Baker, with a south-west steeple, an apsidal end and geometric tracery. Of the original medieval church, only a flushwork south porch survives.

Moreton, St Mary the Virgin: The church was given by William Scobies to the monastery of St Stephen at Caen in Normandy at the time of the Conquest. The nave and chancel are early thirteenth century, built of flint. The west tower was built or rebuilt in 1787; it is of brick with diagonal buttresses and battlements, and in Victorian times received cement rendering. The church was much restored in 1867. The square Purbeck marble font of c.1200 is noteworthy, and should be compared with that at Fyfield, with its decorations of arches, fleur-de-lis and sun, moon and whorl.

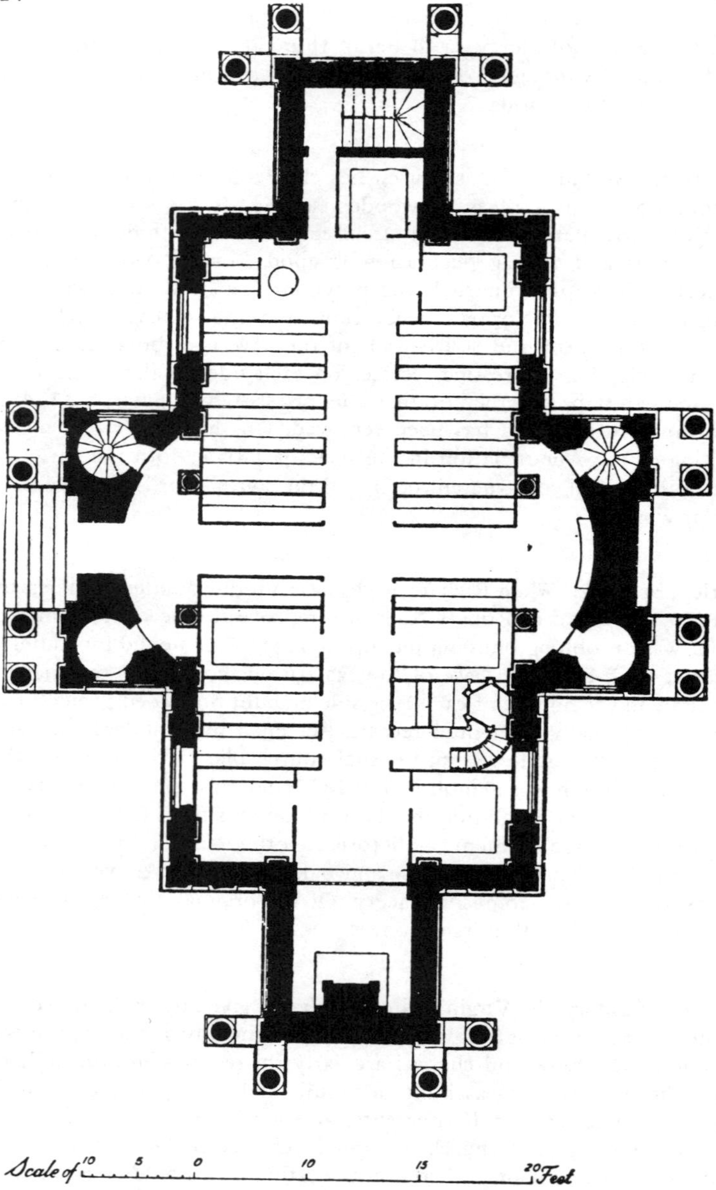

Plan of Mistley

Mountnessing, St Giles: The church stands beside the Georgian Hall south of the village. It has one of the many interesting belfries to be found in south Essex. This belfry is accommodated within the west bay of the nave as an independent structure; it stands on six large posts with cross beams, with arched braces and trellis strutting above. There are half-octagonal responds with moulded capitals on the east pair, and bracing struts from each aisle. The nave is thirteenth century, with a south aisle of the nineteenth century. The piers to the arcades are circular and their capitals moulded; from between the stiff-leaf foliage of one a face of a shrew peers out, her mouth bridled. The early nineteenth century chancel is brick, as is the west wall of the nave, dated 1653, with cramps securing the belfry timbers. There is a good painted eighteenth century reredos to the altar, and communion rails of the same period.

Mucking: The Saxon word 'ing' means a settlement in the marshes. The church of St John the Baptist was rebuilt in 1849 except for the chancel. This has an east window of the Perpendicular period, and a thirteenth century arcade to a previous north chapel blocked, the lancet windows re-used. The nave arcade has a circular pier of the thirteenth century, on which is carved stiff-leaf foliage with 'green men' peering out. There is a good monument of 1607 in alabaster to Elizabeth Downes, who had four husbands.

Mundon, St Mary: At the time of writing, the fourteenth century nave and eighteenth century brick chancel of this pretty isolated church are in danger of collapse. The sixteenth century belfry has been restored; it is an interesting late example of Essex carpentry, though small, on four posts and round the square a semi-octagonal aisle with pent roof. Also of great interest is the north porch, which is an example of early seventeenth century carpentry; there is wind bracing in the lower walls to keep the porch in contact with the main structure, and good carving of trailing vine-leaves on the four-centred arch; as well as octagonal pendants and a square gable finial.

Navestock, St Thomas the Apostle: This church stands in a pretty churchyard set on the edge of a park where the Waldegrave family once lived; their house was demolished long ago. The nave has a plain Norman doorway in the north wall. A south aisle with its stone arcade and circular piers was added in the thirteenth century; its eastern pier is made of oak and almost fluted – a very rare phenomenon. The splendid timber tower on the axis of this aisle may have been constructed at the same time. It was so well built that it stood up to the blast of a land mine which fell just to the south-west in the churchyard in 1940. The tower stands on four heavy oak posts, and arched braces meet in the centre on a foliage boss; aisles north, south and west run round the tower base, making it one of the finest timber towers in Essex. The chancel was rebuilt in the mid-fourteenth century, and there are good windows in the Decorated style, including the east window. On the walls are numerous monuments to the Waldegrave family; many of them are interesting and well carved – note the tablet recording that a (natural) daughter of James II married the first Lord Waldegrave. There is also a good monument of 1653 to John Greene. The organ dates from 1840. Note that the ironwork in the original Norman north door was transferred to the new door.

Nazeing, All Saints: Standing in its secluded churchyard and looking over the Lea valley, this church was once owned by King Harold and was later given to the monks of Waltham Abbey. The nave is Norman and the rere arch of one window is still visible. The chancel, north aisle and the porch with its tile-on-edge floor are all fifteenth century. The piers of the arcade are four shaft and four hollow, good of their period, with moulded arches. The early sixteenth century west tower is perhaps the best feature of the church, with its pleasing red brickwork and dark diaper pattern, diagonal buttresses and stair turret. The fifteenth century font is octagonal, with quatrefoils carrying shield. There are some wall monuments in the north aisles, including one by T. Harling (1823) of a figure by an urn.

Netteswell, St Andrew: This small thirteenth century flint church, with its tiled roof and fifteenth century belfry, stands engulfed in Harlow New Town. The chancel has lancet windows; the other windows are of the Perpendicular period. West of the south porch is an interesting brick panel with the arms of Abbot Rose of Waltham Abbey (1497); King Harold had given Netteswell to the abbey of Waltham in the eleventh century. The weatherboarded belfry has four-arched openings on each face, and a broach spire.

Nevendon, St Peter: This small stone church was much restored in 1875, but the building still has two fourteenth century doorways. The bell turret rests on the tie beams, which are fifteenth century.

Newport, St Mary the Virgin: This is quite a big church, which belonged to the college of St Martin-le-Grand in London during the thirteenth century. Although the tower with pinnacles and battlements is mid-Victorian, the chancel crossing and transepts are thirteenth century, and there are still lancet windows. The south arcade has octagonal piers of the fourteenth century; the quatrefoil north arcade piers are fifteenth century, with decorated capitals. The big handsome porch, embattled and with a room above it, is fifteenth century, as is the nave clerestory; the brick clerestory to the chancel is sixteenth century. Inside are an interesting and unusual thirteenth century font, and a screen of the fifteenth century. A rare church treasure is a thirteenth century chest, which could be used as a portable altar. Its front is decorated with circles, lozenges and shields; and the lid opens to form a reredos painted in oils, depicting the Crucifixion, the Virgin Mary, and Saints John, Peter and Paul. Also noteworthy are the old oak lectern, and some fourteenth century stained glass figures of St Katherine with her wheel and St Michael in the north transept. There is a fine early eighteenth century wall monument in the chancel to the Dents of Shortgrove, just north of the village.

North End (near Ford End), Black Chapel: Possibly built by Augustinian canons in the fifteenth century, this is a rare example of a timber-framed medieval chapel, with a priest's house attached, set at right angles to the nave and chancel. The oak structure is interesting. Inside, the chapel was given an early nineteenth century Gothick look and a west gallery; it is furnished with box pews. The fifteenth century oak pews remain on the north side, as well as a simple screen.

Cold Norton, St Stephen: The twelfth century church became ruinous, and was taken down in 1853 and replaced by one designed by Pritchett. Pulpit and lectern are made out of the old oak beams. There is a brass to a lady of 1520.

Norton Mandeville, All Saints: This small church in a quiet isolated parish dates from Norman times, when the great Mandeville family were given large tracts of land in Essex by William the Conqueror. The church was altered in the fourteenth century; the tracery of the windows is in the Decorated style, and the belfry could be fifteenth century. The king posts to the nave roof on braced tie-beams are good; and there is a Norman font of Barnack stone, which is massive and square with angle columns, set round with medieval tiles.

Black Notley, St Peter and St Paul: The church is still set in the countryside, although Black Notley is now a suburb of Braintree. The flint church of Norman times, with Norman windows and plain doorways, was much restored in 1879. The west belfry with 5 bells is carried on eight sturdy posts with arched braces and trellis strutting. On the south door is ironwork of the twelfth century. Inside can be seen the remains of the stairs to the rood loft, and there is a floor slab to Sir Walter de Wydenal, parson here in the twelfth century, with its inscription in Lombardic letters. There is some fifteenth century stained glass in a north window. Outside the south wall of the church is the tomb of John Ray (1628-1705), the local blacksmith's son who became a world famous naturalist, laying the foundations for Linnaeus and his system.

White Notley, St Ethelreda: The church dates from Norman times. It once had an apsidal chancel; the chancel arch dressed with Roman bricks is Norman, and there are round-headed niches, and traces of a south chancel doorway. The chancel was altered in the thirteenth century, and the south aisle added with circular piers, followed by the north arcade with octagonal piers. There is much interesting timberwork in the church. The south porch is fourteenth century work, and the south door of the same century. The timber belfry is noteworthy; it was constructed in Henry VII's reign, and stands independently on four tall posts with its cusped arch. The nave roof is of the same date. The font is octagonal, of the Perpendicular period, and there is a thirteenth century stained glass portrait of a saint or king in an older window, cut from a Saxon headstone.

Great Oakley, All Saints: The church, which is well situated, has a west tower which was built of septaria and repaired in eighteenth century red brick, with a white weatherboard upper stage. The nave, without aisles, is twelfth century, with a Norman window in the north wall and a long chancel of the fourteenth century. The east window is later, with four lights and panel tracery filled with Victorian glass. There is a pretty fourteenth century north doorway, enriched with carvings of angels. The font is twelfth century Purbeck marble standing on five shafts.

Little Oakley, St Mary: The church looks out towards Hamford Water. It has a west tower of Tudor brick, with a west doorway having shields in the spandrels, and a frieze of shields below the west window whose upper part was not completed. The nave is Norman. The fourteenth century chancel has good work of the Decorated period, with a window of three lights, reticulated tracery and two steeply canopied niches with crockets and finials; the piscina is decorated in similar fashion, and the other windows have good tracery. On the south side, the priest's door is placed in the middle of a buttress.

North Ockendon, St Mary Magdalene: This church stands to the west of the village. The building is Norman, with a fine south doorway with columns; the arch over, decorated with zig-zag, is stilted. The north aisle and north chancel chapel are later, of the Early English period. The piers vary in date and style; two bays have a circular thirteenth century pier, and the north chancel chapel has a quatrefoil pier of the Perpendicular style. The east arch is fifteenth century, as is the chancel arch. Of much interest are the numerous monuments to the Poyntz family, who were lords of the manor from about 1350, inheriting it from the Baudwin family. There are brasses and a fine alabaster tomb chest, with effigies of Sir Gabriel Poyntz and wife (1607) perhaps carved by Gerard Johnson, a famous Dutch sculptor, together with other important monuments to them. Also to be noted is a thirteenth century stained glass window of a female saint (St Helen?); and the pulpit, which is probably seventeenth century.

South Ockendon, St Nicholas: Standing by the village green and opposite the seventeenth century pub, this church was much restored in 1866. The round west tower is one of the six remaining in Essex. It was built of flint in the thirteenth century; and has been somewhat reduced in height, now standing only 37 ft high. The north doorway, which is late Norman twelfth century, is very beautiful; it has three orders and the middle columns have spiral fluting and shaft-ring enrichments. The capitals are carved with volutes and foliage, and the arches are also decorated lavishly with chevrons and billets. Inside, there are some brasses, including one (headless) to Sir Ingram Bruyn of 1400; also an alabaster monument to Sir Richard Saltonstall, Lord Mayor of London, of 1602. His wife was of the famous Poyntz family of North Ockendon.

Chipping Ongar, St Martin of Tours: Close to the Norman castle (only the earth mound and moat now remain) stands this good example of an early Norman parish church. Apart from the Victorian south aisle, vestry and porch, the church dates from about 1100 and is built of flint rubble and re-used Roman brick. The six original Norman windows may be seen at the east end, arranged in two tiers, replaced later by an early fourteenth century window — the stained glass is by Leonard Walker (1929). The lancet windows in the north wall of chancel and nave are original; a Norman doorway, now blocked, is also visible, with the stoup for holy water beside it. An unusual feature is the recess with window in the chancel north wall, where an anchorite lived in medieval times; he could take part in services, watching the altar from his cell through the small window (cf. Lindsell and Chickney). Parts of the chancel roof trusses are Norman, including the scissor braces to the rafter couples with notch-lapped joints, and the V struts above the collars; there were later additions and alterations. The nave roof with tie-beams and king posts is fourteenth century. At the west end is a Georgian gallery on Tuscan columns.

The church has a good early seventeenth century pulpit. In the chancel are fine communion rails; there are two wall monuments, one to Mrs Mitford by Nollekens, and one to Nicholas Alexander, perhaps by Edward Stanton, both of the eighteenth century. South of the altar are two black slabs, which mark the graves of Jane Pallavicini, daughter of Sir Oliver Cromwell, uncle to the Protector, and her son; the Pallavicinis were rich seventeenth century Italian bankers.

High Ongar, St Mary: The church has a twelfth century nave built of flint rubble, and a thirteenth century chancel with a brick tower of 1858 (similar to St Germain's, Bobbingworth); this replaced a wooden tower with shingled spire. Both north and south doorways to the nave are Norman; the south one is particularly fine and ornate. The thirteenth century lancet east windows contain two interesting stained glass armorial shields of 1536, with the initials of Henry VIII and Jane Seymour; at this time Henry owned the neighbouring Forest Hall estate. In his *History of Essex*, Wright records the nave roof as having been painted with 'clouds, stars and the rising sun', but this was all obliterated in 1855. On the chancel walls are two good monuments, one to Richard Stane of Forest Hall (1714), and one to a member of the Earl family who was a rector of the parish.

Orsett, St Giles and All Saints: The church stands in a village still relatively unspoilt. Built mostly of flint, it has a Norman nave and a handsome south doorway, with volute capitals and tympanum carved with diapers; close to it is a small Norman window. Partly thirteenth century, the north aisle seems to have been enlarged in the fourteenth century when the chancel was also built. The windows are of that century. The later west tower was rebuilt in brick with a north-west turret in the seventeenth century, and crowned with a small spire. The rood screen is Ninian Comper's work of 1911, and the north and south chancel screen by Nicholson is also modern; there is a fifteenth century choir screen. There are a number of good brasses and monuments to be seen, including a semi-recumbent figure of John Hatt (1658), and several of the Baker family, including one carved by Westmacott to Richard Baker (1827). Also noteworthy are five Italian panels in high relief of the eighteenth century, set below some stained glass by Kempe. In the churchyard is a fine tomb to Samuel Bonham of 1745, of unusual design. The church was much damaged by fire in 1926.

Paglesham, St Peter: The nave and chancel are Norman; original windows survive on the north side, although restored. A grey west tower was added in the fifteenth century, with diagonal buttresses and battlements; its west window of three lights has panel tracery. In the chancel, a scalloped bowl, possibly Norman, is used as the piscina; and there are two carved seventeenth century chairs.

Panfield, St Mary: This is a small village church, built of flint in the fifteenth century but a good deal restored. It has a nave, chancel and a west belfry on stout posts, with three quatrefoil openings to each side and shingled spire over. The south porch is a good example of mid-fifteenth century carpentry, with its traceried sidelights, six on each side. Inside, there is a tomb recess on the north wall of the nave; a pulpit, on which panels of sixteenth century tracery have been re-used; and some good fifteenth century stained glass of two saints in a north window in the nave.

Great Parndon, St Mary: The church stands in a rural backwater on the south-west fringe of Harlow New Town, with three old chestnut trees to shade it. The chancel nave and tower are fifteenth century; the nave and chancel are undivided and contain good windows of the period. The south brick transept is eighteenth century, and the north Edwardian, while the north porch is new but pleasing. The octagonal font of the Perpendicular period has a stem with tracery, and a bowl with quatrefoils. The brass in the chancel to Rowland Rampston (1598) is good.

Little Parndon, St Mary: This Victorian flint church lies on the north fringe of Harlow New Town. It has an apsidal east end and a picturesque belfry with brick nogging between the studwork. Inside, there is a marble monument to Sir Edward Turnour, who represented Essex in the Commonwealth Parliament and became Speaker of the House of Commons.

Pattiswick, St Mary: This is a small church, with nave and chancel of equal height, and a western bell turret. The nave is thirteenth century and the chancel fourteenth century. Of interest is the roof to the nave, with its tie-beam and octagonal king post, and with its capital ornamented with three scroll mouldings; it probably dates from the mid-fourteenth century. The west bell turret is carried on two straight tie beams. The north porch also has a good roof.

Pebmarsh, St John the Baptist: The church is mostly fourteenth century; the nave, aisles, chancel and west tower, and windows date from this period. The piers to the arcades have semi-circular shafts to the arches and semi-octagonal shafts to the nave. The sedilia are elaborated with crockets and finials. In Tudor times, the tower was embellished with red brick battlements (with diaper work). Pinnacles and a south porch were added, which is quite elaborate, with a stepped gable; the church was also given battlements. Inside is a very fine early brass of 1323 of Sir William Fitzralph, complete in his armour, of a style just post-Bannockburn. Some of his heraldic glass is in the north chancel window; other Victorian glass by Clayton and Bell is in the East window, and there is modern glass in the east window of the north aisle. Inside, the flint rubble walls have been scraped of most of their plaster.

Peldon, St Mary the Virgin: The big west tower, with buttresses, battlements and stair turret, is of Kentish rag-stone of the early fifteenth century. The nave, also of stone, has sixteenth century brick buttresses and clerestory, with windows of two lights; the brickwork contrasts agreeably with the stone. The chancel is an addition or rebuilding of 1859 in white brick with flint and stone. Inside is an octagonal font of the thirteenth century, and a fine hammer-beam nave roof, constructed no doubt at the same time as the Tudor clerestory.

Pentlow, St George: The west tower is one of the six remaining round towers in Essex; it is a late example from the fourteenth century, with very thick walls (cf. Bardfield Saling) seemingly added on to the nave. This is Norman, with a west doorway of the period which has columns with scalloped capitals and a bear's head over the arch. The chancel also is Norman, with an apse having three windows, as is customary. The north chapel is Tudor with its stepped brick gables, and it has a good tunnel vault, beneath which is the tomb chest to the Kempe family with three recumbent effigies of 1609. There is another tomb chest in the chancel to the Feltons (1542), and a big Norman font whose sides are decorated with leaves and crosses, together with a fifteenth century font cover.

Pleshey, All Saints: The church is more interesting historically than architecturally. Here at Pleshey Castle, once the centre of the de Mandevilles' Norman estate, Richard II arrested his uncle the Duke of Gloucester who had married Eleanor, co-heiress of the last Bohun, Earl of Essex. The Duke was led away to eventual execution. The flint church was rebuilt in 1868 to Chancellor's designs. Only the crossing-arches remain of the medieval church, which was cruciform in plan, because of its foundation as a college of priests in 1393. The central tower and stair turret are of good Victorian design. There are fine monuments inside to Samuel Tufnell of Langleys (1758) and to Sir William Joliffe (1749) with urn and cherubs' heads.

Pitsea, St Michael: The church stands on a hill with a good view towards the Thames. The west tower dates from about 1500, but is much restored; the rest was rebuilt in 1871 to designs of Sir Arthur Blomfield.

Prittlewell, Annunciation of the Blessed Virgin Mary: Standing just south of the old Cluniac priory, this large church dates from Norman times. Parts of an early arch built with Roman bricks may be seen in the nave, and two small Norman windows, now blocked, are also visible. There is no north aisle, and the arcade of the south aisle is partly cut through the Norman wall, forming three bays with octagonal piers; the other bays are fifteenth century with lighter octagonal piers, two bays of which form the south chancel chapel. The south windows are big late Perpendicular with three lights. The large west tower of Kentish ragstone dates from about 1470, with three-light bell openings and battlements decorated in flint and stone; similar decorations are found on the two-storey south porch and elsewhere on the building. There is some interesting sixteenth century stained glass, perhaps German, in the east window of the south aisle; and a fine carved south door of the same period.

Purleigh, All Saints: This church, with its wide views, has been restored with aid from the United States since Lawrence Washington, George Washington's ancestor, was rector here in the seventeenth century. The fine west tower, with its bands of flint and stone with some chequerwork, has ornamented angle buttresses; like the chancel, it is fourteenth century. The south porch is of Tudor brick, with a four-centred opening and two-light windows east and west. The arcades in the nave have thick octagonal piers; the chancel has windows of the fourteenth century, and piscina and sedilia have ogee arches and cusping. In the heads of some windows is stained glass of the fourteenth century, tabernacle work. The handsome pulpit dates from the early eighteenth century, and there are large paintings of Moses and Aaron by I. Fairchild on the walls.

Quendon: The church is very trim and tidy and stands just off the main road. It has no known dedication, but dates back to the thirteenth century. Externally the building looks very restored from 1861, with its new weatherboard belfry of 1963. The interior is pleasing, with sturdy thirteenth century circular piers to north and south arcades of three bays; there are niches each side of the altar. The chancel was rebuilt in the sixteenth century, and its roof brightly coloured. On the north wall is a fine monument of 1685 to Thomas Turner of Quendon Hall, and there are two good floor slabs to the same family. The eighteenth century organ case is thought to have come from Jesus College, Cambridge. There is no old stained glass in the church except for the two-light window over the chancel arch; the nineteenth century east window is by Ward and Hughes.

Radwinter, St Mary the Virgin: The church seems large for so small a parish; it was extensively rebuilt in 1870 by Eden Nesfield, whose work is also evident in the village. The church was reconstructed of knapped flint with bands of tiling, and only the unusual south porch is medieval; it is fourteenth century timber work with an upper oversailing storey, but Nesfield doctored it with parged panels. The west tower was added in 1887. Inside, the north and south arcades survive from the original; also the chancel arch and the fourteenth century nave roof, with good tie-beams, braces and king posts. The chancel roof is Victorian, as is the elaborate metal screen. The Flemish reredos is of the sixteenth century, with much carving; and there are some fine Italian paintings in the north aisle.

Ramsden Bellhouse, St Mary: The name 'Bellhouse' probably derives from the Belhus family, who once owned the manor. The church was rebuilt in 1880 with a red brick chancel and nave of rag-stone. It has a fine belfry of the Essex variety with a white weatherboarded and shingled spire, standing on four posts and braced in the usual way from north to south; round it are three small aisles north, west and south, and there is a good west doorway. It is all probably late fifteenth century; including the south porch.

Ramsden Crays, St Mary: The church is prettily set, up a long lane and remote from the village. It was built of rag-stone in 1871, but the windows are probably re-set fifteenth century. The west belfry is of white weatherboard, with a shingled broach spire.

Rawreth, St Nicholas: Apart from the west tower, the church was rebuilt in 1882 to designs of Ernest Geldart, rector of Little Braxted; flushwork adds to the composition, with flint, stone, and so on in the porch. Inside is a brass of 1576 to Edmund Tyrell and his wife; he was a member of the influential Essex family whose monuments may be seen at East Horndon and elsewhere.

Rayleigh, Holy Trinity: The church stands on an eminence close to the old castle. There is Norman work in the chancel, but the building was mostly re-fashioned in the fifteenth century, with a fine west tower having diagonal buttresses, stair turret, west doorway and three-light window over. The south side, all embattled, has a beautiful brick porch with two-light side windows, trefoil arched corbel frieze, and good brick vaulting inside; it shelters the south doorway, which is thirteenth century and came from the earlier church. The aisle windows are of the three-light Perpendicular variety. The arcades inside have piers with four shafts and four hollows; and there is a good chancel arch. In the south chancel chapel built by William Alleyn (1517) lies his monument, a tomb chest with richly cusped quatrefoils, set in a recess. The rood stairs may still be seen and the old screen at the end of the north aisle. There is a brass of 1418 to John Barrington and his wife.

Rayne, All Saints: Although the nave and chancel were built in Victorian red brick in the 1840s, the west tower is a handsome example of Tudor brickwork and unusual in its design. It was built in 1510 by Sir William Capel, a Lord Mayor of London, who lived at Rayne Hall just north of the church. The tower with its blue brick diaper work has buttresses with four set-backs, and is crowned by pinnacles. At its base is a frieze of quatrefoils; over the west window is a blank stepped gable with a finial, and below the bell openings another frieze of castellations; at the top are the customary battlements. The substantial stair turret on the south side is topped by an unusual stepped pinnacle.

Rettendon, All Saints: The church, with its fine fifteenth century tower, has wide views to the south. The chancel with its sedilia and piscina is thirteenth century; the rest of the church was built in the Perpendicular period. The north aisle has octagonal piers and a roof of good early Perpendicular carpentry work, with arches to the collars, and to the tower diagonal buttresses and stair turret. On the east wall of the chancel chapel is a very sumptuous monument of 1727 to Edmund Humphrey by Samuel Chandler, in veined marble; there are four standing figures and one semi-reclining with cherubs. Also noteworthy are some poppy heads on the chancel stalls, depicting animals, and several sixteenth century brasses to earlier members of the Humphrey family. A stone slab of about 1200 has carvings of birds and foliage.

Rickling, All Saints: The nave of this small flint church is Early English; a deep splayed lancet window remains on the west wall. The tower, south aisle and chancel are fourteenth century, the tower having low diagonal buttresses and battlements. Inside, the piers to the south arcade are quatrefoil, and the arches have a quadrant and hollow-chamfer moulding. Set in the fine chancel arch is a fourteenth century screen; the shafts have shaft rings, and the tracery is of squashed ogees. In the chancel north wall is a low tomb chest under a big ogee arch; and on the south side is an oblong tomb chest, the sides decorated with quatrefoils with shields. The pulpit is a good example of fifteenth century work, with fine panel tracery. The modern reredos was carved by Flemish craftsmen.

Ridgewell, St Lawrence: The church is fifteenth century, with a west tower which has angle buttresses, with flint decoration at its base, battlements and a stair turret. The piers to the north arcade have semi-polygonal shafts, and the north chancel chapel has an octagonal pier. The nave roof is very good work of the fifteenth century, arched to the collars and with short hammer beams on alternate frames; there is leaf ornament carved along the wall plates. The screen's dado is noteworthy, and also the arcading in the vestry wall, which must be re-used thirteenth century work.

Rivenhall, St Mary and All Saints: Recent archaeological investigations have shown that this site has been occupied since before Roman times. There was a Roman settlement here, and the remains of a large Roman villa lie beneath the church; on its foundations was built first a wooden Saxon church, then one of stone which was incorporated in the medieval and later reconstructions. The church was rebuilt in 1838 by Lord Western of nearby Felix Hall, Kelvedon. At the same time a tall west tower was added, with polygonal buttresses and battlements; inside, the church is plain, with a coved ceiling. The stained glass is outstanding, and was installed in 1840 by the rector, who brought it back from France. The twelfth century panels are said to have come from the church of St Martin at Chênu in Sarthe. The east window has four large roundels with borders, representing a Majesty, the Virgin and Child, the Announciation and an entombment of the Virgin, all late twelfth century. A knight on horseback inscribed 'Robert Lemaire' is thirteenth century. The Adoration of the Magi is fifteenth century, and there are other panels elsewhere of different dates, a superb collection unparalleled elsewhere. There are some fine monuments, including one of 1608 to Ralph Wyseman and his wife Elizabeth, granddaughter of Lord Rich (see Felsted); and others to the Western family, Thomas Western (1699), William Western (1729), and one of 1844 in the Gothick style to Lord Western.

Rochford, St Andrew: The Tudor church is related in style to nearby Rochford Hall, once the home of Anne Boleyn's father. It has a fine west tower of brick with diaper work, angle buttresses, with a south-east stair turret, a big three-light window of brick, and battlements. Over the west doorway are set the arms of the Botelers, Earls of Ormonde. The south side of the church is battlemented with stone and flint chequerwork. The chancel has a big five-light east window; south aisle and north chapel windows have three lights. The north aisle is Victorian and the red brick north chancel chapel has unusual half-timbered gables. The arcades inside have octagonal piers and double chamfered arches; there is a brass of 1514 to Mary Dilcok.

Abbess Roding, St Edmund: Roding derives from the Saxon 'ing', a settlement, and Hrotha, a family name. There were nine Roding (pronounced Roothing) villages, of which eight survive. This parish is named 'Abbess', because in early times both church and manor were owned by the Abbess of Barking. The dedication suggests a Saxon foundation. Built of flint, the church has a fourteenth century nave, and fifteenth century chancel and roof. It was much restored in 1867, when the west tower was built. Inside is a square late Norman font with interesting decorations; a medieval screen with ogee arches and tracery over; and a Georgian pulpit and tester. Some fifteenth century glass in the south chancel window depicts a bishop and St Margaret (?). There are also good Jacobean wall monuments to Sir Gamaliel Capel (1613) of Rookwood Hall nearby, and to Lady Luckyn (1633) with cherubs, possibly carved by Epiphanius Evesham. Note the hour glass near the pulpit.

Aythorpe Roding, St Mary: The church is set amidst cornfields. Its walls are cement rendered, and its spire is shingled on a weatherboarded belfry. With their deeply splayed lancet windows, nave and chancel seem to date from the thirteenth century, and possibly also the unusual belfry which is carried on transoms with arch braces. The construction of the square turret is similar to Bradwell near Coggeshall, and is thought to be late Norman. Each wall of the turret has saltire bracing.

Beauchamp Roding, St Botolph: The Beauchamp family owned this parish in the thirteenth century. The church stands in rural isolation; perhaps the village was moved after the Black Death; it is dedicated to a Saxon saint. The building has a fourteenth century nave and a fifteenth century chancel; the west tower has diagonal buttresses and battlements. The chancel tie-beams with arched braces rests on stone corbels, strangely carved. In the nave's south wall are the stone stairs to the old rood loft. The pull-out steps to the raised pews at the back of the nave are unusual.

Berners Roding: The name 'Berners' derives from the family of that name; the church has no known dedication. The building is small and isolated, with only the Hall for a neighbour. It dates from the fourteenth century, with two windows of that period; the east window has good brick tracery of the sixteenth century. The small timber belfry has one bell of 1594.

High Roding, All Saints: The church lies in farmland to the south-west of the village. It has a small flint nave and chancel of the thirteenth century, with the south porch a little later, and a Victorian belfry. The south door is bound with medieval ironwork, dating probably from the thirteenth century; the nave roof seems fourteenth century. There are some pieces of fourteenth century stained glass in the windows. The octagonal font is of the Perpendicular period; the pulpit has some traceried panels of about 1500.

Leaden Roding, St Michael: The parish is named 'Leaden' perhaps because the church was the first thereabouts to be roofed in lead. At the end of a path flanked by yews is a Norman doorway, set in the south side of the Norman nave and chancel. The church is built of flint with a shingled broach spire, (like Aythorpe Roding) which is set on a weatherboarded belfry of the fifteenth century. The belfry is carried on posts with low braces and cross strutting. The windows are mostly renewed. Inside is a sixteenth century pulpit which stands on a trumpet-shaped stem. The communion rails are of the seventeenth century.

Margaret Roding, St Margaret of Antioch: A small church built of flint set in a pretty churchyard, consisting of chancel and nave with a belfry with one bell on its west wall. The nave is Norman with walls 3 ft thick; there are several Norman windows with wide splays inside and a Norman doorway north and south, the south one being a fine example of one of several elaborate doorways to be found in Essex. It is of two orders, the outer columns ornamented with zig-zag fluting, and scalloped capitals and moulded bases; the tympanum, a modern replacement, has trellis pattern diaper work and segmental soffit. There is other elaborate carving to be found round some window heads and at the west quoining. The chancel was rebuilt about 1400, and contains an elaborate recess on the north wall of the late fourteenth century and an unusual sedilia on the south wall. There are Victorian paintings on the walls of evangelists and saints. The font is octagonal, early fifteenth century, each face with circle and quatrefoil and shield within. The thirteenth century oak chest should be noticed, and also the late twelfth century ironwork to the south door.

White Roding, St Martin: This church has a Norman nave with Norman doorways north and south, three splayed Norman windows, and a Norman arch to the chancel. There are Roman bricks in its quoins – the village lies just west of the Chigwell–Dunmow Roman road. There was considerable Victorian restoration to the church; but the chancel is Early English, the battlemented west tower with diagonal buttresses was built around 1500, and the porch is Jacobean. Worth noting also are a Purbeck marble Norman font, a south door of great antiquity, probably Norman; stone stairs to the old rood loft; a king post roof to the nave, possibly dating from 1250-1300; and an elegant eighteenth century wall monument to John Maryon. In the churchyard near the porch is a good early nineteenth century tomb with Doric columns.

Roxwell, St Michael and All Angels: The fourteenth century nave and chancel were extensively rebuilt in 1854 and a north aisle added, plus a belfry in 1891. Of interest is the screen, fashioned from an organ case built in 1684 which was once in Durham Cathedral, with its classical and Gothic detail. In the west window is some good stained glass of 1600 from Germany; and in the chancel are two monuments to the Branston family, one of them a Lord Chief Justice, and the other to Mary Byng (1744), who lived at nearby Skreens, now demolished.

Roydon, St Peter: The church is set in a pleasant village. It is built of flint with a west tower. The nave is thirteenth century, with its lancet window on the south wall in Decorated style and a Perpendicular window beside it. The north aisle of the fourteenth century has good windows of its period with ogee tracery, and the arcade piers have octagonal and double chamfered arches over. The octagonal thirteenth century font is noteworthy, with four men at the corners wearing rolled brim hats. The plain heavy screen is fourteenth century, with five ogee arches each side. In the chancel are brasses to Thomas Colte (1471), who was rewarded by Edward IV for his bravery in the Wars of the Roses with a gift of the nearby Nether Hall estate. Jane Colte was Sir Thomas More's first wife. Note also the good king post roof to the nave and some interesting hatchments.

Runwell, St Mary: The church is mostly of the Perpendicular period; but the chancel was lengthened in 1907 and the screen is 1909. The west tower with diagonal buttresses, battlements, stair turret and recessed spire is fifteenth century; the nave has arcades with short round columns of the thirteenth century. There are splendid fifteenth century north and south porches of timber, with king posts and fine tracery in the quatrefoils, and trefoils set in the spandrels of the arches. Inscribed in the spandrel of the south porch is the name of John Abbott. In the chancel are brasses of Eustace Sulyard (1547) and his wife, and other monuments to the family.

Saint Osyth, St Peter and St Paul: The parish church stands close to the priory founded by St Osyth in the seventh century. Legend relates that St Osyth was the daughter of Frithewald, King of East Anglia; she married the son of Sigeberht, the first Essex king to become a Christian. She left her husband in order to found a nunnery, and years later, marauding Danes raided her religious foundation and she was beheaded on refusing to renounce Christianity. Subsequently a great priory grew up on the site, becoming an Augustinian abbey, which was later dissolved by Henry VIII. This parish church is of particular interest, apart from its association with the abbey, because it has a remarkable nave built early in the sixteenth century, with brick piers and arches (cf. Chignal Smealy, St Nicholas, of similar date) with an elegant hammer-beam roof over. The chancel was not rebuilt, but is part of the older thirteenth century church; this was quite big, and had transepts with east chapels whose circular piers with attached shafts may be seen. There was originally a Norman church here; the west tower is a fourteenth century addition to the original nave. The two large monuments in the chancel are to the 1st and 2nd Lord Darcy, who came to live in the priory in late Tudor times; and there is a brass plate to the Countess of Rochford (1773) who succeeded the Darcy family. The octagonal font bears the sword of St Paul, the keys of St Peter and a carving of St Osyth.

Saffron Walden, St Mary the Virgin: There was no doubt a Saxon church here in the days of Edward the Confessor, when Ansgar, the royal master of horse and an important nobleman, was thegn of Walden. A Norman church must have replaced the wooden Saxon structure after William the Conqueror granted Walden to the de Mandeville family, among forty lordships in Essex, for the Normans were enthusiastic builders of parish churches, as well as abbeys and castles. The church was probably cruciform in plan, with a central tower; as was the later church of the mid-thirteenth century, parts of which survive in the arcades of the present chancel and in the arches from the aisles to the chapels. These arches would have opened into the thirteenth century transepts, and the aisles would have been narrower than the present

Facing page: Saffron Walden

fifteenth century ones. The vaulted crypt, partly under the south porch, also formed part of the early medieval church. It is divided into four bays and the arches are single-chamfered; the ribs spring from semi-octagonal responds. The carvings under the east windows of the north aisle are also taken from the earlier church and have been re-set.

The building became unsafe after a fearful storm at Candlemas in 1445; many churches were badly damaged, and it is recorded that St Paul's in London was set on fire. It was decided to rebuild first the tower, which was finished about 25 years later, and then the nave, joining the new tower to the old chancel. By 1500, the north and south aisles and the south porch were also completed, followed by the north porch, the nave clerestory and the flanking turrets. After this the chancel was altered and re-roofed, a clerestory being added. Finally in 1526 the side chapels were altered; the newly rich Lord Audley completed the south chapel in about 1544. It suffered in the Civil War, when it was used as an officer's mess by the Parliamentary garrison in 1647.

The church has remained the same ever since, except for the spire which was built in 1832 by Thomas Rickman (renowned as the author of *The Principles of Gothic Architecture*). This replaced a wooden lantern, lead covered and 'mean in appearance' according to Lord Braybrooke. Rickman also designed New Court, of St John's College, Cambridge, in the 'Gothick style'.

Well situated on a hill overlooking the town, the church is 183 ft long and 80 ft wide (Thaxted is also 183 ft long); so it is one of the largest and finest in Essex. The building is worth comparing with the Chapel of King's College, Cambridge, since we now know that much of the work on the nave at Saffron Walden, as at King's, was the responsibility of John Wastell. A famous master mason of his time, he worked at Canterbury Cathedral for Archbishop Morton and then at Cambridge, Bury St Edmunds and Peterborough; he came from East Anglia, and died in 1515. Saffron Walden church was completed by his successor, Henry Semark.

The chancel of about 1250 retains its original quatrefoil piers, giving a clue to the appearance of the whole cruciform thirteenth century church. The walls above were raised to form the clerestory in about 1510, with its windows set in pairs; and the sanctuary was raised to accommodate the vault for the bodies of the Earls of Suffolk (the Howard Vault). The roof, in six bays, is thought to have come from another religious building, and was put in by the first Lord Audley; it is low-pitched and ornamented with foliage bosses, with figures of saints in the wall brackets. The faded colouring is pleasing.

The altar's reredos is modern, and so too the screen with rood-loft

Facing page: Saffron Walden, from Wright's *Essex*

over, designed by Sir Charles Nicholson in 1924. The five-light east window dates from Butterfield's work of 1876. The design of the organ case is partly Gothick of 1825, and partly Victorian of 1885 by Bodley.

The north and south chapels were rebuilt in about 1526, the north one having a doorway of the period with four-centred arch and moulded jambs. Just east of it, lies a tomb chest to John Leche (1521), the vicar from 1489 to 1521, who with his sister worked so hard to complete the rebuilding of the church. Over the altar hangs a copy of Correggio's painting 'The Holy Family', given by Lord Howard in 1793.

The final work to the structure of the church, except for the addition of the spire, was the alteration to the south chapel by Lord Audley in 1544, who died in that year and whose tomb is now in this chapel. It was in the chancel until 1793, when many alterations were made to the church, including the new east window to the chapel. The tomb is of black Belgian slates (touche), and is very beautifully carved; compare the Marney tomb at Layer Marney, and the de Vere monument at Castle Hedingham, possibly by the same craftsmen. Thomas Audley rose to fame in Henry VIII's reign, and eventually became his Lord Chancellor; he unscrupulously amassed a great fortune, mostly through the dissolution of the monasteries, including the abbey of Saffron Walden, on the site of which stands the great house of Audley End.

The nave is a fine example of the Perpendicular style. Begun around 1497, it is 54 ft high, and consists of seven bays; the western bays are incomplete and die into the tower's east wall. The piers are lozenge shaped, with four attached shafts, and only those facing the arches have capitals; the nave shafts run up and have capitals only where the roof springs. The spandrels are decorated with tracery in the style of many Suffolk churches. The 13 clerestory windows have mullions on each side which run down to form panels below. The roof, like the chancel, is low-pitched and much adorned with bosses and tracery, and at its east end is more elaborated to form a celure (canopy of state) over the rood. The original colouring is now faded. The Royal Arms of Charles II are placed over the tower arch.

The fine chancel arch, cusped and panelled, has a doorway each side, leading to stair turrets which gave access to the rood loft. They end in polygonal turrets, much akin to those at King's College, Cambridge, and suggest the influence of John Wastell. The north and south aisles are each as wide as the nave; they are roofed with tie beams, braced with long carved brackets dating from about 1520; no doubt the three east bays of each aisle originally formed chapels. In the north aisle below the three eastern windows are set carvings from the earlier church, consisting of twelve recesses with carved canopies of the fourteenth century. They are very interesting; the middle bay has shields which bear

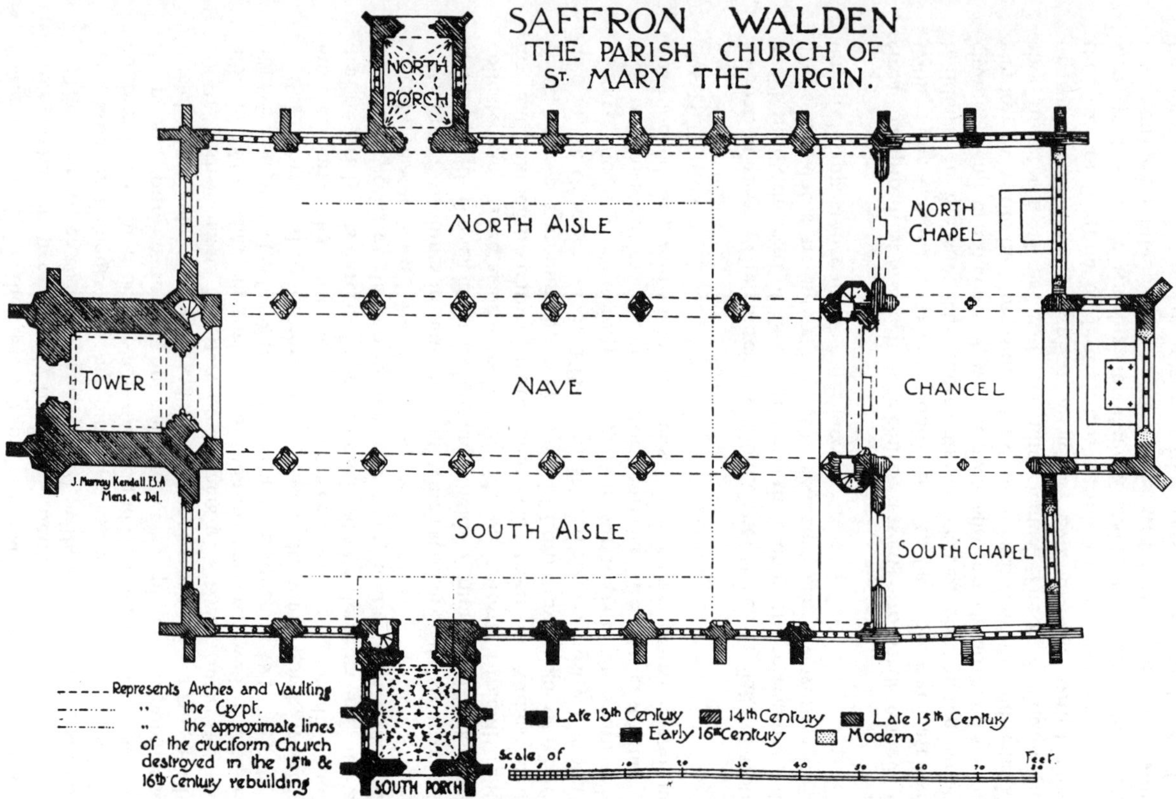

Plan of Saffron Walden

the instruments of the Passion, and the eastern one has carvings of King David with his harp, the Resurrection, Abraham's Sacrifice, etc. These latter carvings are perhaps early fifteenth century.

The west tower was built about 1470, with set-back buttresses and decorated battlements and big pinnacles, almost with turrets at the corners, but without a spire. On the ground floor may be seen vaulting shafts and springers for a stone vault never completed (cf. porches at Littlebury, a mile or so away). The octagonal stone spire, rising nearly 200 ft, with crockets and tiers of dormers plus flying buttresses was built in 1831, when the top stage of the tower was renewed. The tower holds a peal of twelve bells, four of which were added in 1914.

Both north and south porches are closed; the south porch, which is more elaborate, has an upper chamber over a two-bay fan vault, a good deal restored; it is externally embellished with battlements and turrets. The north porch of about 1500 has one storey and a stone vault with carved bosses; it is used now as a vestry.

Church furnishings include the font, which is octagonal, late fifteenth century, with the usual quatrefoils and shields. A number of brasses are collected and fixed against the north aisle wall, mostly fifteenth century and sixteenth century figures; and apart from the Audley tomb chest, there is a monument to two sons of Lord Braybrooke who both died in the Crimean War in 1854. The stained glass is mostly Victorian or later; the only pre-Reformation glass to survive is in the south aisle west window, said to be a portrait of Henry VI. The great east window was blocked until mid-Victorian times, when it was opened up and the tracery renewed.

Salcott, St Mary: The church was rebuilt after the earthquake of 1884 which shook this part of Essex, although the arch of the tower survived. The south doors are interesting early sixteenth century work, with a linen-fold appearance in the outer face.

Great Sampford, St Michael: The church was given to Battle Abbey by William the Conqueror. There would seem to have been at least two buildings on the site. The south chancel chapel, part of the earlier church, is thirteenth century, with its two-light east window and sexfoil window over; the building is otherwise fourteenth century, and remarkably fine for a village, with splendid chancel. The east window has unusual tracery and is flanked outside by two buttresses with niches; the cross of St John of Jerusalem is traced in flint – was the church associated with the Knights Hospitallers? Inside, the chancel has seats under cusped pointed arches on both sides, with a piscina and sedilia on the south side. The north arcade of four bays to the nave (1320) has quatrefoil piers with shafts in the diagonals, similar to Thaxted; the south arcade has octagonal piers of a later date, and there is an interesting arch to the south chapel with excellent carvings in the capitals. There are also traces of a stone screen between chancel and nave (cf. Stebbing and Great Bardfield of similar date). The recess in the south wall of the chapel has a nicely crocketted gable and niches to both sides.

Little Sampford, St Mary the Virgin: The church is built of flint and stands on the hillside. The building is mostly of the fourteenth century; work was interrupted by the Black Death in 1349. It has a good small west tower, with set-back buttresses and chamfered angles between which form the four polygonal pinnacles above (cf. Great Dunmow). The fourteenth century nave has a clerestory of quatrefoil windows on the north side; and piers to the north aisle which are lozenge shaped, with four shafts and without capitals. The chancel is fifteenth century. Its east window is in good Perpendicular style, as are the other windows; this was built by the Greene family, who came into property here by marriage in 1450; they also built the north porch. The south porch, in brick, is seventeenth century, and the screen is early sixteenth century. There are some interesting monuments on the north wall of the chancel, including one to Sir Edward Grene of 1556, with a matching one opposite but unlettered; also to William Twedy (1605) and his wife, who are depicted kneeling. Amongst others is a fine figure of Bridget Peck (1712), reclining and holding a book. Note the hatchments to the Enstall family.

Sandon, St Andrew: Set in a trim churchyard with some handsome tombs, the church is of considerable interest. Nave and chancel are built of flint, pudding stone and Roman brick, all of which contrasts agreeably with the Tudor brick west tower and porch. The nave is Norman, with a north aisle added in 1350 whose piers are of Caen stone. The fine tower and porch are possibly the work of the builder employed at Hampton Court by Cardinal Wolsey, then lord of the manor of Sandon. The diaper work in dark bricks resembles St Andrew crosses. There are battlements on corbel tables, and a handsome stair turret – note the unusual brick dome to the tower and the brick vault in the porch. In the church is a fine pulpit of Henry VII's reign, complete with pedestal. The nave has substantial fragments of a single hammer-beam roof of the mid-fifteenth century, similar to Gosfield. Note the piscina in the north aisle, and a brass of 1588 in the chancel. The Pax, a rare survivor from medieval times, is now in the Victoria & Albert Museum.

Shalford, St Andrew: This fine parish church stands amongst lime trees near the upper Blackwater. It was built in the fourteenth century, and has several interesting features. Some of the windows with straight heads suggest the future Perpendicular style; they have some good tracery. Inside, the piers to the north and south arcades have four shafts, with keels in the diagonals (cf. nearby Bardfield Saling) and two-centred arches. The sedilia has cusped arches on polygonal shafts, and is not unlike that in Fyfield church. Of great interest are the three recesses for tombs, which are large and beautiful; all date from the fourteenth century, with cusped ogee arches, crockets and finials. We do not know their history; but the coats of arms on the shields of that in the chancel resemble some fragments of fine fourteenth century glass in the east window, which relate to the Norwood family. Also good are the octagonal font with coats of arms in the shields, the screen and the south door. There is an unusual altar front with banners of fine straw-plaiting.

Sheering, St Mary the Virgin: This church stands just above the Victorian Gothic rectory, on a hill sloping down to the brook. It is built of flint, with a Norman nave, a thirteenth century west tower, and chancel and south porch in early Perpendicular style; the north aisle was added in 1902. The south door to the nave is good late fourteenth century, with vertical mouldings and a moulded rail across. Also of considerable interest is the nave roof, which has an unusual design. The stained glass in the top of the east window is rare late fourteenth century, depicting the Coronation of the Virgin with attendant angels and two censing angels.

Shelley, St Peter: This is a flint church of 1888 by Habershon and Fawckner, thirteenth century in style. The building stands amongst trees near Shelley Hall, to the north of Chipping Ongar.

Shenfield, St Mary the Virgin: The church lies secluded and away from the main road. It has a white weatherboarded belfry; and a shingled spire with sturdy Essex posts, and bracing of the fifteenth century to support it, visible from the nave. The interior is a little gloomy, but the good Victorian east window and chancel south window by Kempe have fine colouring. There is an interesting timber north arcade of six bays, with four attached shafts and hollows for each pier, and four-centred arches (cf. Theydon Garnon and Upshire which is perhaps a copy). Note also the alabaster reclining figure of Elizabeth Robinson (1652) under the belfry; and the three hatchments with their armorial bearings in the north aisle.

North Shoebury, St Mary the Virgin: The church was built in the thirteenth century with lancet windows. The south aisle was subsequently demolished; its octagonal piers and arches are still visible outside. The chancel is low and wide; the west tower, also built in the thirteenth century, was later given diagonal buttresses with a stepped pyramid roof. The square bowl of the font stands on five supports, with fleur-de-lis carved in the top corners. The coffin lid, with a foliated cross and lettering, is thirteenth century.

South Shoebury, St Andrew: The nave and chancel are Norman and are built of flint, rag-stone and septaria. There are north and south doorways, the south one as usual being more elaborate, with columns and billeted hood moulding. Later, windows of the thirteenth century and Perpendicular were inserted and a fourteenth century west tower built, with diagonal buttresses; the brick battlements are eighteenth century. The Norman chancel arch inside has interesting arched recesses on either side and also on the north and south nave walls; these probably housed side altars in medieval days. The nave roof is good, with octagonal king posts, cambered tie-beams and wallpieces of the fourteenth century.

Southchurch, Holy Trinity: This area is now a suburb of Southend. The old Norman church with its south doorway became the south aisle of a bigger church, when in 1906 a new nave was built on its north side to designs of Ninian Comper. In 1932 a chancel was added on by F.G. Eden. The old Norman north door was moved to the west end of the new building, and other portions were re-set. The fifteenth century belfry remains in position on its eight posts. The fourteenth century tomb recess and Easter sepulchre are interesting.

Southend: Southend grew as a seaside resort in Victorian times. Its older churches belong to the neighbouring parishes engulfed in this conurbation; but the more recent churches should be mentioned.

St Albans, Westcliff, is an interesting design of Sir Charles Nicholson and Corlette; it was built about 1900 in flint with red brick dressings. It has a south-east tower, arcades with square piers and a painted roof.

All Saints, Southchurch Road 1888, was designed by Brooke and enlarged in 1934. The building is of red brick, without a tower; the east end has two tiers of lancet windows.

St Erkenwald, Southchurch Avenue, was designed by Sir Walter Tapper in 1905. It is built of yellow brick, and is tall with lancets in the Early English style.

St Margaret, Leigh, by Sir Charles Nicholson (1931) has arcades of Tuscan columns, an apsidal east end and painted roof.

Southminster, St Leonard: This large church has been much altered through the centuries. The nave was built in Norman times of stone, and has a Norman doorway and west window. It was heightened and given a flint clerestory in the fifteenth century, when a fine porch was added with a stone tierceron vault, side windows and richly canopied niches. A west tower was built in the fourteenth century and ornamented with flint and stone battlements. In the eighteenth and nineteenth centuries the nave was altered again, this time in brick, when the chancel and transepts were given plaster rib vaults, none of which is very satisfactory. There is an octagonal font of the Perpendicular period, and there are some brasses of 1560 and 1634. One of Nelson's chaplains became vicar here after Trafalgar.

Springfield, All Saints: The church lies in a leafy suburb of Chelmsford. It is built of flint, with some pudding stone and Roman brick; Chelmsford was a Roman town. Perhaps Oliver Goldsmith worshipped here, for he lived for a while just opposite. The nave is Norman, the chancel and tower fourteenth century; the tower was partly rebuilt with brick in late Tudor times. Inside is a beautiful font of the Early English type (c.1220); its foliage carvings are of the stiff-leaf variety, and some of the stalks are carved into circles with trefoils. The fifteenth century screen is much restored. There is a seventeenth century painting of Moses.

Stambourne, St Peter and St Thomas: One is much impressed by the sturdy Norman west tower, which is built of flint with very thick walls, and incorporates much Roman brick, especially in its round-headed windows; like many Norman towers it is unbuttressed. An arch opens into the nave; this is fifteenth century, and shows the patronage of the McWilliam family who are commemorated by the interesting glass in the east window, where Henry McWilliam and his wife kneel. There is heraldic glass above in the tracery. The north arcade of three bays has octagonal piers, and the roof to the north aisle of about 1525 has rafters with five roll mouldings worthy of note. Also good are two niches with canopies to the east jamb of the nave south window; and in the chancel chapel, a niche with a shield over, bearing the McWilliam arms. The screen has ogee arches and panel tracery above; the dado is painted with figures of saints, as is often found. The porch is sixteenth century.

Great Stambridge, St Mary and All Saints: Perhaps the walls embody Saxon work, for there are small round-headed windows, now blocked, in the north walls; these are thin, and unlike Norman walls. The south aisle was added in the late thirteenth century; its piers are octagonal and the arches double chamfered. The fifteenth century tower of stone has a brick parapet. The porch is interesting work of the same century, as is the octagonal font.

Stanford-le-Hope, St Margaret of Antioch: The church has a Victorian tower designed by the industrious Parson Geldart of Braxted; it is placed at the east end of the north aisle. There is also a Victorian west front. The nave has two Norman windows; the piers of the north arcade are Early English, alternately circular and octagonal. The south arcade was built in the following century, like the chancel, which has a fourteenth century sedilia and ogee-headed recess opposite. The screen is of about the same date. The font is thirteenth century. There are monuments to the Fetherstone family of the eighteenth century, and an unusual baroque tomb to James Adams of the same period in the churchyard. The church contains good Victorian stained glass windows, some by Kempe.

Stanford Rivers, St Margaret of Antioch: A pleasant avenue of lime trees leads to the west door of this church. The nave is twelfth century, with round-headed Norman windows. The belfry is an interesting example of fourteenth century timberwork, with its four posts and elaborate intersecting bracing to north and south. The nave and chancel roof are also good. The chancel is of the Decorated period and the clerestory windows are sixteenth century. Fronting the west gallery are nine tracery panels from the original screen. The font of Barnack stone is a cumbersome thirteenth century octagonal example with arcading round the top. The heavy communion rail dates from the time of Archbishop Laud; there is a good brass of 1584 on the south wall, and the old oak pews are worthy of note.

Stansted, St Mary the Virgin: The church has a rather stern Victorian flint exterior, with a west tower of 1692; but the interior is full of interest. The building was re-fashioned in 1888, but retains fine Norman doorways south and north, the latter re-sited when the north aisle was added; both have three orders of columns, scalloped capitals, and arches with zig-zag and saltire cross decorations. Inside is a fine Norman chancel arch with much zig-zag decoration and unusual Norman ball motifs. The chancel retains some fine tall shafted arcading of the thirteenth century; and on the north side an interesting arch with some stiff-leaf carving. The font is late thirteenth century, and rather cumbersome. There are a number of very good monuments in the church; in the north chapel lies a knight in armour with his legs crossed, reputedly Roger de Lancaster (early fourteenth century). There is a splendid marble monument to Sir Thomas Middleton, Lord Mayor of London, of 1631; he lies on a sumptuous sarcophagus with black marble columns each side. Then there is a recumbent alabaster effigy of Hester Salusbury, daughter of Sir Thomas Middleton, wearing fashionable clothes of the period (1614); this work is attributed to Epiphanius Evesham, and is beautifully executed. There are also some other good monuments worthy of note.

Stansted, St John the Baptist: Stansted's other church is a Victorian building in red brick by Caroë of 1889. The design is in the Perpendicular style; it is fairly elaborate, with a south-west tower, whose porch is complete with gargoyles and pinnacles and stair-turret. Inside, a west gallery is supported on four-centred arches.

Stanway, St Albright: The church is dedicated to an eighth century East Anglian king (Alberht). It is situated on the Roman Stane Street. The nave is Norman, with use of Roman brick in the openings; and the south arcade of about 1500 was brought from the church of St Runwald in Colchester. Of considerable interest is the nave roof's scissor bracing, possibly as old as the nave. The rest of the church, chancel, south aisle, south chancel chapel and belfry are the result of Gilbert Scott's restoration in 1880. There is some stained glass of 1892 by Kempe in the windows. Just south on the other Roman road lie the interesting ruins of the medieval church of All Saints, with a tower containing bands of brick and flint work. Perhaps this church became ruinous during the fighting around Colchester at the time of the Civil War.

Stapleford Abbotts, St Mary: The old church was rebuilt in 1861 to designs of T. Jeckell of Norwich, with crazy-paving stone walls and Gothic windows; the rather squat brick tower at the west end is earlier, and dates from 1815. Interesting is the north chapel in red brick (1638), built for the Abdy family of nearby Albyns, with round-headed windows, a fireplace for the squire, and monuments; these include a fine one to Sir John Abdy of 1758, with a cherub holding an oval medallion. There is also a good stained glass figure of Edward the Confessor in the north vestry of the fourteenth century. The early seventeenth century pulpit is noteworthy.

Stapleford Tawney, St Mary: The church is set amongst lime and beech trees and looks across the valley to Theydon Mount. The building, of flint, is early thirteenth century, but it was drastically restored in the 1860s, when a north vestry and south porch were added. The lancet windows have been mostly restored, but the old blocked doorway in the nave north wall can be seen from outside. The belfry, of typical Essex timber construction, is probably fifteenth century, with its braced tie-beams and saltire cross braces north and south. The stone coffin near the south porch is twelfth century; another lies outside on the north side. The spire is shingled, the belfry weatherboarded. There are numerous monuments inside to the Smith family of nearby Suttons; also notable are the seventeenth century pierced altar rails.

Stebbing, St Mary the Virgin: This is a mid-fourteenth century church of exceptional interest and beauty, situated at the south end of the village, with a cluster of picturesque cottages and houses around. It has a west tower and south porch, and good window tracery in the Decorated style. Inside, there are five-bay arcades north and south with piers of an unusual shape; these have polygonal shafts with round ones in the diagonals; the head stops to the arches are interesting. Between nave and chancel is a famous stone screen, filling the chancel arch with its beautiful tracery, characteristic of the Decorated style (c.1340). There is one other stone screen like this in Essex at Great Bardfield, a few miles east of Stebbing, but a little later in date (1380); and a similar one at Trondheim in Norway. The screen is worth studying, with its ogee arches, quatrefoils, ball-flower decoration; and not least four quaint figures at the springing of the central arch. Also very fine are the flat-pitched nave and chancel roofs, constructed in the fifteenth century, together with the clerestory. The brass to Margaret de Ferrers (1390) commemorates a local Norman family who achieved riches by following William the Conqueror. Noteworthy are the eighteenth century communion rails; the old stone stairs to the rood loft; and fourteenth century iron bound chest, made of one piece of wood.

Steeple, St Lawrence: The church was rebuilt in 1884 by F. Chancellor, who was responsible for a number of Essex churches, such as Ford End and Pleshey. This one is in the Early English style, with cusped lancets. Materials from the old church were re-used, the yellow septaria being mixed with bricks which produces an unusual effect. The medieval doorway was also re-used. There is a tile-hung belfry which rises above the nave roof.

Stifford, St Mary: The church is mostly thirteenth century, including the timber framing to the spire surmounting the short west tower. The nave has a two-bay south arcade with circular pier, and the responds to the arches have interesting corbels; the east one is still coloured and represents a golden-haired youth, crowned. The south chancel chapel has lancet windows. The north doorway is Norman, and contains an interesting door, with thirteenth century ironwork. The construction of the spire with its use of curved timbers is very good work of the same century. There are a number of good brasses, including one to Ralph Perchehay, a rector (1380), John Ardalle, who died in 1504, and members of the Lathum family (seventeenth century).

Stisted, All Saints: The church was much restored in 1844, and a new tower built at the east end of the south aisle – this odd arrangement is also found at Ford End. The nave is late twelfth century, with circular columns in the arcades, some having good foliage carvings to their capitals. The chancel is a little later in date; it has five stepped lancet windows (renewed) at the east end, which contain some interesting pieces of sixteenth century Flemish stained glass. The windows in the aisle walls are fourteenth century. There are early Victorian monuments to the Savill–Onley family, who were squires of the parish.

Stock, All Saints: This well-kept village church has at its west end a timber belfry, one of the group of Essex timber belfries; it has dark weatherboarding (vertical) below and contrasting white weatherboarding (horizontal) above, and is capped by a shingled broach spire. Over the west doorway in the belfry are three wooden tracery panels; and there are wooden tracery windows on the north and south sides as well. The upper part of the belfry has an extension on the east side; inside, it is braced on all sides with trellis strutting above, as well as bracing at ground-floor level; these timbers may be thirteenth century. The south porch is also medieval timberwork, with ogee arch openings to both sides. The north aisle of three bays has octagonal piers and is fifteenth century, with a king post roof on tie-beams and fine wall plates. The chancel is Victorian, but it has interesting modern decoration and contemporary stained glass in the east window; the figures on the rood screen are carved by Gwynneth Holt. The interesting brass of 1574 is to Richard Twedye, who provided money for building and maintaining the almshouses opposite the church.

Stondon Massey, St Peter and St Paul: This is a good example of a small early Norman church; it was built by the de Marci family – hence the name Massey. There may once have been an apsidal east end. Nave and chancel have original windows deeply splayed, and Norman doorways plain and unmoulded on both sides. The late medieval belfry is carried on sturdy oak framing; in it hang three bells. The north chapel was added in 1874, built in the Early English style; the oak screen of simple design with its ogee arches is late fifteenth century. The font is in the octagonal Perpendicular style, and the pulpit (1630), with strap decorations and diamonds banded, is a good example of its period. There are brasses of 1573 to Rainold Holingworth and his wife, and to John Carre (1570) with his two wives. The composer William Byrd (1543-1623) lived nearby at Stondon Place, and although a Roman Catholic, may lie buried in the churchyard beside his wife.

Stow Maries, St Mary and St Margaret: The name 'Maries' indicates a marsh. The church was built in the fifteenth century of flint, stone and septaria; it was later heightened with Tudor brick and given a corbel table on trefoil arches. The chancel was raised higher than the nave, with brick stepped gables. There is a white boarded west bell turret. Inside is a brass of 1602 to Mary Browne and her seven children.

Strethall, St Mary: The church is set remotely in undulating country and is not to be missed by connoisseurs. It has a Saxon nave of the eleventh century with an unusual chancel arch, which should be compared with the late Saxon work at St Benet's, Cambridge, only 15 miles north of Strethall. The mouldings and decorations of both arches are worth studying. On the outside of the nave here at the west end may be seen the long and short quoins which the Saxons liked to use. The west tower and chancel are later, fifteenth century work; and in the latter is a brass to a priest of the fourteenth century, and a Tudor tomb chest. A Norman font on columns stands under the tower, in which hang two bells, one bearing the name of William Revel, which dates it to 1350-60.

Sturmer, St Mary: Both the nave and the north doorway, with its lintel decorated by chequers, are eleventh century Saxon work. The Normans constructed the south doorway, with columns having scalloped capitals, and zig-zag decoration over; grotesque heads project from the jambs, and the tympanum is carved irregularly with rosettes and crosses. They also built the chancel. Lancet windows were later inserted at the east end; a west tower was added in the fourteenth century and a south porch was built of brick with crowstepped gable in Tudor times. Of importance is the nave roof, a double hammerbeam; the pierced tracery panels are rather poor; a vine-leaf trail is carved along the wall plates and pendants fixed to the principal collars; it is possibly the work of Thomas Loveday, who lived at Sudbury during Henry VIII's reign and worked on Gestingthorpe church roof.

Sutton, All Saints: This is a Norman church with interesting features, including a sturdy Essex belfry of the fourteenth or fifteenth century. There is a fine early thirteenth century south doorway with three orders of columns. A good Norman chancel arch has one order of columns, the capitals scalloped, and there are some Norman windows in the nave and a lancet window of the thirteenth century in the chancel. The weatherboarded belfry rests on stout posts, with curved braces and trellis strutting from east to west. The south door, with its counter-rebates, is a rare thirteenth century type; the porch sheltering it is also unusual, dated 1633. The font is of thirteenth century Purbeck stone, with shallow pointed arcades to each side.

Takeley, Holy Trinity: The church stands on its own, north of Stane Street, the Roman road; close to the new airport of Stansted. The building is of flint, and also contains a good deal of Roman brick. The nave is probably twelfth century. The chancel was rebuilt in the mid-thirteenth century, when a south transept was added. This was then thrown into the present south aisle of the mid-fourteenth century, with an arcade of octagonal piers and double-chamfered arches. The west tower with its good doorway and three-light window over is fifteenth century, as is the south porch. The church was much restored in 1874, when an organ chamber was added and a new east window inserted. Inside there is a spectacular fifteenth century font cover, tall and much ornamented with crockets and buttresses; also a fine pulpit with a trumpet-shaped base of the same period.

Tendring, St Edmund King and Martyr: The church has a Victorian rag-stone tower of 1876 and a south aisle of the same period. Inside is some very interesting fourteenth century timberwork; the hammer-beam roof truss near the west end is most unusual and is surprisingly early in date. It is supported on the framing of the north and south doors which have good tracery details, one with circles containing mouchettes. The nave roof with its raised tie-beams is also unusual, and is comparable with Middleton. The nave and chancel are thirteenth century, and the north timber porch dates from the fourteenth century. There is a monument of 1615 to Edmund Saunder in alabaster, the figure kneeling in prayer.

Terling, All Saints: Set prettily on the village green, the church has a handsome tower of 1732, built of brick with stone quoins and round-headed openings. It is crowned by a shingled spire; the original steeple fell in 1730. The chancel is thirteenth century with one lancet window visible. The nave is of a later date, with arcades, four bays of octagonal piers; the north aisle was renewed in the nineteenth century, but there remains a fine fifteenth century timber porch on the south side. The church has a good thirteenth century octagonal font, with two blank pointed arches to each side; and there are brasses of 1558 and 1584.

Great Tey, St Barnabas: Here stand the remains of a very important church. In Norman times the parish had connections with the royal family; Eustace, earl of Boulogne, was lord of the manor and his grand-daughter, Matilda, married King Stephen. The church was cruciform in plan, with a crossing tower which is a Norman characteristic (cf. Fyfield, Waltham Abbey). Because of its size, the parish in 1829 decided to pull down most of the nave, leaving the magnificent tower, the chancel (mostly fourteenth century), a transept and just the stump of the nave. The tower is in four stages, with Roman brick dressings. In the second stage are coupled groups of three arches; there are two windows in the third, and bell-openings with a colonette in the fourth with side windows. A circular stair turret stands at the north-west corner. The chancel windows are good examples of fourteenth century tracery, as are the sedilia and the transept windows. In the south porch a circular pier of the Norman nave can be seen.

Little Tey, St James the Less: A small Norman church; the nave and chancel are not divided by a chancel arch. The east end is apsidal but has a gable roof over it, giving it a top-heavy appearance. The timber belfry is a later addition, and contains one bell dated 1701. There are round-headed Norman windows and doorways to north and south, the latter as usual more ornamented; the tympanum is decorated with lozenge diapers.

Marks Tey, St Andrew: The nave is Norman; it has a plain north and south doorway and a small south window with Roman brick surrounds. The chancel is fourteenth century; its interesting south porch dates probably from the mid-sixteenth century, with unusual chamfered mullions, diagonally set. Also of interest is the west tower, which was damaged when Colchester was besieged in 1648 during the Civil War; the upper part was replaced by a timber construction, of saltire bracing with a spire framed in; it was given vertical weatherboarding including battlements. The octagonal fifteenth century font is very remarkable; it is made of oak, with tracery panels on the stem and bowl.

Thaxted: The church is dedicated to St John the Baptist, St Mary and St Lawrence (patron saint of the cutlers). This is probably the finest church in Essex; its history is particularly interesting because of its association throughout the middle ages with the Norman, Plantagenet and Tudor dynasties.

In Saxon times the manor was owned by Wisgar. After the Conquest it was given by William I to Richard Fitzgislebert, who was a grandson of Geoffrey, the natural son of the first Duke of Normandy. Richard was therefore William's cousin, and doubtless for this reason received rich rewards for his services to the king; he was given this manor, in addition to the college and castle of Clare on the Suffolk border. His son became the first Earl of Clare, assuming the name de Clare; the family remained powerful for many generations, and were patrons of the church at Thaxted. Their close connection with the Plantagenets – a successor, Gilbert de Clare married Alice, a niece of Henry III, and later Joan, daughter of Edward I – ensured that Thaxted came to posses such a splendid church.

Gilbert de Clare's descendant and heiress Elizabeth de Clare married William de Burgh, and their grand-daughter married Edward III's son, Lionel Duke of Clarence. The title 'Duke of Clarence' was adopted as it incorporated the word 'clarentia', signifying the Clare estates. The daughter of this marriage, Philippa, married a Mortimer, the Earl of March; and a grand-daughter Anne Mortimer, who married the Yorkist Earl of Cambridge, became the grandmother of Edward IV. Edward's daughter, Elizabeth of York, married Henry VII, victor of Bosworth; and for this reason Henry VIII granted the manor to his first wife, Catherine of Aragon, as part of her dowry. These royal connections greatly influenced the design of the church.

The prosperity of Thaxted in medieval times resulted from the cutlers and the cutlery industry. The records of the London Guild refer to 'Thaxted, an Essex town where cutlery had long flourished'. Their work included the manufacture of knives, swords and daggers, with handles elaborately worked in gold, silver and ivory. The cutlers' houses stretched from Thaxted to Cutlers Green, which lies on the Debden Road. The wool trade no doubt enhanced the prosperity of the town, which was as important as its neighbour Saffron Walden.

There have been three churches in Thaxted. A Saxon one is recorded in the time of Edward the Confessor; the building was sited not far from the present church, and was probably entirely of wood, and

Thaxted

Thaxted: interior of nave

thatched. It is said to have burnt down in the fourteenth century, but its name is commemorated in the present church in St Catherine's Chapel.

The neighbouring monks of Tilty Abbey, founded by the Cistercians, derived much income from Thaxted until about 1262, when their own abbey was finished; not until then could the people of Thaxted set about building a larger church for themselves, on the same site as the present one. Grants were obtained from the college at Clare in Suffolk, and from the lord of the manor who at the end of the thirteenth century was Gilbert, Earl of Clare. In the fourteenth century, Elizabeth de Clare, the heiress of the de Clare estates and a great benefactress, who founded Clare College at Cambridge, probably helped the townsfolk to enlarge their church.

The nave piers are the oldest part of the present church, and were built around 1340; they are quatrefoil in section, with shafts in the diagonals, and may be copies of Cambridgeshire or Northamptonshire work. The two-centred arches are quadrant moulded, and have hood mouldings with interesting head stops. These formed parts of the older church which Edmund Mortimer later wished to enlarge, as it is thought; this building was cruciform in plan, but had a smaller chancel and transepts than the final rebuilding. Mortimer died of the plague in 1382. It is interesting to note that he rebuilt the nave of Great Bardfield church in a neighbouring parish in memory of his wife Philippa, the daughter of Lionel, Duke of Clarence; she died a few years before him.

Next the south transept was rebuilt during the later fourteenth century. This was financed partly by Elizabeth of Clare, or by her son the Earl of Ulster; it is called the chapel of St Catherine, but was originally dedicated to St Anne. The architecture is plainer, and perhaps little money was available for building at that time; although the cutlers' guild was formed towards the end of this century it had not amassed great wealth. The arcading has seven seats below the south window, with richly crocketted ogee arches, alternately pointed and coupled. The canopied niche in the west wall may have held a figure of St Anne, which was later replaced by one of St Catherine, after Catherine of Aragon visited the church with Henry VIII in 1521. On a pillar adjoining the south aisle is a carving of St Catherine between two wheels. The south transept was enlarged and the south porch built about 1361, this latter for Lionel, Duke of Clarence, son of Edward III who married Elizabeth de Burgh, grand-daughter of Elizabeth of Clare, and heiress to the de Clare estates. It bears his ducal coronet and arms in the niche on the south face. This porch is of much interest, with its three doorways, its vaulting, a priest's chamber over and good windows. In those days the church porch, particularly to the south, was frequently used for secular as well as religious purposes, and parts of the marriage and baptismal ceremonies would take place there. This porch, like the whole of the south of the church, lacks the rich detail lavished on the north side, which was built and embellished later on by richer patrons and townsfolk. The gargoyles nevertheless are of interest and there are good figures carved along the string courses.

About 1400 the north transept was enlarged; the seven seats of the sedilia suggest it was a guild chapel, connected with the cutlery trade. John Ffan, a member of a well-known family in this trade, was buried at the crossing; and Aberfurth, church warden in the early sixteenth century, who came from a long line of cutler-husbandmen, was also the warden of their guild. It may also have been a singers' chapel, for there is a charming figure high on the north wall playing a one-string violin; and outside is a figure of David with his harp, while on the other side of the north window, Goliath holds a large club. The canopied niche on the west wall perhaps held a figure of St Lawrence; it is fifteenth century. The reredos on the east wall, with a head of Christ on its frieze and censing angels either side, is very beautiful.

The north aisle was next widened, and the north porch added. The manor of Thaxted had now been inherited by Cicely of York, who had married Richard, Duke of York, a descendant of Edward III through the Mortimer family; she was the Duke of Clarence's daughter, Philippa having married Edmund Mortimer. Cicely of York's son became Edward IV, and the royal connection is evident in the north porch, whose two shields over the doorway bear the royal coat of arms. Though twice restored, this porch – and indeed the whole north side of the church – is much enriched. The canopied niche between the upper windows no doubt contained a statue of the Virgin Mary. The roof is vaulted, and the bosses show the reputed arms of Wisgar, the Saxon thane and subsequent owner of the manor. There is a handsome north-west turret staircase which leads to a muniment room over; the turret is embellished with figures and adds much to the composition, being higher than the porch itself. There are figure friezes below the battlements on this north side, with numerous gargoyles and pinnacles which add to the rich effect.

The west tower with its steeple was probably added next; its overall height is 181 ft, just two feet less than the length of the church. It was struck by lightning in 1814, and had to be rebuilt; the restoration was faithful to the original at the insistence of Lord Maynard, who financed the operation. Possibly the original masons came from Cambridge or Northampton, as its form is unlike anything in Essex, with its tiers of dormer windows, its four flying buttresses connected to the pinnacles, and its battlemented tower with set-back buttresses linked polygonally in their angles.

Thaxted, from Wright's *Essex*

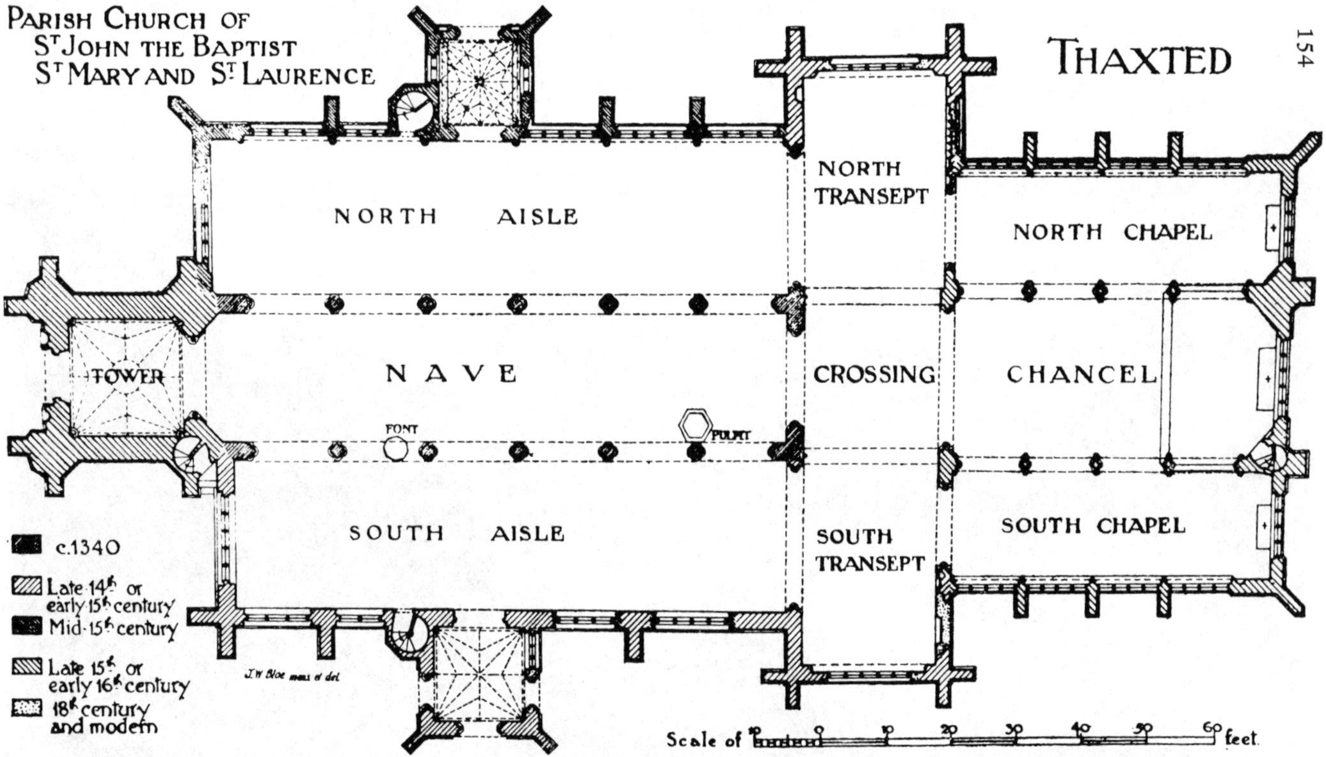

Plan of Thaxted

On the vaulting inside the tower may be seen the arms of the Earls of March and Ulster – Anne, mother of Richard Duke of York and grandmother of Edward IV was a Mortimer, and possibly a Mortimer began the construction of the tower. The bosses are carved with the instruments of the Passion, and on one is depicted the pelican in her piety. At the end of the fifteenth century the tower held only two bells; now there are eight.

The chancel with its north and south chapels seems to have been the last part of the church to be completed, together with the clerestory, in the late fifteenth century and early sixteenth century. Henry VIII gave the manor to Catherine of Aragon as part of her dowry, and he probably helped to finance the final building work; there are a number of Tudor emblems to be found in the church, including the portcullis, the fleur-de-lis and Catherine's own insignia.

The chancel arcades, of four bays each side with pierced spandrels, are very beautiful. The piers are somewhat complex in section, and thin shafts and hollows frame the arches. The clerestory and roof are fairly plain.

The chancel chapels both have similar straight-headed windows with panel tracery; and the east windows have glass by Kempe of the 1900s, depicting figures connected with the church, such as Gilbert de Clare. The north chapel's roof – the Thomas of Canterbury chapel – has an interesting painted ceiling. The fragments of early sixteenth century glass in the four north windows should be carefully noted; particularly the figure of St Christopher, second from the east, which has good background detail, including a fifteenth century ship with its sails, a mill with water wheel – perhaps Tilty Mill – and a bell tower. There are numerous badges of the House of York, including the white rose and golden falcon; the coat of arms of Edward IV quaters Geneville which occurred on his marriage to Elizabeth Woodville in 1465. Perhaps the king gave this window, as he descended from the Mortimers.

There is more fine glass in the south transept, St Catherine's chapel, where a panel of a knight bears the Mortimer coat of arms on his shield; this is late fourteenth century, and may be in memory of Edmund Mortimer, Earl of March, who died of the Black Death. This panel is all that remains of a larger window which illustrated the Mortimer lineage in the form of a Jesse window. There is other interesting old glass in the south aisle, where there are four panels of the Creation; these are fifteenth century, but were re-set in 1907.

The carved roof bosses in the church should also be noted. They are of the Tudor period, and bear the coats of arms of families closely connected with the church; in the nave roof are the sun in splendour (Edward IV), a shield with the de Vere mullet, a shield with lion

HOUSE OF CLARE & DESCENDANTS

Richard Fitzgislebert (son of Gislebert & grandson of Geoffrey, natural son of Richard, 1st Duke of Normandy) = Rohaise, daughter of Earl of Buckingham

Gilbert, 1st Earl of Clare = Adeliza, daughter of Earl of Claremont

Richard, Earl of Clare = Adeliza, sister of Earl of Chester

Roger, Earl of Clare = Maud, daughter of James de St Hilary

Richard, Earl of Clare = Amicia, daughter of Earl of Gloucester (heiress to this earldom)

Gilbert, Earl of Gloucester & Clare = Isobel, daughter of Earl of Warwick

Richard, Earl of Gloucester & Clare d.1262

Gilbert (the Red) Earl of Gloucester & Clare, d.1295 = (1) Alice, niece of Henry III (2) Joan, daughter of Edward I

Gilbert, Earl of Gloucester & Clare killed at Bannockburn 1314 | Eleanor | Margaret | Elizabeth = John de Burgh (1) Earl of Ulster (2) de Verdun (3) Roger Damory

Edward III = Philippa of Hainault | William de Burgh, Earl of Ulster, d.1340

Edward the Black Prince | Lionel, Duke of Clarence* = Elizabeth de Burgh, ward of Edward III

Philippa = Edmund Mortimer, 3rd Earl of March

Roger, Earl of March = Eleanor Holland

Edmund | Anne = Richard, Earl of Cambridge d.1415 (son of Edmund, Duke of York who was 4th son of Edward III)

Richard, Duke of York = Cicely Nevill

Edward IV = Elizabeth Woodville

Elizabeth of York = Henry Tudor (VII)

Henry VIII = Katherine of Aragon

* Edward III created the title Duke of Clarence for his son Lionel by incorporating the name Clare.

rampant between two bird-bolts (York), a pomegranate (Catherine of Aragon) and so on. In the south aisle, the last roof to be finished, are more fine bosses, including carvings of the reefed knot of the Bourchiers, pomegranate and grapes of Catherine of Aragon, Tudor portcullis, rose of York and many more.

The church is remarkably uncluttered with tombs and memorials to the great personages connected with it; the Mortimers and others of royal birth would have had their tombs elsewhere. For this we can be thankful and so enjoy the light and spacious interior, as so little of the medieval stained glass has survived.

The font cover in the north aisle is fifteenth century, and would have been richly coloured and gilded. It is worth comparing with those at Littlebury and Takeley, the latter late medieval, the former sixteenth century. The pulpit is fine late seventeenth century work with garlands at its angles; the staircase up to it is taken from another building. Of the same period are the screens to the north and south chapels. The communion rail dates from about 1700 with its twisted barley sugar stick balusters. There is a good brass of c.1480 in the chancel to a priest, wearing academic dress. The dearth of other monuments is unusual.

Theydon Bois, St Mary: The church stands on the edge of Epping Forest. It was built of Victorian red brick in 1850 by Sydney Smirke, with a south-west tower and copper-clad spire. The old church stood on the Abridge road. The modern pulpit is by Paul Waterhouse.

Theydon Garnon, All Saints: This is a church of charm and interest in a rural setting. It has a fine west tower, with an inscription on the south wall dating it 1520 which commemorates its benefactor Sir John Crosby. It is built of red brick with blue headers interspersed, and has buttresses, battlements and a good north-east stair turret. This is one of a number of fine brick towers in this part of Essex (cf. North Weald or Epping Upland). The north aisle is also of brick (1644); the date is conveniently inscribed on the east gable. The chancel, built of flint, is thirteenth century; the restored east window dates from the fifteenth century. The nave has two south-facing dormers, which are rather picturesque and seem to be early nineteenth century. Inside, there is a five-bay timber arcade with octagonal piers (1644) and round arches (as at Shenfield). The pulpit is elegant early eighteenth century work. There is a fine brass to William Kirkeby, rector (1458); and in the chancel two tomb chests and some excellent wall monuments, including one to Sir John Archer (1682) of Coopersale House, and another to his adopted son William (1739). Amongst other interesting items in the

Theydon Garnon, from Ogborne

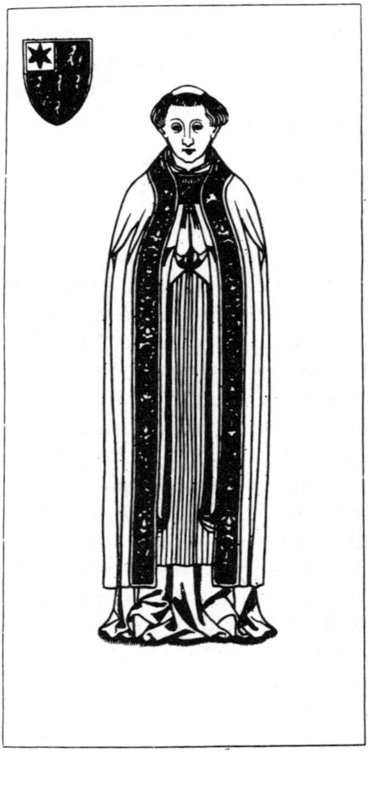

Theydon Garnon:
brass of William Kirkeby, 1458

church are some good hatchments and the royal arms of George III. The nave roof is very good of its kind, and dates from the mid-thirteenth century.

Theydon Mount, St Michael: This small church was built in 1611-14 by the Smith family of Hill Hall nearby, a beautiful Elizabethan house which stands forlornly across the park. The nave, chancel, west tower and porch are all of subdued rose-red brick. The tower is well proportioned, with diagonal buttresses, battlements and small spire. The staircase turret on the south side is very charming, with its segmental gable; together with the adjacent porch, it forms an excellent example of the best brickwork of its period. Inside, the chancel is cluttered with monuments to the Smith family which are worth studying. Particularly interesting is the one to Thomas Smith (1577), who was secretary to Queen Elizabeth. He lies on his side under a coffered arch flanked by Ionic columns.

Thorpe-le-Soken, St Michael: Most of the church was rebuilt by W. White in 1876. The fine Tudor west tower remains, of red brick with blue diaper work; it has diagonal buttresses and bell openings, also with brick tracery. Inside, the font stands on a Norman plinth. The fifteenth century screen with intersecting ogee arches is noteworthy. In the chancel beneath a canopy lies the recumbent effigy of a knight of Edward I's reign, dressed in chain mail, his feet resting on a lion.

Thorrington, St Mary Magdalen: The church is approached through a farmyard. There is a fine west tower of 1480, built of knapped flint with diagonal buttresses; it has a three-light west window, two-light bell openings and battlements; and is not unlike its neighbour at Brightlingsea. The date of construction is recorded on a brass in the floor of the tower, to the benefactors John and Margery Deth. The south porch of the fourteenth century, which is flint and septaria, contains old tiles as dressings to openings and quoins. Inside, the north arcade is Victorian. There is a late medieval font, and a brass of 1564.

Thundersley, St Peter: The church stands on a hill on the outskirts of Southend and Rayleigh. It has a chancel of 1885. The nave and narrow aisles date from the early thirteenth century; the piers are circular, with capitals having stiff upright leaves. The west window is of the three-light Perpendicular type, with panel tracery. The belfry, which is good of its kind, stands on a system of stout posts behind the west window. The small octagonal font has quatrefoil panels.

Grays Thurrock, St Peter and St Paul: The church was rebuilt and extended westwards in 1846. The present building includes portions of the original Norman church which was cruciform, with round-headed arches; as well as some thirteenth century work. Inside stands a font of the octagonal Perpendicular type with quatrefoil panels. There is a brass of 1510. A tablet of 1875 commemorates the boys and master of the training ship 'Goliath', destroyed by fire that year in the Thames.

Little Thurrock (or East Thurrock), St Mary the Virgin: The building has a Norman nave, with a restored chancel arch and a plain Norman south door. The chancel is fourteenth century; it contains the sedilia, which has shafts with moulded capitals and pointed arches. There is a Victorian arcade of three arches between the nave and west tower. The pulpit dates from 1700. The church was restored in 1878.

West Thurrock, St Clement: The church lies on the marshes by the Thames, with a large factory nearby. It was much visited in the middle ages by pilgrims on their way to Beckett's shrine at Canterbury. The west tower of the fifteenth century with its stripes of flint and stone, and seventeenth century brickwork at the top, is good to look at; it stands where once there was a circular nave, which is very unusual. The present nave originally formed the chancel; aisles were added to the north and south around 1200, and in the thirteenth and fourteenth centuries chancel and north and south chapels were added for pilgrims. Amongst the monuments are a brass of 1584 to Humphrey Heies and his son, and two alabaster figures of Sir Christopher Holford and his wife (1608). There is also a stone coffin lid of the thirteenth century, and some rare fourteenth century tiles with eagles and fleur-de-lis.

Tilbury near Clare, St Margaret: This is a lonely church. The nave and chancel are fifteenth century; the west tower is of brick with blue diaper work, diagonal buttresses, battlements and stair turret, built by a de Vere in 1519. There are fragments of Tudor wall paintings in the nave, depicting a man and a horse in front of a brick-nogged house; and stencilled Victorian decoration on the chancel arch. The south door in two halves is good, and so is the porch with original roof. The pulpit is Elizabethan, with plaited ornament.

East Tilbury, St Catherine: The church stands near the river; its tower and south aisle were demolished by Dutch shot during the war of 1667, when Dutch ships sailed up the Thames. The building has a blocked Norman window; it was enlarged in the thirteenth century, and the chancel has three stepped lancet windows at the east end and lancet windows north and south. The north arcade of the nave with four bays is good late twelfth century work; the piers are alternately circular and octagonal, and the capitals are scalloped with angle volutes. A new west tower, begun as a war memorial in 1917, has yet to be completed.

West Tilbury, St James: Somewhere near here, the Venerable Bede tells us, St Cedd founded a religious settlement when he brought Christianity back to Essex in the mid-seventh century. This is the probable site of his church, standing high and looking over the river Thames. There is Norman work in the nave walls, but the tower is modern.

Tillingham, St Nicholas: The Dean and Chapter of St Paul's have owned this manor since Christianity came to Essex. There is a Norman doorway into the nave, and a Norman font on which leaves are carved. The chancel has stepped lancet windows of the thirteenth century at the east end, and lancet windows on north and south sides; also sedilia and piscina. The south arcade has octagonal piers of the fourteenth century. The west tower with angle buttresses and west window dates from the same century although the battlements are later. There is a brass of 1584 to Edward Wiot.

Tilty, St Mary the Virgin: Tilty Abbey was founded in 1153 by Maurice Fitz Geoffrey and Robert de Ferrers for Cistercian monks; nearly all traces of the abbey have vanished except for this, the chapel outside the abbey walls (cf. Little Coggeshall), which survives as the parish church and stands in solitude. The chapel was originally a simple rectangular building of 1220, with lancet windows on the south side. A chancel was added in 1330, with beautiful tracery in the windows, particularly in the east window of five lights, with its flowing design and niches each side on the outside wall. Inside, the piscina and triple sedilia with their cusped arches are noteworthy. There are some good sixteenth century brasses in the church, and a hatchment of the Maynard family on the chancel beam. The cupola is early nineteenth century.

Tiptree, St Luke: This church was built in 1855 by E. Christian. It is of red brick, and has an apse but no tower.

Tollesbury, St Mary: The massive west tower of the church, which is Norman, probably rests on a Saxon base; the upper portion is late Tudor brickwork, together with the buttresses and battlements. The nave is also Norman; the chancel was rebuilt in Victorian times. The eighteenth century font was purchased with the fine of a man who swore in church, and has an amusing inscription – 'Good people all I pray take care, that in ye church you do not sware, As this man did'. The stained glass in the east window is by Kempe (1902). There are brasses to Thomas Freshwater and his wife (1517) and also a good monument of 1654 to Jane Gardiner.

Tolleshunt D'Arcy, St Nicholas: This is a church of the Perpendicular period. The west tower has diagonal buttresses and battlements; and the south porch, of Kentish rag-stone, shelters a fine medieval door. Inside on the coved ceiling, are some charming paintings of flowers by the Victorian parson Geldart of Braxted. The D'Arcy family who lived in the cottage next door during the fifteenth and sixteenth centuries are commemorated in some interesting brasses and monuments, including a marble monument of 1593 to Thomas D'Arcy and his wife Camilla. Also to be noted is a German or Flemish brass of c.1400, depicting the Virgin and Child, St Bartholomew and St Philip. Two of the brasses are palimpsets of older brasses.

Tolleshunt Knights, All Saints: The church is remote, and stands up a lane. The nave and chancel are fourteenth century, and the bellcote Victorian. In the chancel lies the stone effigy of a fourteenth century knight in armour, holding his heart in his hands. The font dates from the same century, as does the nave roof, which has interesting wall plates and tie-beams.

Tolleshunt Major, St Nicholas: This small church, built of pudding stone and septaria, seems out of proportion with its fine west tower. This was added by Beckingham, of neighbouring Beckingham Hall; it is in deep red Tudor brick with blue diaper work. In 1888 the industrious Parson Geldart of Braxted designed the south porch. The roofs appear to be original fifteenth century work, and in the nave are two niches with brick canopies over. The font, placed against the south wall, is half an octagon, with shields and roses of the fifteenth century.

Toppesfield, St Margaret of Antioch: The church is dominated by the large west tower. A tablet on the west face records that it was built in 1699, and commemorates the rector who gave £100 towards its building and the bricklayer, Daniel Hill. The building is of red brick with black headers; it has round-headed windows, and an unusual parapet formed of two half round depressions and a central battlement to each side, with a fine obelisk to each corner. The rest of the church is fourteenth century, with a south aisle and arcade of octagonal piers. In the chancel are cusped arches on the south wall for the sedilia; in a recess stands a tomb chest. There is an interesting monument to Dorcas

Smyth (1633) by John Colt, with carvings representing various virtues, such as a beehive for Industry. Some stained glass of the fifteenth century in the south aisle depicts the coronation of the Virgin. The north and south porches are fifteenth century, the north one of timber.

Great Totham, St Peter: The building stands in a trim churchyard. The tower is built of septaria and pudding stone; and the belfry, neatly shingled, has two cinquefoil lights of oak tracery to each face. Nave and chancel are fourteenth century and the north aisle is Victorian. There is some seventeenth century armorial glass in the west window, some medieval painting in the north-east corner of the nave, and a brass of 1606 to Elizabeth Coke and her daughter.

Little Totham, All Saints: Although small, the church has interesting features. The north and south doorways are Norman; the north one is plain, as so often the case, but the south one is unusually decorated; the two orders of columns have blocks with rosettes carved thereon, and the voussoirs are also elaborately carved. Chancel and nave have lancet windows, arranged in step formation at the east end. A large west tower of flint was added in 1527, and finished with a weather-bound top on a frame of unusual construction. The octagonal fifteenth century font is carved in a way not often seen. Also noteworthy is the seventeenth century monument to Sir John Samms and his wife, two figures kneeling opposite each other, and the thirteenth century north door with its ironwork.

Twinstead, St John the Evangelist: The church was rebuilt in 1860 in red brick, with a mixture of yellow and black. There are trellis patterns inside, and a triple arch to the chancel. The fine colouring in the east window is by Hardman. There is a good brass of 1610 to the Wyncoll family with five daughters. An early bell hangs in the bellcote.

Ugley, St Peter: The church is isolated, and stands amongst chestnut and yew trees. It has a handsome Tudor brick west tower with battlements and diagonal buttresses. The west portion of the nave is thirteenth century; nearly all the rest was built of flint in 1866. The church includes some masonry bought from the ruins of nearby Bolington church.

Ulting, All Saints: This small church, near the river, is mostly thirteenth century, including the nave and chancel. It was much restored in 1873 when the north porch was added. The wooden turret and spire are fifteenth century. The nave roof is noteworthy, with its arched collar frame, as are the good wall plates and wall pieces. The font is an interesting thirteenth century octagonal example, with one blank arch on each side; the angles of the octagon are chamfered.

Upshire, St Thomas: The church was built in 1902 by Sir Thomas Buxton, who wished it to resemble a typical Essex church. It has a weatherboarded belfry and shingled spire. The rest of the building is rather in Voysey's style, with a pebble-dash exterior, buttresses and dressing stone from Chilmark, Wiltshire. The north arcade of timber is a rough copy of that in Shenfield church; the chancel ceiling has plaster panels, producing a pargetted effect. The fittings are pleasantly art nouveau. The church has a fine view across the valley towards Nazeing.

Vange, All Saints: After the Conquest, the manor was held by Bishop Odo, William I's step brother. The small church is Norman, with a blocked Norman window in the nave and a square font of the same period with zig-zag motif on one side. The church was restored in 1837.

Virley, St Mary: The ruins of this medieval church form part of the rectory garden; it has an interesting chancel arch.

Great Wakering, St Nicholas: The church is built of rag-stone, septaria and flint. It has an early Norman nave with blocked north and west windows against which was built a later Norman tower. The shingled broach spire is Tudor. The arch into the nave is one-stepped and has simple imposts. The chancel has lancet windows of the thirteenth century; the nave roof has tie beams arch-braced beneath and octagonal king posts with moulded capitals. Against the tower is a Tudor two-storey porch, which is very unusual. Perhaps it was erected to provide accommodation for the priest who came to minister from Beeleigh Priory.

Little Wakering, St Mary the Virgin: The fine west tower was built through the generosity of the Bishop of Norwich in about 1420, and his crest – a pelican – stands on the west doorway with a three-light window over it. The tower has niches on either side and diagonal buttresses, with chequered battlements and a shingled spire. Nave and chancel are Norman. There is a small window in the chancel, and a good tomb recess of the thirteenth century in the nave north wall. The doorway and stairs to the rood still exist.

Waltham Abbey, Holy Cross & St Lawrence: We learn from a treatise on *The Finding of our Holy Cross*, written by a canon of the abbey in the twelfth century that a church was built here by Tovi during the reign of King Canute. Tovi, one of Canute's chief advisers, owned land at Montacute in the West Country. A cross of stone with miraculous powers was discovered here by divine instruction, it was transported to Waltham where Tovi had a hunting lodge, and a church was constructed to house the sacred object with two priests appointed to minister. Tovi died about 1042 and Edward the Confessor, who succeeded as king, gave the manor to Harold, son of Earl Godwin. Harold was brother-in-law to Edward and also Earl of Essex. In 1060, Harold refounded the church as a college of twelve secular canons, and appointed Wlwin as dean; he provided an income from local manors, and set about rebuilding the church on which he lavished considerable sums of money.

When it was finished, he arranged a service of dedication, to which he invited king Edward and the queen, his sister, and Cynesige, Archbishop of York, amongst other great men of the land. We read that the feasting and celebrations lasted eight days, and that the king confirmed Harold's gifts to the church with a charter, written in gold. We also learn that king Harold went to this church to pray before marching south to do battle with the invading Normans in 1066, and that the holy cross gave a sign warning him not to go. Two canons followed the king, and after his death at Hastings, they brought his body back to Waltham and buried him there with great honour. This holy cross or rood became an object of worship and pilgrimage and the war-cry of Harold and the Saxons at Hastings was 'Holy Rood'. The cross, which was large and made of black marble, with a figure of Christ on it, seems to have disappeared at the time of the abbey's dissolution in Tudor times, and there is now no trace of it.

The canon speaks well of William I's subsequent treatment of this church, although he gave the town and land which had been bestowed on the dean and canons, to his favourite Walcher, Bishop of Durham, who was murdered in 1080 because of his insolence and cruelty in Northumberland. Afterwards Henry I gave the estate to his two queens, who in turn handed it back to the canons.

Henry II visited Waltham several times. As an act of expiation for his part in the murder of Thomas Becket, he was ordered by the Pope to found three abbeys; in fact Henry re-founded three existing abbeys, one of which was Waltham. In 1177 he dissolved the Anglo-Saxon college of secular canons, and founded a college of sixteen canons of the order of St Augustine, giving the church a new name, St Lawrence.

In 1184 the abbot was 'mitred', an honour conferred by the Pope on the heads of important religious houses. Waltham grew to become one of the largest and richest abbeys in England; the abbot was a peer of the realm, sitting like a baron in Parliament. Such dignitaries lived in palatial

Waltham Abbey: interior

lodgings, entertained royalty and had parks and manor houses as well as conducting their religious duties. For instance the Abbot of St Albans dined on a dais fifteen steps high, and the monks serving him sang a grace at every fifth step.

Henry greatly enlarged the original abbey. To the Norman nave and crossing he added a choir longer than the former nave, larger transepts, and a retro-choir, together with the other buildings such as cloisters, chapter-house and dormitories, which accompanied a large establishment of this kind. When finished, the abbey was comparable with St Albans, Bury St Edmunds and Evesham. Its architectural merit would have been considerable, but we know nothing of its style because in 1540 it was surrendered to Henry VIII and pulled down – one of the great acts of vandalism for which he was responsible. All that is left of the building is the Norman nave west of the original crossing, with a lady chapel and west front of the fourteenth century a west tower, built in the reign of Mary Tudor; and the Victorian alterations of Burges to the east end.

The nave consists of arcade, triforium (gallery) and clerestory, in the customary style of the major Anglo-Norman churches. The great puzzle is how much of this impressive building is the work of Harold and how much the work of the Normans. Experts have had difficulty in arriving at a satisfactory answer. There is a description of Harold's church in *The Finding of our Holy Cross* before Henry II re-organised the abbey, which mentions the elaborate ornaments, vestments, relics and so on which Harold gave to his church. A manuscript now in the British Museum lists 'amongst other rich gifts, seven caskets, three of gold and four of silver gilt, enriched with gems, filled with relics; four censers of gold and silver, eight gold candlesticks and four of silver, four crosses of gold and silver, studded with jewels, five chalices, two of gold and three of silver, another cross of silver, two suits for the priests, covered with gold and gems, and four altars with relics, one of gold and three of silver'. The relics are described as of inestimable value, having wrought many miracles. The four altars suggest that Harold's church was a fair size.

Harold was the richest man in England next to his brother-in-law, Edward the Confessor; he was able, hard-working, religious and well-travelled. He would have seen what was being built in Normandy, at Jumièges for instance, or at Westminster where King Edward was building his abbey. Edward began its construction in 1050, adopting the fashionable style of Normandy. His new abbey of Westminster was consecrated in 1065 just before his death, when it was far from complete, with only choir, transepts and two bays of the nave; the whole church and cloistral buildings were not finished until 1163. Its plan and

Waltham Abbey, from Wright's *Essex*

general scheme derived from Bernay and Jumièges, and it had an east end of three parallel apses, a central tower, two western towers, and a nave of double bays with alternating compound piers and cylindrical columns, twelve bays in all. Its total length was 332 ft.

Clearly the Norman style influenced English architecture before the conquest of 1066. Edward employed English craftsmen to build his abbey and Harold presumably did likewise; but work may have proceeded slowly because of the difficulties in obtaining and transporting materials such as stone from Caen. Waltham was only a small hamlet in the royal forests north of London, and we know from the Domesday survey that the population of the 19 surrounding parishes comprised only 2 priests, 513 villeins, 451 bordari, 58 serfs and 18 freemen. Harold's ambition to rebuild Tovi's church (of which the herring-bone work on the south-east corner of the existing building remains) may have only been partly realised. He probably adopted the custom of starting work first on the chancel, then the transepts, crossing and nave; so at the time of his death, the western parts were perhaps incomplete. Durham Cathedral, with which Waltham bears many similarities, was started in 1091 and not finished until 1133, and this was remarkably quick by medieval standards. Durham may be an improved version of Waltham: the layout of the naves have much in common, such as composite piers alternating with round ones. The grooving on the columns is most interesting as it is uncommon; but the comparison of Waltham, Durham, Norwich, Lindisfarne, Dunfermline and the crypt of York should give an indication of dates. In a manuscript of about 1050, now in the British Museum, two rows of columns are shown ornamented in the same way, and the drawing is supposed to relate to Waltham; so grooving in columns may have started earlier than is supposed. Zig-zag decoration is much in evidence at Waltham; this form of decoration is not supposed to occur in England before 1100 but it can be seen in German Romanesque churches – Speyer Cathedral dates from 1030; so the style could have appeared over here prior to William's invasion.

In the *Life of King Harold*, written in the early twelfth century, there is mention of work going on in the abbey during the years 1125-6 in Henry I's reign, and we know Henry I's two wives were benefactresses of the abbey but no details are recorded, and the work may have been necessary maintenance. On the other hand this may be a reference to the completion of the nave, because examination of the original fragments of timber forming the nave roof revealed that the church had a ceiled roof, consisting of a tie-beam to every rafter couple, wall plates set at the centre of the walls and a frame design which included two collars, notch lapped at their ends; the lower collars were braced with notch-lapped soulaces (short timbers triangulating the conjunctions of rafters and collars but beneath the collars). The approximate date of these roof trusses seems to be mid-twelfth century, roughly contemporary with the reference.

Certainly the east bay of the nave differs in some respects from the others; the zig-zag ornament goes deeper into the soffits of the arches, and the corresponding clerestory windows differ from the others; details are dissimilar to the more westerly bays, suggesting this end was later in date. The arches and piers to the clerestory are different; it would seem that this was the last part of the nave to be finished; possibly it required rebuilding at some stage, for the larger churches were seldom built without interruptions. Henry II's vast additions to the abbey church were not finished until 1242; ships were bringing marble to it in 1229. Its final length was 400 ft, so in its great days it was one of the largest churches in England.

Further alterations were made during the thirteenth century when the stone vaulting to the aisles was found to be thrusting the outer walls apart; it was removed to relieve the strain, a wooden ceiling taking its place. In the next century a chapel was added on the south side, west of the south transept; now called the Lady Chapel, it stands on a vaulted undercroft of two bays, the ribs chamfered, and lighted by small windows. The chapel externally has bands of flint and stone, windows with tracery in the Decorated style, and between them buttresses embellished with niches. Its west window is unusual, being straight-headed; inside it has a pretty three-light arcade with pierced spandrels. On its east wall is a fine wall painting of the same century, depicting the Doom; this was plastered over during the Reformation and was only uncovered again in 1876 when the whole chapel was restored.

At much the same time as the Lady Chapel was built, it was decided to reconstruct the west front of the Abbey which may have had twin west towers in the Norman grand style. At any rate these, if they ever existed, were taken down and the central Norman door was removed and replaced by the beautiful existing doorway, which is deep enough to allow diagonal seats over which are vaulted niches. Over the doorway is a gable, in the spandrel of which is a quatrefoil containing a head of St Lawrence. Unfortunately the Tudor west tower obscures most of the rest of this re-fronting, but the beginning of blank shafted niches can be seen under the tower arch. At the end of the north and south aisles may be seen the windows which replaced the original Norman ones; and the outer doorway of the Tudor tower incorporates work of this period, with its three orders of columns, carved capitals and fleurons in the arches.

Just before all this work was undertaken, an attempt had been made to gothicise the Norman arches at the west end of the nave, by sub-

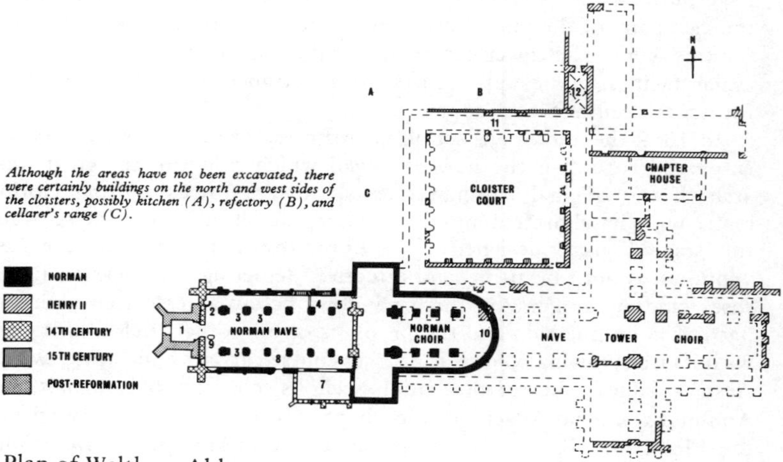

Plan of Waltham Abbey

stituting pointed arches for the round ones; but it was discovered that the structure of the abbey was being weakened, and the work was stopped. The life of the great abbey continued undisturbed throughout the fifteenth century, and the townsfolk were allowed to use the nave for their worship. An earlier abbot had built a low wall dividing this from the crossing; the choir and other parts of the building were kept exclusively for the use of the monks; and there was also a rood screen, the sawn-off ends of which can be seen protruding from the walls high up in the triforium.

In 1534 Henry VIII broke off relations with the Pope and set himself up as Head of the Church of England; two years later he ordered Thomas Cromwell to organize the dissolution of the monasteries. All those in Essex were suppressed and although Waltham, because of its importance and size, was the last to be plundered and destroyed, its end came. Henry had thought of making Waltham into a cathedral, but instead handed it over to a court favourite, Anthony Denny, for him to demolish. Finally in 1552 the great central tower just east of the present altar fell, bringing down all the bells and choir with it. The townsfolk were allowed to retain the nave as their parish church; and in 1556, to save it from collapse, they built the west tower from the stones and materials of the demolished buildings, the tower acting as a large buttress to the nave, which had been weakened by the removal of the east parts of the once great church; the abbey bells were sold to pay for this work. The tower has irregular flint and stone chequer work and ashlar facings in the upper parts. As mentioned, the west doorway is fourteenth century work re-set.

In 1859 the Victorians set about restoring the abbey. W. Burges was employed to design the new east wall which now fills the great west arch of the original Norman crossing tower. Burges' curious Gothic style, with its short columns and clumsy detail may be criticised; but the stained glass, designed by E. Burne-Jones in 1861 for the east windows, is both beautiful and effective, depicting the Creation in the rose window; and in the three windows below a Jesse tree with the patriarchs on one side and the prophets on the other. Below this glass with its rich glowing colours is a string course carved to illustrate two of Aesop's fables. The reredos, by T. Nicholls, contains four panels; the Annunciation, the Angel and the Shepherds, the Visit of the Magi and the Flight into Egypt. During the same restoration a new nave ceiling was installed, painted by Sir Edward Poynter; the lozenge design contains the signs of the Zodiac, the Labours of the Months, the Four Elements, the Past and the Future; it is a version of the Norman ceiling in Peterborough Cathedral, where can be seen the customary early Norman way of building with vaulted side aisles and flat timber ceilings to the nave. This ceiling successfully provides colour which would otherwise be lacking in the nave.

Of the many interesting monuments in the abbey, the most imposing is the one to Sir Edward Denny, who died in 1599; he was a soldier of Elizabeth I and knighted for his exploits in Ireland. He with his wife below recline on shelves, beneath a coffered arch with Fame and Time in the spandrels. It is carved by Isaac James and Bartholomew Adye. Nearby is a recumbent effigy of Lady Elizabeth Grey, cousin to Lady Jane Grey, the nine days' queen – all that remains of a tomb now destroyed. Another unusually well carved tomb chest is to Captain Robert Smith (1697). His ship, a merchantman called 'Industria', is carved with a wealth of detail; it sails on its alabaster sea, and cherubs on either side mourn.

Also good is a monument of 1763 to James and Hester Spilman – a sarcophagus, a grey obelisk, a cherub and heads in profile. There is a memorial to Thomas Leverton, a renowned architect of the early nineteenth century, on which a woman weeps by an urn. Amongst mural brasses, the most noteworthy is to Thomas Colte with his wife and ten children (1559).

The only old screen is at the east end of the north aisle and is early fourteenth century work. The font, near the main door, is of plain

Purbeck stone; it is now octagonal, but was originally square and probably dates from the late twelfth century. The pulpit is a handsome mid-seventeenth century one, with tapering pilasters at the angles and elaborated panels.

Of the many splendid monastic buildings that once surrounded this great abbey, practically nothing remains. There survives a short length of vaulted passage leading off the north-east corner of the cloisters, which lay on the north side of the choir. The gatehouse still stands, a fourteenth century building with a carriage and pedestrian entrance; it contains some early brickwork which is of considerable interest because of its date (cf. Little Coggeshall). There is also a bridge leading up to the gatehouse, probably built in the same century.

Well-kept gardens now occupy the site where for centuries the monks carried on their daily round; and the foundations of some of the abbey's demolished walls can be seen.

Great Waltham, St Mary and St Lawrence: This village church stands with old houses grouped around. It has a surprisingly large nave, 32 ft 6 in. wide, and a west tower with Roman bricks in some of the quoins. The Norman building was much restored by Chancellor in 1874 and given a north aisle. The south arcade is of the Perpendicular period, although it was much altered in the Victorian restoration. The sixteenth century nave roof is good, with its tie-beams and hammer-beams with figures of angels and other carving. The well-known and resplendent monument to Sir Anthony Everard of Langleys and his wife, seventeenth century, can scarcely be missed; the two figures recline beneath a coffered arch. Also of great interest is the medieval heraldic glass in the west window of the south aisle, bearing three coats of arms of the Bohun family of nearby Pleshey Castle. The fifteenth century carved pews in the south aisle are unusual.

Little Waltham, St Martin: This village church is built of flint. The tower and nave are Norman, with a good Norman south doorway, columns with scalloped capitals, and a Norman window on the south wall. The tower was rebuilt after collapsing in the sixteenth century, using a good deal of Tudor brick, and it is now surmounted with a small cupola. The chancel dates from the Perpendicular period. The whole church was much restored in 1883, when the north aisle and organ chamber were added, and chancel and nave were re-roofed. There is a thirteenth century dug-out chest of sycamore wood, and a brass of 1447 to John Maltun, both worth examining.

Walton-on-the-Naze, All Saints: The present church of 1873 was designed by H. Stone. The old church was engulfed by the sea in 1796, and an interesting memorial of the occurrence is preserved in St Paul's Cathedral, in the prebendal stall distinguished as *Prebenda consumpta per mare* (Prebends eaten up by the sea), because the estates about the church belonged to the Cathedral.

Great Warley, St Mary the Virgin: In 1904 a new church was built thanks to the local benefactor, Evelyn Heseltine, to designs of Charles Townsend and interior designs of Sir William Reynolds-Stephens. Like the church at Hascombe near Guildford, its roughcast exterior shows the influence of Voysey, and the interior the fullest development of Art Nouveau. The nave walls are panelled in walnut, and the roof, a wagon-vault, is decorated with broad bands of silver. A conventionalised rose-tree and lily are much used in the decorations, the lily being the flower of the Virgin Mary; the rood screen, for instance, is composed of six brass rose-trees which flower freely at the top. All the detailing is in the same style; the font, pulpit, lectern, organ case, altar-rail, even pendant lights, use a variety of material for their effects. The chancel is apsidal. The figure of Christ in the centre panel stands on a coiled serpent; the vault has a vine decoration rising in low relief. This is perhaps the most complete Art Nouveau church in England.

Great Warley, Christchurch: This suburban church of 1855 by Teulon is built of Victorian red brick.

Little Warley, St Peter: This small church is awkwardly placed just south of the London–Southend road. Its brick west tower dates from 1718. The fifteenth century nave is built of stone, and the windows have Perpendicular tracery. The chancel is much buttressed, and was partly rebuilt in the nineteenth century; it has some good Tudor brickwork similar to Little Warley Hall, which stands immediately south of the churchyard, and is worth a glimpse. Inside on the chancel north wall is a fine monument to Sir Denner Strutt (1641) who lies on a shelf with his first wife above while sturdy cherubs hold aside the curtains. On the other side reclines his third wife, Lady Strutt (1658); and in the nave, carved in alabaster, is Father Time (seventeenth century). There is also a brass to Anne Terrell (1592).

North Weald, St Andrew: This is a fourteenth century church of flint and some Roman brick. It has a fine Tudor brick tower of which there are several in this part of Essex, with a beautiful brick arch into the nave. There are good windows in the flowing Decorated style, particu-

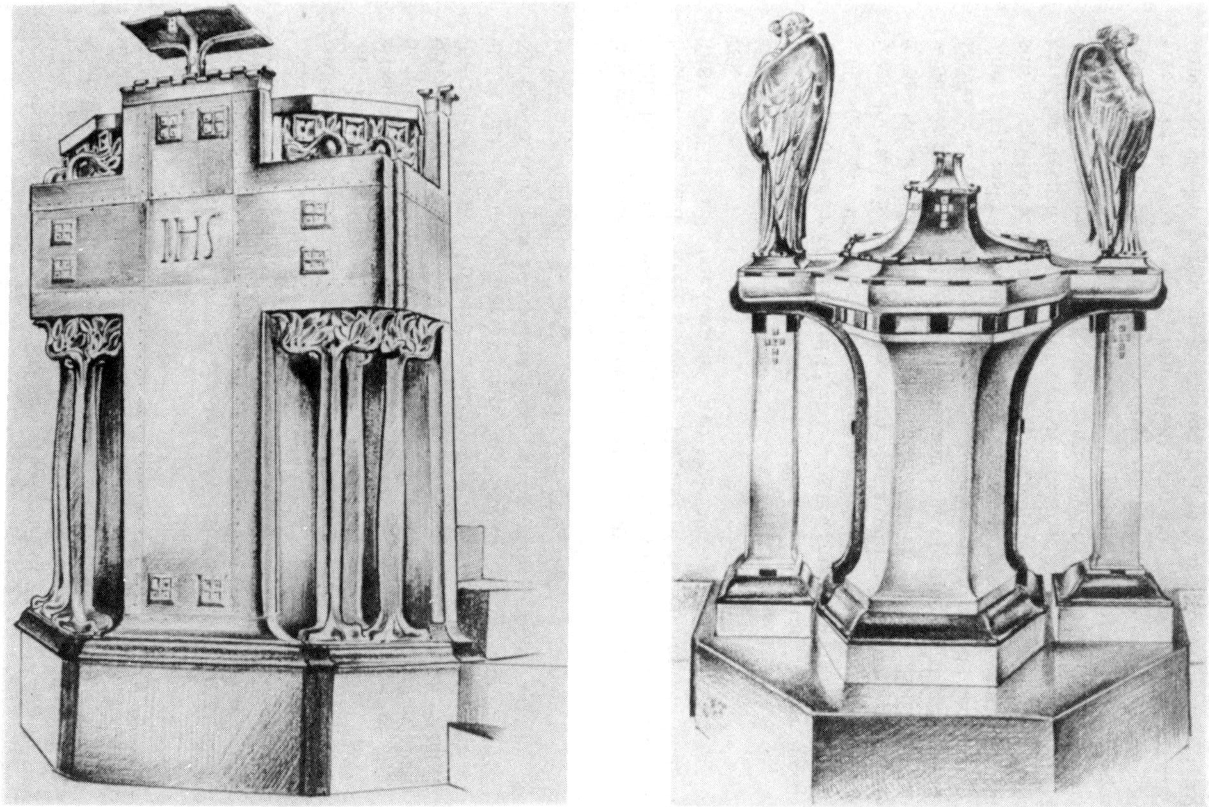

Great Warley: art nouveau pulpit and font

larly in the south-east chapel. The stained glass of its east window is by Kempe. After a serious fire in 1964, the old screen was moved to a Norfolk church and new glass to the east window inserted. There is some good medieval glass in the north side of the nave. A brass of 1606 shows the Larder family.

South Weald, St Peter: The rebuilding of 1868 to a design by Teulon obliterated most of the original church. The big west tower of c.1500 remains, and a fine Norman doorway into the south aisle; it has columns carved in zig-zag, a tympanum decorated with squares cut into two triangles, and zig-zag decoration on the arch. The south aisle with circular piers is a copy of its thirteenth century predecessor. The tower is ashlar faced, with a stair turret; the rest is of flint with some stone bands. Inside, there are some fine old brasses near the font, which is seventeenth century. In the south chapel are numerous monuments to the Tower family who lived at nearby Weald Hall, now demolished; and also a fine big one with sarcophagus and obelisk to Hugh Smith (1757). Note two fine Flemish stained-glass panels in the west window of the tower.

Weeley, St Andrew: The sixteenth century tower is of rose-red Tudor brick, built with unusually large bricks; it has diagonal buttresses and battlements, and a west doorway. The rest of the church was built in 1881 by Robins in late Perpendicular style, with red brick to match the tower.

Wendens Ambo, St Mary the Virgin: The parish name 'Ambo' means both the Wendens (Great and Little). This is a small and very interesting village church. The west tower, surmounted by a 'spike', is Norman. A west doorway is ringed with Roman bricks (which came no doubt from a nearby Roman villa), and has a plain tympanum. The Norman windows are interesting, especially the bell openings with colonettes. Inside, the tower opens into the nave with a plain round-headed arch. The south aisle has round piers of the early thirteenth century, with simple capitals and bases. The octagonal columns to the north aisle are early fourteenth century, but the aisle itself is a modern rebuilding of 1898. The chancel is thirteenth century, with some lancet windows. The clerestory to the nave was added in about 1500; the brick Tudor windows were inserted later, perhaps to light the rood loft. The rood screen of five bays dates from 1500; and the pulpit, with its tracery panels of similar period, is exceptional. The brass to a knight of 1410 (Sir William Loveday?) is noteworthy. The remains of a cycle of wall paintings in the chancel, depicting episodes in the life of St Margaret, are a rare treasure. The fourteenth century font has a wooden domed cover of about 1600.

Wethersfield, St Mary and St Mary Magdalene: The church lies close to the village green. Some of the building is possibly Saxon. The squat tower is early thirteenth century, with small lancet windows and pointed arch into the nave, some of which is also thirteenth century. Its south arcade has circular columns and good stiff-leaf carving on the east respond; the octagonal piers to the north arcade are probably of a later date. The window tracery in some instances resembles that at Shalford in its late fourteenth century decoration. The clerestory and roof are fifteenth century. The screen is delicate, with ogee arches and tracery over; and there are some fragments of fourteenth century stained glass worth studying in the nave. In the fourteenth century chancel, darkened by its more recent stained glass, is a fine piscina. There are also interesting alabaster effigies to Henry Wentworth (?) and his wife (1482) of nearby Codham Hall. In the aisles are beautiful wall monuments to the Mott family (c.1760), and to Joseph Clarke (1790).

Wicken Bonhunt, St Margaret: The church, built of flint, has a thirteenth century chancel with lancet windows. A south window has good Early English shafts, and there is still a scratch dial outside on the south-east wall. The tower, nave and porch were rebuilt in 1858 by the rich parson to his own designs in 'Decorated' Gothic style, with much stained glass, which makes the church gloomy. The monuments to the Bradbury family of nearby Brick House are worth examining; that on the south chancel wall was carved by H. Scheemaker (1731). In the village there is also the small Norman chapel of St Helen's; the nave and chancel contain original windows.

Wickham Bishops, St Bartholomew: The parish is so called because it was once the residence of the Bishops of London. The previous church became ruinous, and a new one was built in 1850 to disigns of Ewan Christian. It is of freestone with a tall steeple and is quite pretentious.

Wickham St Paul, All Saints: The parish is called St Paul because of its appropriation in medieval times to the Dean and Chapter of St Paul's Cathedral. The church stands close to Wickham Hall. Its main interest is a fine Tudor tower of 1505, in red brick with blue diapers, built, we learn from a will, for £20. It has diagonal buttresses, a stair turret, battlements and pinnacles. Over the west doorway is a brick window of three lights, with intersecting tracery.

Widdington, St Mary: The church in this small pleasant village was very largely rebuilt in 1872. Little remains of the original building, except a Norman window on the north chancel wall, the fourteenth century east window, and an interesting south window in the chancel. This has good dog-tooth decoration of mid-thirteenth century, and shafts with excellent carved capitals of the stiff-leaf type. There is a little stained glass of a sundial (1664) in a north window, a screen of 1907 by Sir Guy Dawber, and a brass on the wall of a civilian (1460).

Widford, St Mary: This church was built in 1862 at the expense of Arthur Pryor of Hylands nearby; it replaced the previous building on its site. It is of Kentish rag-stone, with a freestone spire which rises to a height of 145 ft. There is a rich Victorian east window and other Victorian and Edwardian glass; a heavy stone pyramid stands in the churchyard to Lady Falkland (1776) by E. Pearce, designed by G. Gibson.

Great Wigborough, St Stephen: This church is finely situated with Abberton reservoir to the north and Peldon church across the valley. It was mostly rebuilt with old materials, such as septaria, after the earthquake which shook this part of Essex in 1884. The nave roof has Victorian hammer-beams with gilded angels; the porch is also Victorian. The font is of the Perpendicular period, with shields in quatrefoils in the usual style.

Little Wigborough, St Nicholas: This church has little to keep it company. The fifteenth century nave, chancel and west tower were all much restored after the earthquake of 1884. Inside there is much Victorian ironwork.

Willingale Doe and Willingale Spain: These two churches stand together in one churchyard, with a row of lime trees to separate them; a layout unique in Essex and very rare elsewhere.

St Andrew's on the south side is in Willingale Spain. The name of Spain derives from the family of de Hispania who lived at Spains Hall, Finchingfield, after the Norman conquest. It is the smaller and older of the two. The flint nave has some Norman windows and two Norman doorways north and south; and there are Roman bricks in the quoins. The white weatherboard belfry rests on a tie-beam with four arched braces; it dates from the fifteenth century, as does the chancel. The octagonal font is fourteenth century, with tracery on the stem and quatrefoils on the bowl; note the interesting twelfth century ironwork on the north door.

St Christopher's on the north side is in Willingale Doe. The name comes from de Ou, a knight of Henry II's reign who owned the manor. It was much restored in 1853. The building is of flint. Its main interest lies in its monuments and brasses. On the chancel south wall is a large monument of 1641 to Robert Wiseman and his wife, with a semi-reclining figure between Corinthian columns and two kneeling figures above, very good of their kind. There is a good brass to Sir Thomas Torrell (1442) of nearby Torrells Hall, and two interesting brasses, one each side of the altar. The font is octagonal, Perpendicular in style.

Wimbish, All Saints: The church has Wimbish Hall and the old rectory as its neighbours. There is a Norman nave, and fine south doorway with columns, the inner pair carved spirally, the outer ones plain, sheltered by a fifteenth century porch. One Norman window remains, near which is thirteenth century blank arcading on the south external wall. Inside is a good thirteenth century north arcade of four bays with quatrefoil piers. The rest of the north aisle was restored in Victorian times; the chancel too is Victorian, and the tower, which was pulled down in 1883, was never rebuilt. There is a fifteenth century screen at the east end of the north aisle, near which lies a beautiful, if sadly mutilated, brass of 1347 to Sir John de Wantone and his wife. The figures were originally set in an octofoil of ogee arches.

Witham, St Nicholas: The south doorway alone survives from an earlier Norman church, with its columns and zig-zag ornament. The rest of the church is fourteenth century, except for the two chancel chapels, which are fifteenth century. The west tower has diagonal buttresses, a window with tracery of the Decorated period and battlements. The aisle windows are of the same century, and also the east window with ogee reticulation, although this was later renewed. The piers to the four-bay arcades are square, with attached demi-shafts; the arches above have double-wave mouldings. The screen has cusped ogee arches, with cusped arches at the top. The monuments include one of 1592 to Francis Harvey and his wife, facing each other at a prayer desk; a tomb chest with the recumbent effigy of John Southcotte, an Elizabethan judge; and a good alabaster bust of William East (1726).

Wivenhoe, St Mary the Virgin: The old church had to be rebuilt after the Essex earthquake of 1884, to designs of Hakewill; although the early sixteenth century west tower remains with its diagonal buttresses. Inside, there are good Tudor brasses to Viscount Beaumont, his wife (who later married Lord Oxford) and her chaplain.

Wix: The priory, one of the many monastic foundations in Essex, was dissolved by Cardinal Wolsey; this small church was formed from the south aisle of the priory church. It was much rebuilt in the eighteenth century, but an arcade is visible in the north wall with thirteenth century octagonal piers.

Woodham Ferrers, St Mary the Virgin: The de Ferrers family, who owned the manor in the thirteenth century, built this church in about 1250. It has a nave with clerestory, aisles of three bays, chancel and belfry; the Tudor tower has been demolished. The piers to the bays are alternately octagonal and circular, the arches double-chamfered; the aisle windows have two-light Decorated tracery. There is a good fifteenth century south porch of timber, with six cusped openings each side. The belfry rests on tie-beams without posts or wall-pieces. Over the chancel arch inside hangs a painting of the Doom, with Christ seated centrally and angels on either side. There is a noteworthy monument of 1619 to Cecilie Sandys, wife of the Archbishop of York, who lived nearby at Edwins Hall; the background is charmingly carved with flowers.

Woodham Mortimer, St Margaret: The church was rebuilt in the nineteenth century, except for the nave's south wall, which has a Norman window and the rear arch of a doorway. The heavy font bowl is probably Norman too. There is a small brass of 1584 to Dorothie Alleine, a child of three, in Elizabethan dress. The tomb chest of Peter Chamberlen, physician to the early Stuart kings, is in the churchyard.

Woodham Walter, St Michael: According to Wright, the Essex historian, this church was rebuilt by Thomas Radcliffe, Earl of Sussex, who owned the manor of Woodham Walter as well as that of New Hall. Churches entirely built in Queen Elizabeth's reign are rare; this building, of rose-red brick with crow-stepped gables, shows traces of once having been plastered outside. Theydon Mount church, also entirely of brick, is a little later in date (1611). The walls are buttressed, and the windows straight-headed with cusped lights. There is a large octagonal font with tracery on the stem; and the windows contain a few pieces of old stained glass. The bell turret with shingled spire is Victorian.

Wormingford, St Andrew: The building stands in a pretty churchyard looking down to the Stour valley. Its west tower is good Norman work, with original windows and bell openings topped by a seventeenth century brick parapet. The nave is also Norman; the north arcade with octagonal columns dates from the fourteenth century. The church was restored in Victorian times, and given quite an elaborate roof of soft woods with panels of pierced tracery.

Wrabness, All Saints: There are superb views from here across the water to Suffolk. This small church consists of nave and chancel only; the eighteenth century bell-tower is a separate wooden structure in the churchyard, housing the one bell. The old north doorway in the nave is Norman, and the decorative fifteenth century south doorway is set within an older Norman doorway. In the porch wall is a thirteenth century coffin lid. The hammer-beam nave roof of the Perpendicular period is unexpected; an octagonal font of the same period is very defaced.

Writtle, All Saints: Just off the village green stands the church, built of rag-stone rubble, flint and some ironstone; it is quite large for a village. The church dates from Norman times. The west tower was rebuilt in 1802; the nave arcades and clerestory date from 1879, and only a few of the circular pillars are original thirteenth century work. The two porches are early fourteenth century, and there are some good windows in the aisles from the Decorated period. Inside stands the original much-weathered Norman font. There are remains of wall paintings with St George and the Dragon over the north door. A stairway leads to the rood loft near the font. The church contains a number of very interesting brasses, wall monuments and floor slabs. In the chancel, which was baldy damaged by fire in 1974, are particularly good monuments to Edward Elliott and his wife (1595), to Sir Edward Pinchon by Nicholas Stone in 1629, portraying an elaborate pastoral scene with angels. On the chancel south wall is a fine memorial to Sir John Comyns (1759) of nearby Hylands, signed by H. Cheere. The stained glass windows are mostly Victorian; but the nave roof of about 1480 with its bosses and angels is a fine one. It is interesting to note that Writtle church once possessed five chantry chapels, where in the middle ages Mass was said regularly for the souls of the departed.

Great Yeldham, St Andrew: The church dates from the fourteenth and fifteenth centuries, with a north arcade rebuilt in Victorian times. The south porch is the lower portion of a large tower begun in the fourteenth century and never finished, but given a stepped brick gable. Another tower was built in the following century, with angle buttresses, three-light bell openings, stepped battlements, pinnacles and small figures of angels. There is an Elizabethan pulpit, and a fifteenth century screen, with figures of saints painted on part of the dado; also a brass of 1627 to Richard Symonds and his family. The south door is also noteworthy.

REDUNDANT CHURCHES

Alresford: damaged by fire, preserved as monument.

Asheldham, St Lawrence: now a youth centre.

Berechurch: craft workshop, except Audley chapel.

West Bergholt, St Mary: maintained by Friends of Friendless Churches.

Chickney, St Mary: maintained by Friends of Essex Churches.

Colchester, All Saints: museum.
Holy Trinity: museum.
St Giles: masonic hall.
St Martin: theatre.
St Mary on the Walls: theatre.

Harlow, St John the Baptist: arts centre.

East Horndon, All Saints: maintained by the Friends of Essex Churches.

Frating: converted into house.

Kelvedon Hatch, Old Church: residential use.

Little Oakley, St Mary: converted into house.

Langdon Hills, St Mary: converted into house.

Latchingdon, St Michael: converted into house.

Leyton, St Edward: Elim Pentecostal church.

Mundon, St Mary: maintained by Friends of Friendless Churches.

Netteswell, St Andrews: community centre.

Shellow Bowells, St Peter & St Paul: converted into house.

West Thurrock, St Clement: crafts workshop.

Tolleshunt Knights, All Saints: leased to Greek Orthodox Church.

Wickham Bishops Old Church: maintained by Friends of Friendless Churches.

Witham, All Saints: youth centre.

KEY TO MAP

A
B
C
D
E
F
G
1
2
3
4
5
6
7
8
9
Cambs
Herts
London
Hadstock
Gt Chesterford
Lt Chesterford
Littlebury
Strethall
Elmdon
Chrishall
Ashdon
Sturmer
Ashen
Helions Bumpstead
Steeple Bumpstead
Ridgewell
Birdbrook
Tilbury
Saffron Walden
Hempstead
Radwinter
Wimbish
Stambourne
Toppesfield
Wendens Ambo
Debden
Newport
Widdington
Wicken Bonhunt
Langley
Arkesden
Clavering
Gt Sampford
Lt Sampford
Finchingfield
Wethersfield
Thaxted
Lt Bardfield
Rickling
Berden
Quendon
Ugley
Henham
Mannden
Elsenham
Stansted
Birchanger
Farnham
Chickney
Broxted
Tilty
Gt Easton
Lt Easton
Gt Bardfield
Shalford
Lindsell
Bardfield Saling
Panfield
Stebbing
Bocking
Braintree
Gt Dunmow
Rayne
Takeley
Lt Canfield
Lt Dunmow
Felsted
Barnston
Gt Hallingbury
Lt Hallingbury
Gt Canfield
H Roding
North End
Ford End
Hatfield Broad Oak
Aythorpe Roding
Lt Leighs
H Easter
Pleshey
Gt Waltham
Sheering
White Roding
Leaden Roding
Good Easter
Lt Waltham
Hatfield
Harlow
Matching
Margaret Roding
Mashbury
Abbess Roding
Chignal Smealy
Roydon
Lt Parndon
Latton
Lt Laver
Roxwell
Gt Parndon
Netteswell
High Laver
Beauchamp Roding
Broomfield
Springfield
Magdalen Laver
Berners Roding
Fyfield
Willingale
Writtle
Chelmsford
Nazeing
Moreton
Widford
Gt Baddow
Epping Upland
Bobbingworth
N Weald
Shelley
Norton Mandeville
Epping
Waltham Abbey
Theydon Mount
H Ongar
Blackmore
Margaretting
Theydon Garnon
Greensted
Chipping Ongar
Ingatestone
Upshire
Theydon Bois
Stamford Rivers
Stondon Massey
Fryerning
Stock
W Hanningfield
Stapleford Tawney
Doddinghurst
Buttsbury
H Beech
Navestock
Mountnessing
Abridge
Loughton
Kelvedon Hatch
Billericay
Downham
Chigwell
Lambourne
Stapleford Abbotts
Shefield
Bentley Common
Hutton
Ramsden Bellhouse
Ramsden Crays
Chigwell Row
Brentwood
Ingrave
Childerditch
Gt Burstead
Nevendon
S Weald
Lt Burstead
Lt Warley
Gt Warley
Basildon
E Horndon
Laindon
Dunton
Vange
Bulphan
Langdon Hills
Fobbing
Pitsea
N Ockendon
Horndon on the Hill
S Ockendon
Stanford-le-Hope
Corringham
Mucking
Stifford
Orsett
Aveley
Grays Thurrock
Chadwell St Mary
Lt (E) Thurrock
E Tilbury
W Thurrock
W Tilbury

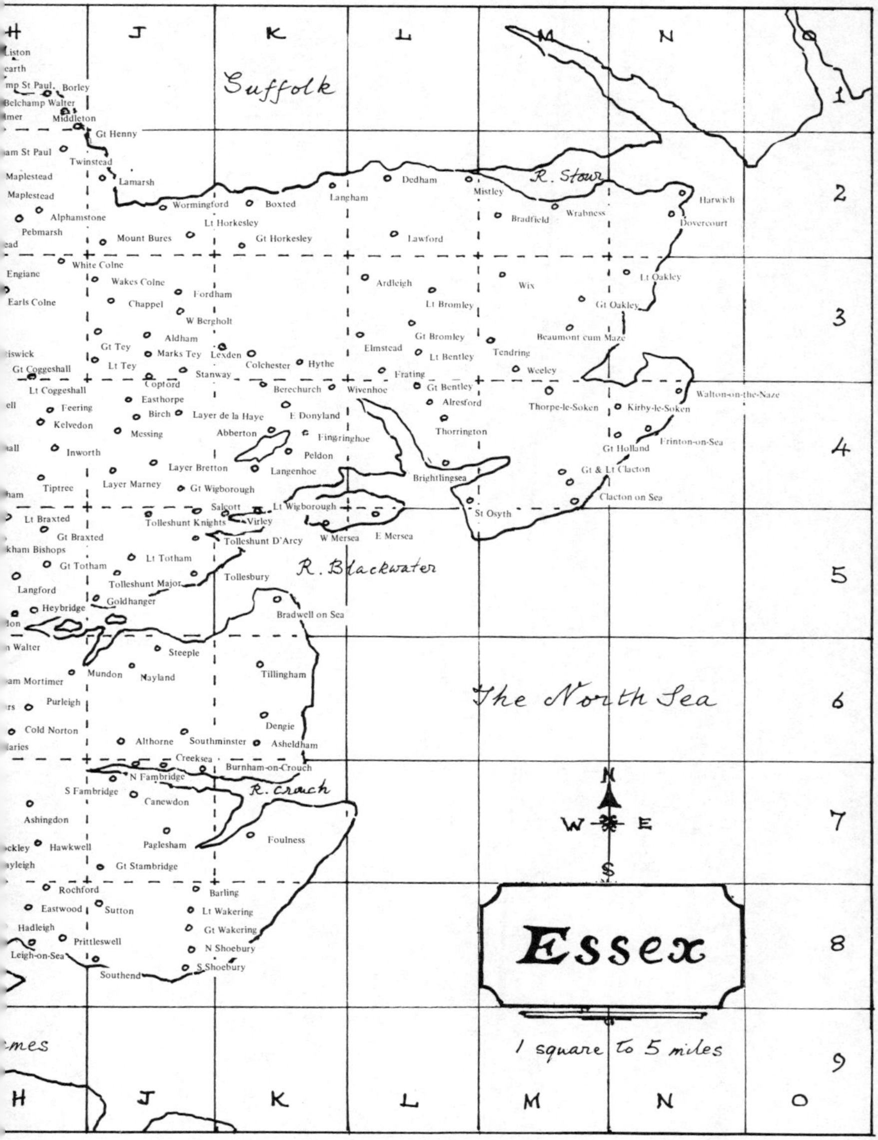

Suffolk
R. Stour
R. Blackwater
R. Crouch
The North Sea
Essex
1 square to 5 miles
N
S
W
E
H
J
K
L
M
N
O
1
2
3
4
5
6
7
8
9
Borley
Belchamp Walter
Middleton
Gt Henny
Twinstead
Lamarsh
Wormingford
Boxted
Langham
Dedham
Mistley
Harwich
Dovercourt
Wrabness
Bradfield
Lawford
Lt Horkesley
Gt Horkesley
Mount Bures
Alphamstone
Pebmarsh
White Colne
Wakes Colne
Fordham
Chappel
W Bergholt
Aldham
Gt Tey
Lt Tey
Marks Tey
Lexden
Colchester
Hythe
Stanway
Copford
Earls Colne
Gt Coggeshall
Lt Coggeshall
Feering
Kelvedon
Inworth
Tiptree
Easthorpe
Birch
Messing
Layer de la Haye
Abberton
Berechurch
E Donyland
Fingringhoe
Peldon
Langenhoe
Layer Bretton
Layer Marney
Gt Wigborough
Lt Wigborough
Salcott
Virley
Tolleshunt Knights
Tolleshunt D'Arcy
W Mersea
E Mersea
Ardleigh
Lt Bromley
Gt Bromley
Elmstead
Lt Bentley
Frating
Gt Bentley
Wivenhoe
Alresford
Thorrington
Brightlingsea
St Osyth
Wix
Tendring
Weeley
Beaumont cum Moze
Lt Oakley
Gt Oakley
Thorpe-le-Soken
Kirby-le-Soken
Walton-on-the-Naze
Frinton-on-Sea
Gt Holland
Gt & Lt Clacton
Clacton on Sea
Lt Braxted
Gt Braxted
Gt Totham
Lt Totham
Tolleshunt Major
Tollesbury
Langford
Heybridge
Goldhanger
Bradwell on Sea
Steeple
Mundon
Mayland
Tillingham
Purleigh
Cold Norton
Dengie
Althorne
Southminster
Asheldham
Creeksea
Burnham-on-Crouch
N Fambridge
S Fambridge
Canewdon
Ashingdon
Hawkwell
Paglesham
Foulness
Gt Stambridge
Rochford
Barling
Eastwood
Sutton
Lt Wakering
Hadleigh
Gt Wakering
Prittlewell
N Shoebury
Leigh-on-Sea
Southend
S Shoebury